The Economic Consequences of the Severn Bridge and its Associated Motorways

by E.J. Cleary and R.E. Thomas

Bath University Press

The economic consequences of the Severn Bridge and its associated motorways

Mr E. J. Cleary (Swansea)

Professor R. E. Thomas (Bath)

This report has been prepared, under the joint directorship
of the above, at the University of Bath, and the University College
of Swansea and the Newport and Monmouthshire College of Technology.

Bath University Press

BATH UNIVERSITY PRESS

1973

0 900843 24 1

Preface

The opening of the Severn Bridge in 1966 provided a rare opportunity to assess what effects such a road crossing would have on the life and trade of parts of Wales and the South West Region where in some cases road distances were reduced by up to 50 miles. The South West Economic Planning Council and the then Welsh Economic Council agreed to sponsor jointly a research project to carry out such an investigation and this was commissioned by the then Department of Economic Affairs in association with the Welsh Office. The University of Bath, the University College of Swansea and subsequently the Newport and Monmouthshire College of Technology were invited to undertake a joint study having the following terms of reference:—

1. The Severn Bridge Research Project will be an investigation of the effects of the Severn Bridge and its associated motorways on the economy of the Bristol Channel area. It will comprise —

(1) An examination of existing studies of comparable situations and of relevant theoretical models to predict likely consequences.

(2) While closer analysis in (1) above may suggest other areas of early impact, the following areas will be studied to trace the early course of change:—

(a) the pattern of traffic flows, both road and rail

(b) the distribution network both in terms of stockholding and control

(c) labour mobility and recreational travel, including shopping

(d) changes in land values

(3) A wider analysis of the industrial structure of the area to give a basis for assessing the longer run consequences of the improvements in communications. To a degree the Bridge is likely to weld the present separate economies of South East Wales and the Bristol area into a single new economy.

2. The main object of the investigation will be to increase understanding of the extent and rate of change of the industrial structure of an area, under the impact of a sharp improvement in communications. While in part the course of events, and hence this study, will be determined by the particular industrial structure of the area studied, the conclusions will have relevance to possible future investment in communications elsewhere, such as at Deeside and Humberside. By tracing the course of change, it may be possible to assess at an early stage the benefits that will result from the Bridge and so provide a firmer basis for decisions relevant to the future development of the area as a whole. At points specific information relevant to policy making should emerge, for instance, para 1 (2) (a) above, should make possible an estimate of the saving of resources made possible by the Bridge.

The research team submits this report as a limited attempt to evaluate one of the outstanding engineering feats and communication changes in Britain in the present century. It is, above all, a study of a long-awaited opportunity and the way in which two very different communities have taken their first steps to take advantage of this great improvement in road communications.

The report is being published in order to make the information which it contains more generally available, however, it must be emphasised that none of the Government Departments supplying data for the study, nor the Councils that sponsored it are in any way committed to the findings or opinions expressed therein.

Acknowledgements

Any research project which gathers information on a large scale generates so many debts of gratitude that it is not possible to acknowledge them all individually. While the Severn Bridge Project is in this category, there are some debts that we wish to acknowledge specifically.

We thank Professors R C Tress and W M Williams for their initiatives and help in setting up the project. Traffic surveys at the Bridge depended heavily on the help of the Gloucestershire County Surveyor and Chief Constable and all their staffs. Mr J G Reeks, the Bridge Manager, despite our continual efforts to disrupt the smooth running of his organisation, was always generous in his help as were his staff. Mr T R Newman was a most helpful point of contact with the Ministry of Transport in our survey activities and in other areas. Elsewhere in our work we benefited from the efforts of the Road Haulage Association, the Monmouthshire County Surveyor, the Cardiff Planning Officer, the Tay Bridge Authority, British Rail, the Ministry of Agriculture, the Bristol City Engineer Surveyor and Planning Officer, the County Planning Officers of Gloucestershire and Somerset and the main bus companies, notably the Bristol Omnibus Company and Red and White Services.

We could not have conducted the surveys of industry and distribution without the great assistance of the staff at the Atlas Computer Laboratory at Harwell and also the Computer Unit at Bath University.

We were also helped by the many manufacturers, distributors and hauliers who responded to our questionnaires and the large number of motorists and householders who kindly endured our inquisitions. To these must be added those students of the School of Management at Bath University who have assisted in many subsidiary studies.

Our particular thanks are also due to those civil servants at the Office of the South West Economic Planning Council and Board and at the Welsh Office, who had oversight of the project and whose advice and suggestions were very helpful to us.

Mr Gethin Williams, Newport and Monmouthshire College of Technology, made available the results of his work on the effect of the Bridge on the fatstock markets and on rail freight.

We wish to thank those who gave secretarial and administrative help, Mrs P Ingram (Newport), Mrs C Morgan (Swansea), Mrs O M Sur and Mrs P Locke (Bath).

Lastly the Councils of University of Bath, the Newport and Monmouthshire College of Technology and the University College of Swansea who gave the various members of the research team a home.

The Research Team comprised:

University of Bath
Professor R E Thomas
Mr R K B Hubbard
Mrs S M Hubbard (1967–69)

University College of Swansea
Mr E J Cleary
Mrs S H Spence
Mr J Diamond (1966–67)
Mr M L Taylor (1967–69)

Newport and Monmouthshire College of Technology
Miss P A David

The Economic Consequences of the Severn Bridge and its Associated Motorways.

CONTENTS

Introduction, History of the Severn Bridge, Economic Structure of the Estuarial Area and Survey Methods

Introduction

1.1 The Severn Estuary has been a barrier to movements since the beginning of recorded time. Up to the nineteenth century the crossing was a hazardous one because of the strength of the tides and the dangers of shifting sandbanks. In the nineteenth century when the railway became a dominant means of inland transport the first Severn Bridge and then the Severn Tunnel created new links between the expanding industrial area of South Wales and the main centres of population in Southern England. But when the growth of road motor transport rose to a position of dominance in inland transport in the middle of the twentieth century the barrier presented by the Severn led to renewed pressure for the creation of a road link. The opening of the Severn Road Bridge from Beachley to Aust in 1966 therefore created new links not only between the two regions fronting the Bristol Channel but between each of them and other parts of Britain. A change in communications on this scale with savings of up to 49 miles in distance and proportionate savings in travelling time clearly held the prospect of substantial changes in the fortunes of the two regions immediately connected. The investigation of the effects of the Severn Bridge was inaugurated with the principal objectives of quantifying the savings for the nation resulting from the Bridge and assessing its impact on the economies of South Wales and the South West of England.

1.2 Precedents for studies of this kind are hard to find. There had been a limited pilot study of the effects on firms in the Bristol area of the change in road communication which would emerge with the completion of the Bridge and the two motorways, the M.4 and the M.5, which were to intersect north of the city of Bristol. The Economic Planning Councils for the South West of England and for Wales commissioned a more extended study to start in October 1966. The investigation was to take three years and be undertaken jointly by Bath University, University College of Swansea and Newport and Monmouthshire College of Technology.

1.3 The investigation had three main features. First, there was to be an examination of the existing studies of comparable situations and of relevant theoretical models that might offer lines of enquiry or bases of predicting likely consequences. Second, certain studies were to be made of immediate changes, notably the pattern of traffic flows of road and rail, the distribution network and labour mobility and recreational travel. Third, it was hoped that further studies could be undertaken into

such topics as land values and other consequences of the Bridge and the movements created by it. Not all these enquiries have been pursued mainly because of the difficulty of obtaining data on some topics such as land values. The main studies of traffic and of industry and distribution, together with studies of household expenditure by a sample group of Bridge users, form the backbone of this report. In addition, the research team has taken the opportunity to collect as much relevant information as possible both in the course of its normal investigations and through the good offices of local authorities, private individuals and, in particular, the sponsoring departments.

1.4 Accordingly this report sets out the main conclusions and data resulting from the investigations conducted from 1966 to 1969. The remainder of this chapter is concerned with the history of the Bridge, the economic structure of the regions immediately adjacent and an outline of the survey methods used. Chapter 2 deals with previous studies and the extent to which these have been of some assistance. Chapter 3 then deals with the traffic flows, whilst Chapters 4 and 5 examine these in further detail in respect of light vehicles and the commercial transport industry as a whole. Chapter 6 examines the effects on industry particularly in terms of new raw materials and new connections, whilst Chapter 7 looks at the distribution network. Chapter 8 then attempts to estimate the benefits derived from the Bridge, and Chapter 9 sets out the main conclusions of the study as a whole with some projections as to likely future effects of the Bridge and its associated motorways. Map A, at the end of this report, provides general information about the areas adjacent to the Bridge, i.e. mainly the eastern part of South Wales and the northern part of the South West region.

The History of the Severn Bridge

1.5 Economic ties between South Wales and Bristol have existed since mediaeval times and the Severn Estuary has always been a barrier to the growth of these ties. The estuary narrows from 8 miles wide between Nash Point and Clevedon to only 1 mile at the English Stones. This narrowing by a factor of 8 in a distance of 12 miles creates sharp changes in water depth with changing tides and also means that the tides run fast. These conditions make the river crossing difficult and help to shift the sandbanks, further accentuating the difficulty. The alternative to the Beachley-Aust crossing is a 50 mile detour through Gloucester. In these circumstances it is not surprising that with the improvements in materials, technology and engineering knowledge in the late eighteenth and early nineteenth centuries, thoughts turned to putting these improvements to work in eliminating the Severn barrier.

1.6 In 1823 the Postmaster General appointed the engineer Thomas Telford to advise him on measures to improve the mail coach route from London to Milford Haven, the port of departure of the Irish packets. Telford, viewing the narrow crossing at the English Stones with misgivings "One of the most forbidding places at which an important ferry was ever established — a succession of violent cataracts formed in a rocky channel exposed to the rapid rush of a tide which has scarcely an equal on any other coast", first suggested a ferry crossing from Uphill Bay to Sully Island. This, however, would have involved over 20 miles of new roads and was rejected. Telford then proposed a bridge to span the estuary but this proposition was not taken up, though Telford did have a part in the piers for the Beachley-Aust ferry.[1]

1.7 In 1845 Thomas Fulljames became the first of a long line of Gloucestershire County Surveyors to become involved in a project to bridge the Severn. He proposed a railway bridge at the Beachley-Aust crossing but, despite a favourable report on the project by James Walker, F.R.S. to the Lands Commission of the Admiralty and interest from the Bristol and Liverpool Junction Railway Company, nothing came of the proposal. I. K. Brunel at the same time proposed a more modest bridge higher upstream at Awre as part of a rail link from Swindon to South Wales, but the Admiralty ruled out this proposal as a danger to navigation, not the last time that objection was to be raised. The scheme put forward by Samuel Baldwyn Rogers[2] of Nantyglo was altogether more ambitious, amounting to almost a new town as the crossing! He proposed a stone bridge at the English Stones of 21 arches of over 300 feet spans. It included a railway and carriageway, houses, shops, refreshment rooms and "suitable conveniences for a sort of permanent International Exhibition". The scheme did not get beyond the artist's impression stage.

1.8 The last quarter of the nineteenth century saw more substantial progress at least as far as the railway was concerned. In 1879 the single line bridge at Sharpness was completed, but this still left open the possibility of considerable savings via a crossing lower down the estuary. The possibility of such a railway bridge was considered in 1863, the bridge to be built at the New Passage. However, the Great Western Railway rejected this in favour of a tunnel. Work on a tunnel did not begin until 1879 and the work faced considerable geological difficulties and took 7 years to complete, being opened in 1886. This facility met the needs of the then current situation and the picture was not changed until the influence of the motor car became important. The First World War showed the potentialities of that new form of transport and before that war was over schemes were suggested to create a road crossing of the estuary.

1.9 In 1923 a conference of Local Authorities and the Ministry of Transport favoured a bridge at the Beachley-Aust site. There was, however, substantial opposition based on an alternative proposal that would solve the transport problem and at the same time make a contribution to meeting the rapidly growing demand for electricity, by incorporating a road crossing in a barrage. The Government of the day decided more information was needed and appointed a committee to enquire into the proposals for a barrage. This committee did not move rapidly and in 1929 a further conference of Local Authorities expressed disappointment at the lack of progress and created a committee to watch progress. The Severn Bridge Barrage Committee reported in 1931 (though the report was not published until 1933) in favour of the barrage scheme, but the financial crisis of that year was scarcely the best climate to propose a scheme costing £50 million and no action was taken.

1.10 The next move arose out of agitation for a new bridge to replace the existing one over the River Wye at Chepstow. Gloucestershire County Council used the occasion to consider the justification of a Severn crossing. Consulting engineers were commissioned to report on costs and possible sites (Sharpness; Littleton-Sedbury; Aust-Beachley and New Passage-Sudbrook were all considered.) At the same time the Road Improvement Association took up the matter and reported in favour of the New Passage site, which would obviate the need for a new Wye Bridge. In October 1935 a conference of Local Authorities on both sides of the estuary was called by the Gloucestershire and Monmouthshire County Councils and this conference decided to go ahead with a bridge at the English Stones site, subject to Ministry of Transport approval. The Ministry agreed the consulting engineers' plans and, subject to Parliamentary approval, a grant of 75% of the cost, the remaining 25% to be met half by the local authorities benefiting and half by tolls on users. The estimated cost was £2,480,000.

1.11 The Gloucestershire and Monmouthshire Councils promoted a Parliamentary Bill to authorise the project and this Bill went to a Select Committee in April 1936. There were many objectors, who fell into four groups — local authorities such as Gloucester and Bristol, anxious about the effect of the bridge on their commerce; navigational and conservancy interests fearful of the effect on shipping and land drainage; commercial interests directly affected, especially the Great Western Railway and the ferry company; and local landowners who felt a bridge would affect amenities and values in a variety of ways.[3]

1.12 Apart from general apprehension about the damage that a bridge might cause to these diverse interests, the Select Committee spent a good deal of time on the geological consequences to the Severn Tunnel of building a bridge in the close proximity implied by the English Stones site. The possibility of the bridging operation causing leaks in the tunnel was the most concrete objection to the bridge proposal raised during the brief period of the Select Committees Hearings. On 12th May, 1936 the Select Committee, without hearing the main body of evidence, reported that they found the preamble to the Bill not proved and that was the end of the matter.

1.13 A conference in October 1936 found 93 local authorities still in favour of a bridge and there were hopes that when the Government assumed responsibility for all trunk roads, as they did on 1st April 1937, the Government would construct a bridge. Local authorities were soon informed that this would not be so. With rearmament and the approach of war the matter was put aside, although as late as the summer of 1939 the Ministry of Transport agreed to pay three-quarters of the cost of a further investigation into a Severn crossing by Gloucestershire County Council.

1.14 The lack of a road crossing became a serious matter as the war progressed and there was a critical transport bottleneck at the Severn as munitions, coal and other supplies moved out of a South Wales that had full employment at last. Before the Second World War was over, the Welsh Advisory Council of the Ministry of Reconstruction reported (1944) that "The construction of a Severn Road Bridge would be the greatest single contribution to the improvement of transport facilities in South Wales. We regard the provision of the Bridge as so essential to the industrial future of that part of the Principality that we subordinate to it all other questions of the development of communications in that area."[4]

1.15 At the same late stage of the Second World War, a Severn Bridge was being reconsidered in relation to the County Surveyors Society's pre-war scheme for 1,000 miles of motorways in Britain. The Gloucestershire Surveyor, Mr. E. C. Boyce, advocated a bridge at the Beachley-Aust site and this proposal was endorsed by a further joint conference of Local Authorities. In May 1945 the Ministry of Transport decided to adopt this proposal as a government project under the 1945 Trunk Roads Act. Engineers[5] and architects were appointed to produce plans and the project was carried a stage further in July 1947 when an order was made fixing the line of the Bridge (in fact Bridges since the Wye had to be crossed also) and its associated motorway connections from the A.38 north of Almondsbury to the A.48 north of Haysgate. However, this scheme did not reach fruition; the economic difficulties of the late 1940s, devaluation and rearmament forced a cut in public capital investment projects and the Severn Bridge was again postponed.

1.16 Again the Local Authorities met and proposed to sponsor an ad hoc bridge authority to finance the construction of the Bridge, designs for which were now in hand. The construction would be financed from loans to be repaid from toll revenue. However, the Government of the day insisted that any bridge must be a government project and any Private Bill to authorise a bridge authority and construction would be opposed.

1.17 Approval for a Forth Road Bridge in 1958 led naturally to a revival of interest in and pressure for a Severn Bridge and soon afterwards, on 27th September 1960, the Ministry of Transport announced that a start would be made on the Severn Bridge. The 1945 proposals formed the basis for the new scheme and the delay was not without some advantages. The new Bridge would now be part of a wider motorway network, not merely a link between the A.38 and A.48. Further, there were important improvements in design from the lattice girder

proposals of 1945 to a box girder design; this change had a substantial effect in reducing the cost of the Bridge by 20% to 25% compared with the earlier lattice girder design. At long last work on the piers began in 1961 and the Bridge was eventually opened on 8th September 1966.

Economic Structure

South Wales

1.18 Industrial South Wales is essentially a nineteenth century creation; while the roots of industrialisation can be traced much deeper into the past, the rapid growth of population and urbanisation in the area are closely bound up with the expansion of the coal and iron industries in the nineteenth century. The 75 years to 1914 were years of high, though not continuous, prosperity and stand in sharp contrast to the inter-war years of depression. Between the wars South Wales became one of the classic examples of the dangers of industrialisation on a narrow base. The inter-war decline in demand for coal, especially for export, and for iron and steel products led to deep and widespread depression with little respite over the two decades.

1.19 The years after the Second World War saw a determined effort to revivify industrial South Wales. The old industries were to be refurbished and the industrial base was to be broadened by attracting new industries to the area. Much capital was invested in the iron and steel industry and to a lesser extent (especially proportionately) in the coal industry. Both industries were restructured, moving to larger production units. Again the iron and steel industry was most affected.

1.20 Attracting new industry in the immediate post-war years proved highly successful. The end of the war left the British people ill stocked with goods but well stocked with savings. In this situation speed was important to manufacturers in getting back into peace-time business. In these circumstances control of both building licences and the location of new industrial development were effective in attracting (or propelling) new industries into South Wales. Further, many war factories had been built in South Wales, because so much unemployed labour was available and because the relative isolation of South Wales from the London-Midlands-North West industrial axis gave strategic advantages, and these factories now became available for civilian use and occupation.

1.21 Progress in the immediate post-war years was swfit and by the 1950s unemployment in South Wales was at low levels compared with the pre-war situation, if not compared with some other parts of Great Britain. In the 1950s controls on location of industrial development were exercised less rigorously in favour of the pre-war depressed or Special Areas, now the Development Areas. A factory's contribution to exports was now weighed in official quarters in deciding whether to grant an Industrial Development Certificate as well as its contribution to reducing unemployment and the scales tipped in favour of refusing permission to develop outside the Development Areas less frequently.

3

1.22 High levels of unemployment in the Development Areas in the recession of 1958-59 gave a new urgency to industrial diversification; pressure on potential developers to locate their factories or extensions in the Development Areas increased. The Local Employment Act 1960 increased the attractions the Government could offer to those moving to Development Areas which were now defined more closely, only particular towns being eligible rather than almost the whole of South Wales as earlier. This latter restriction was relaxed again as the protection of the depressed areas increased in the 1960s and the whole of South Wales, except the coastal strip around Cardiff and Newport, became eligible for favoured treatment. In addition to the firmer use of the negative power to prevent firms expanding outside the Development Areas, there were increased positive attractions. Higher Investment Allowances were payable in the Development Areas and under the Selective Employment Tax employers in manufacturing industry in those areas received a subsidy on each person employed (the Regional Employment Premium) in addition to the refund of that tax generally available to manufacturers.

1.23 Unfortunately these new attractions to industrial expansion and diversification in South Wales occurred at a time when the run-down of employment in the coal industry was accelerating and increased capital intensity in the iron and steel industry was putting a number of jobs there in jeopardy. The result was that while industry continued to diversify, overall employment was not expanding.

1.24 These various factors have changed the economic structure of South Wales a good deal. The decline in importance of the coal industry is the most notable change. There have been smaller, but still significant, declines in agricultural employment and also in transport and communications, especially the railways. Significant gains are less dramatic in terms of the numbers employed in particular industries, but they are more widespread. Vehicles, chemicals, engineering, textiles and the residual categories, other metal manufacturers and other manufacturing industries are all industries which show substantial post-war growth in South Wales. These gains, together with the relative rise in incomes of the still important coal industry and the renewed prosperity of the iron and steel industry have formed the basis for the expansion of those industry groups tied very closely to local demand. Construction and professional services are two such industries with considerable post-war growth and in the last decade the Distributive Trades can be added.

1.25 The construction of the Severn Bridge fits in well with the developing industrial pattern. The growing industries tend to move a variety of goods to many locations for further processing or sale to final consumers. They are components and materials that require the flexibility of road transport much more than the traditional heavy industries where the railway served their needs well. The expansion of industry since 1920 has been more and more dependent on road transport, and the Bridge with its associated motorways, contributes to reducing the relative isolation of South Wales from some of the more rapidly growing sectors of the economy in London, the South East and Southern England. Yet it is only one influence among many in the industrial structure of South Wales. Changes in technology, patterns of demand, and indeed legislation, are formative influences in industrial structure. Transport is but one influence among many.

The South West

1.26 The South West of England is fortunate in combining a splendid countryside and coastline with an avoidance of the worst scars, physical and social, of the earlier phases of the industrial revolution. While many of the earliest manifestations — and scarring remains — of that revolution are associated with parts of the peninsula, the main outcome was the loss to other regions of what were then the growth industries, textiles, shipbuilding and metal manufacture. The northern half of the region, Gloucestershire, North and Central Somerset and North Wiltshire, had access to the key material of the period — coal — both in Somerset and the Forest of Dean and industries developed in these areas. Indeed the earlier Severn Bridge — the rail link from Lydney to Sharpness — was expressly intended to give better access from the mines of the Forest of Dean to the Bristol area. But the industrial structure continued to be dominated by three features. The first was the role of the port of Bristol as an importer of foodstuffs and raw materials. This was linked to the second, a strong business community trading over a wide area including South Wales, and adapting itself to changes in the fortunes of its enterprises by evolution from one trade to another. The third was the establishment of a strong combination of industries and services.

1.27 The historical role of the port of Bristol continues to be important to both the traditional and newer industries of the sub-region, notably to food, drink and tobacco on the one hand and to chemicals on the other. The innovative role of the business community is seen in the continual inception of new methods, products and enterprise. The evolution from tramways to supersonic aircraft is but one example of this process. Another is the development of new processes and products in traditional industries such as tobacco and footwear. The trading role of Bristol is not a consequence of its size and purchasing power but a factor in its creation.

1.28 The region had a share in some of the industries which declined after the First World War such as coal mining, but the main emphasis in its structure lay in industries which were expanding, and its industrialisation accelerated in the inter-war years as the engineering industry expanded around the aircraft industry. The new mobility of industry which resulted from a combination of electricity and cheaper transport, notably road transport,[6] made the area an attractive one in which industrialists might launch new ventures. Immediately prior to the Second World War, the food, drink and tobacco industries were the largest single group in the Bristol-Severnside area, closely followed by vehicles, shipbuilding and aircraft in which the aero-engine and airframe developments were setting in motion many subcontracting arrangements and leading to important new growth in Bristol-Severnside and Gloucester-Cheltenham. The non-ferrous metal industries concentrated in the Bristol area in 1938 were long established as were the paper and printing trades with their two growth points, packaging and colour printing. While many of these had some historical connection with the port, a feature of many of the newer developments was the combination of technical innovation, business acumen and individual initiative.[7]

1.29 The Second World War accelerated these movements by producing a massive expansion of aircraft and engineering work with a large inflow of new labour and the establishment of many new factories. At the same time, contraction of some other trades was hastened and the sub-region emerged much stronger in manufacturing industry than ever before. Admittedly much of this was dependent on the aircraft industry which had been inflated to meet wartime demands and which was notoriously susceptible to political decisions for both military and civil projects. One important consequence was the presence of factories and labour, much of it highly skilled. Another was the incentive to main and sub-contractors to diversify into other products which would be less dependent on the fate of the aircraft industry. The presence of facilities has been particularly important to the development of Gloucester for example, while the development of new products has been seen among engineering firms in the Bristol-Severnside area. Perhaps even more important was the extent to which firms were based in the region and concentrated their technical development there.

1.30 The 1950s saw the further strengthening of these trends. In the late 1940s and again in the 1960s, governmental controls on the siting of new factories have tended to steer the larger lumps of new factory employment towards the Development Areas but there were some important new moves into the sub-region during the 1950s partly into premises vacated by contractions in the aircraft industry but also with new developments such as ICI at Avonmouth. The newcomers have been particularly important to North Gloucestershire while they have been overshadowed in the Bristol-Bath areas by the growth of indigenous firms, a growth which has included a net export of new jobs to other areas.[8] The northern part of the South West region has, therefore, become more industrial than hitherto. Those industries that are contracting nationally have not always done so in this area; indeed some have expanded and increased their national market share, e.g. footwear. To this must be added the spectacular growth of Swindon as a London overspill centre.

1.31 At the same time the distributive and service trades have also increased in scale and activity. A classification of distributors used later in this study[9] identifies "regional distributors" and shows their relatively strong representation in Bristol. The growth in population with net inward migration reinforces the attraction and importance of the area. The combination of net immigration, low unemployment, high activity rates and largely home-based growth and innovation make it an attractive area for further expansion, a feature reflected in the parallel study of the future of Severnside.

1.32 But such growth involves heavy and increasing demands on transport. The nature and timing of much of this growth means that it is based primarily on road transport and any extension in the motorway network of which the Severn Bridge forms a part, is therefore of significance to the economy of the sub-region. The Bridge offers the opportunity not only to restore some of Bristol's traditional trading roles in respect of South Wales but to develop new linkages in a direction where they have been conspicuously absent, the main connections of the South West North being with the South East and the Midlands. The associated possibility of change through the construction of the M.4 and M.5 motorways with their intersection at Almondsbury are perhaps of much greater significance to the eastern seaboard of the Bristol Channel.

The Effects of the Severn Estuary on the Economy of the Area

1.33 The extent to which the Severn acted as a barrier was clear from the surveys of industry and distribution. In 1966 the principal, if not the dominant, destinations of the output of manufacturers in most trades were London and the South East, and the rest of England and Wales. Only among firms in food, drink and tobacco did a majority despatch 50% or more to their own home region. Only occasionally were there even individual firms for which the region across the estuary had this degree of importance. In fact the great majority did only a little trade with the region across the estuary. The only trades where cross-estuary trade was a significant proportion of business were, however, those where time and speed were important factors in delivery and competition, notably food, drink and tobacco.

1.34 While among manufacturers the position was similar on both sides of the estuary, this was not the case among firms in distribution. In South Wales the great majority had no trade into the South West but among firms in the South West almost 50% had some trade with South Wales before the Bridge. Furthermore the number of such firms in the South West, mainly in the Bristol area, was more than double the number in South Wales. While the Severn may have been a barrier for distributors in South Wales it was less so for those in the South West, partly a reflection of Bristol's traditional role.

1.35 Organisational links between firms operating on both sides of the estuary were the exception. Among manufacturing firms employing 100 or more persons, over 70% had no other plants or depots on either side of the estuary and only 15% had establishments in both South Wales and the South West. The picture emerges of, on the one hand, a changing industrial structure in South Wales with large national concerns and branches of expanding firms based elsewhere and, on the other, of a locally based core of firms, some very large, supplemented by branches of national firms in the South West, each having its own orientation to the rest of the country.

1.36 While this describes the outward flow of products of the two regions astride the Severn, it does not fully reflect the distribution of goods to consumers in those regions. Much of the merchandise is made elsewhere or is imported. Manufacturers play an important part in distribution, but so do specialist distribution firms. Here several types may be distinguished. There are those firms that distribute nationally through one or two centres or through, say 12—15 major centres. Such firms are present in the areas under study, the main concentration of their depots being on the east bank from Bristol northwards. Then there are regional distributors based on centres such as Bristol and Cardiff and lastly there are local distributors in smaller centres. Even before the Bridge, Bristol was clearly the largest distributive centre in either region and Cardiff was clearly the leading centre in South Wales. There was already some competition in South Wales from Bristol but such business had to travel via Gloucester unless rail-borne and the evidence is that very little of it travelled through the tunnel.

Survey Methods

1.37 The study of previous research into comparable situations did not lead to any significant departure from the principal lines of immediate enquiry indicated in paragraph 1.3 above. The study of traffic flows over the Bridge has taken two forms, the analysis of daily traffic and the conduct of surveys of origin, destination and journey purpose — the areas covered by these surveys are illustrated in Map B at the end of this report. Rail traffic data has been obtained from British Railways. The study of the distribution network has taken the form of two surveys of manufacturing industry and distribution — the areas covered are shown in Map C. Further studies arising from the main lines of enquiry have included coach traffic, the effect on road hauliers and interviews with a sample of householders to obtain details of travel patterns. The survey methods used are set out briefly in the succeeding paragraphs while further details are given in Appendix 1.

Daily Traffic

1.38 The fact that tolls have to be paid to cross the Bridge means that there is necessarily a continuous count of traffic day and night, and for this purpose each day begins at 7 a.m. A computer records the class of each vehicle as the toll is collected. A daily record of crossings by vehicle class can be obtained by aggregation of the lane shift totals: this record is marred occasionally by failures of the computer. The pattern of traffic is in general terms very regular and interpolation adequately fills any gaps resulting from computer failures. The aggregation of the totals for each traffic lane for each collector's shift of work forms the basis of the monthly figures of traffic for the various classes of vehicle.

Traffic Surveys

1.39 A series of origin, destination and journey purpose enquiries were conducted. One lane was allocated for interviewing traffic in the direction (eastbound or west-bound) being surveyed on the day — from 6 a.m. to 10 p.m. To obtain a random sample of traffic in the interview lane a police constable was on duty, operating about 100 yards from the toll booth, whose job it was to select the first vehicle passing a given point after an interview was complete, and direct that vehicle into the interview lane. One possible weakness of this system is that the constable, whose normal function is to aid the flow of traffic, will be reluctant to direct vehicles into the interview lane that are approaching the toll area in a different lane and this may be particularly so in the case of heavy vehicles. This difficulty was met by stationing

the constable away from the toll booths so that he could give directions to approaching vehicles as they left the two-lane (in each direction) section of the Bridge to spread into the multi-lane toll area. The problem of balancing the sample for light and heavy vehicles was met by treating them as separate populations. A count was kept of the number of heavy and light vehicles crossing and the light and heavy vehicles interviewed were then grossed up by appropriate factors to represent the two vehicle populations. The density of the sample of vehicles (of either type) varies over the day; when traffic is light early in the morning a large proportion can be accommodated in the interview lane, a much smaller proportion at peak times. The sampling fraction varied from about one-third early morning to one-fifteenth at the busiest times. An hourly record of interviews and the traffic count meant that hourly sampling factors could be used in estimating characteristics of the light and heavy vehicle population from the respective samples. The chief limitation of the interview was time; clearly long delays would make the whole process unacceptable to both the public and the Bridge administration. The result was that the range of questions was very narrow. The same group of trained interviewers was used on each occasion and over the 16 hour day they managed from 800 to 1000 interviews.

1.40 The high traffic densities on summer weekends made it impossible to interview at all without causing unacceptable delay and congestion. The two surveys at these times were made by distributing a numbered reply-paid post-card to one vehicle in every five. The time of distribution of each numbered card and the number of occupants in the vehicle were noted so that hourly sampling fractions of returned cards could be found and used in estimating the population from the sample. The percentage of cards returned varied very little from day to day, always being just under 40%. At the first survey in March 1967 interviews were conducted and cards distributed so that something could be known of the reliability of returned post-cards in relation to inter-views. On one occasion further detail was obtained by requesting the receiver of the card to give his name and address if he was prepared to answer some further questions regarding the expenditures made by the occupants of the car on their journey. The public was very co-operative and refusals at 1% constituted no problem.

1.41 Use was also made of two origin and destination surveys carried out by the Gloucestershire County Surveyor. The first of these was in August 1966, a month before the Bridge opened, and the second a year later. A sample of vehicles crossing a screen line covering the main routes into Wales affected by the Severn Bridge was interviewed.

Household Interviews

1.42 The brief interviews with travellers were supplemented by a series of more detailed home interviews concerning patterns of travel, reasons for travelling and expenditure on journeys. These interviews were conducted in five areas close to the Bridge — Chepstow, Ebbw Vale and Newport to the west and Thornbury and Bristol to the east. In Thornbury and Chepstow a 10%

sample of the whole population of households was drawn from the rating lists. In Ebbw Vale, Newport and Bristol the 10% sample was similarly drawn for selected wards in those towns. Interviews were completed at 92.5% of the 2525 selected households; the lowest percentage of completions in any area was 89.

Road Hauliers

1.43 To provide further details of the movement of heavy vehicles two enquiries were addressed to road hauliers. Soon after the Bridge opened a general questionnaire was addressed to all members of the Road Haulage Association in the South Wales and South Western traffic areas. Since others' experience indicated that a complicated and detailed questionnaire was likely to meet with a low response rate, especially from small firms, this questionnaire was phrased in general terms about commodities carried and routes operated. Detailed questions were confined to size of fleets, licence type and carrying capacities. This first enquiry brought a 35% response rate. For the second enquiry early in 1968, three-quarters of the same Road Haulage Association members were sent a fairly simple questionnaire, although it requested some details of mileage run in a selected week. The remaining quarter was asked to keep logs for each vehicle for the selected week, and this quarter included all those firms which stated in the first enquiry that 10% or more of their operations were on cross-Bridge routes. The response to this second stage enquiry was poor, only 7% of the 'log' firms and 13% of the others responding.

Manufacturing Industry and Distribution

1.44 The traffic surveys and Bridge toll data give a picture of movements across the Bridge, their origins, destinations and types. They cannot of themselves provide information as to the reasons underlying changes that have occurred and surveys were made of firms in manufacturing and distribution. An earlier pilot study conducted in 1965 among a group of firms in the Bristol area had suggested both lines of enquiry that might be explored in a larger survey and types of possible change. The surveys of manufacturing industry and distribution concentrate on certain aspects of possible changes which are discussed more fully in Chapter 2.

1.45 The principal sources of information were two postal surveys of establishments in Orders II to XX of the Standard Industrial Classification (1958) as known to the offices of the Department of Employment and Productivity in the districts surveyed and also certain retail establishments. The first survey was intended to establish the pre-Bridge situation and the intentions and expectations of firms at the time when the Bridge had just been opened: the data was collected in the autumn and winter of 1966-67. The second survey was then undertaken after two full years of use of the Bridge, the data being collected in 1968—69.

1.46 The two surveys used establishments as the main source of data and as more than one establishment may be owned and controlled by the same organisation the analysis refers to "firms". The "firm" is therefore the operating organisation, not necessarily the owning group.

The term "company" is used in some parts of the survey analysis to distinguish the ultimate owning organisation.

1.47 The two surveys differ in scope however. The 1966-67 survey was carried out in two parts, the first part covering South East Wales and South West North and the second part being extended to include the whole of the South West Economic Planning region, exclusive of Poole. The exclusion of industrial South West Wales, the area of Port Talbot-Swansea-Llanelli, was due to there having been a recent survey of that area. Throughout both stages of the first survey, questionnaires were sent to establishments and the letter accompanying the questionnaire offered interviews as a means of clarifying replies and this was taken up by 10% of the firms approached.

1.48 The second survey departed from the first in three respects. First, the areas surveyed now excluded South West South except for the Wellington-Westbury area of Somerset and Wiltshire but included industrial South West Wales. These changes concentrated study on the areas most likely to be affected. Those areas which are common to the two surveys and, therefore, the main source of comparison of intentions and results are as follows:—

South Wales: Monmouthshire, Newport, Cardiff, that part of Glamorgan bounded by Bridgend, Maesteg, Blaenrhondda and Hirwaun inclusive, and the adjacent industrial districts in Brecknockshire. (Map C, Areas 3 to 8 inclusive).

South West: Bristol, North Somerset, North Wiltshire, and Gloucestershire except for the Forest of Dean which was analysed separately being west of the Severn. (Map C, Areas 1 and 15 to 20 inclusive).

The second departure was the extension of the study to a sample of 25% of manufacturing establishments employing 20—99 persons. The first survey had only gone to manufacturing establishments with 100 or more employees and to distributing establishments employing 20 or more. The third departure was in the design of the questionnaire which excluded some matters not usefully reported in the first survey but now included questions on services of various kinds.

1.49 The second survey was deliberately more extensive than had first been planned because of changes in the intervening years, notably the considerable re-classification of firms from distribution to manufacturing that followed the introduction of Selective Employment Tax. The response rate among manufacturing firms was 73% in both regions; among firms in distribution the response rate was 65%. (See Appendix 1A).

Coach Traffic

1.50 Coach traffic was surveyed by questionnaire sent to all licensed operators in the two regions in 1967 and 1968 supplemented by interviews, by an analysis of company records and by a further questionnaire to the largest operators in April 1970.

REFERENCES

1. L. T. C. Rolt, The Severn Bridge; Rolt also refers to an abortive attempt at a tunnel in 1810.

2. S. B. Rodgers, Samerias or Working Benefit Societies and a magnificent Bridge across the mouth of the River Severn at New Passage in Gloucestershire.

3. Including the damage to game that would be inevitable from the poaching that would be implicit in the bringing together of so many navigators for so large a construction! (Minutes of Proceedings before the Select Committee, p.305).

4. Office of the Minister of Reconstruction, Welsh Reconstruction Advisory Council. First Interim Report 1944.

5. Messrs. Mott, Hay and Anderson were one of the firms of consulting engineers. Here was one link with many earlier schemes as this firm had been associated with all the Severn Bridge Projects back to 1923.

6. Bristol industries were the first to obtain "agreed charges" from the railway companies, as an aid to national distribution at a flat rate and as a consideration for not switching to road transport.

7. See J. N. H. Britton "Regional Analysis and Economic Geography: A case study of Manufacturing in the Bristol Regions", (London) 1967.

8. Severnside — a Feasability Study H.M.S.O. 1971 Pp. 75—76.

9. Chapter 7.

CHAPTER TWO

Possible Economic Effects of Major Transport Improvements

2.1 A large literature exists concerned with the economic effects of highway improvements on communities; the vast majority of these published studies refer to highway improvements in the United States. The effects observed in these studies depend on the precise form that the improvement takes and its precise location, with all that the latter implies about history and socio-economic structure. All such improvements are the same in that they bring certain places closer together; all are different in that these places are different. Some of the economic effects of highway improvements are general, founded on empirical evidence drawn from a wide variety of places, other effects are very specific. What can be inferred about the effects of the opening of the Severn Bridge from these studies depends in part on how similar that improvement is to those previously studied. It is very dissimilar. As has been stated earlier South Wales and the Bristol area are two mature, though very different, industrial areas, with for many years quite good rail communications between them but a very poor road link. One distinctive feature of the Bridge lies in the scale of the improvement in the road link; most published studies are concerned with more modest changes. That the two areas should be important enough to warrant a good rail link (not of course only for trade between them) in the 1880s and despite further, though not continuous, growth over the next 70 years should lack a good road link in the 1950s, is a measure of the novelty of the Severn Bridge.

2.2 The benefits of highway improvements are first expressed as a reduction in the costs, in the widest sense, of movement. These benefits start as benefits to users: the driver able to visit friends more cheaply and conveniently, the manufacturer able to transport goods more cheaply, the salesman able to make more calls in a day, the sightseer able to travel to new areas without extra cost. The benefits are transferred in whole or in part to others in the form of lower (at least lower than they would otherwise have been!) prices, speedier and more reliable service and better facilities made possible by the larger markets that the highway improvements create. The benefits spread through the economy in a multitude of ways as those making choices for themselves or others alter their decisions in response to the lower costs of movement via the new facility.

Background

2.3 The first step in a study of this kind is, therefore, an examination of previous studies of the types of change made possible by so major an improvement in transport. In this way the questions originally selected

for detailed study can be extended or modified. Straight comparisons have proved impossible. While comparable changes have occurred in the past, from the Severn Tunnel to the Forth Road Bridge, only the most recent have attracted even the slightest study of their economic implications. Even among the extensive literature on highway improvements, the scale of the change is invariably far less than in the one now considered. Accordingly it is necessary to seek a wider base for analogous situations, starting with studies of inter-regional trade, themselves an extension of international trade, continuing with studies of the location of industry and of changes in transport and ending with specific studies of highway improvements.

Inter-Regional Trade

2.4 One of the difficulties from the very outset is the sparse treatment of spatial relations — or rather its absence — in many aspects of economic theory, notably that of international trade from which inter-regional studies evolved. The effect of the Severn Bridge is to remove an obstacle to the creation of a single market embracing at least parts of South Wales and the South West of England. The creation of a single market in place of two previously separated markets offers the opportunity for new competition among suppliers. Protection previously accorded by the barrier to transport is removed and new sources of competition are created. Firms that previously did not consider selling in the protected market to be worthwhile now find that the boundaries of their market have been extended. They may now seek new trade in the area opened up. As long as they can match or undercut the prices and services offered by existing suppliers within that market they can expand their operations. The direct cost of transport may not always be so relevant as the time factor. It is argued later that the cost of transport is not usually a major factor in the cost of many manufactured goods; it is rather the cost of transport in a time which permits effective competition that is critical. Firms in both areas may now experience new competition in their "home areas" and this may lead to lower prices and/or better service. This assumes equal knowledge of the markets by all competing firms. If this is not so then the extent of new competition is dependent upon the market knowledge and learning speeds of the competing firms, a factor further discussed in paragraphs 2.24 and 2.44 below.

2.5 To the extent that the two regions are part of a national market served by firms that sell in many, if not all, regions then the changes are in their own distribution arrangements. They may not have served one of the two regions previously. Thus a firm might have served the South West as part of a Southern England market but not regarded South Wales as a worthwhile market to enter. The cost of entry represented by marketing, administrative and distributive costs had hitherto been such as to discourage penetration. The creation of a single market means that these costs can now be shared with the region already served, a form of economy of scale, and it is worthwhile to extend operations. This presupposes that one market is in some way more isolated than the other. The proximity of the South West, at least the Bristol-Gloucester-Wiltshire area, to the South East contrasted with the previously isolated position of South Wales, lends some support to this hypothesis.

2.6 Further discussion on these lines poses several questions. To what extent are the two regions self-contained and what proportion of their trade is with one another and with the rest of the country? If the nature of their production is such that they are each closely linked to the rest of the national economy though not to one another, in what activities are changes likely to occur? The answer would appear to lie in those goods and services which satisfy one or more of four conditions:—

(i) They are produced in each region primarily for local consumption in that region.

(ii) They are products in which speed and frequency of delivery are essential.

(iii) They are consumed nationally, or at least in both regions, and are produced for local and national sale.

(iv) They are produced both in the regions and elsewhere — including abroad — but are distributed by firms serving one or both regions.

2.7 It is now possible to extend this analysis in two ways. The first is essentially a re-definition of the two regions linked by the new facility. Hitherto this has implied only South Wales and the South West. Clearly the new facility sets up opportunities for a similar set of changes involving regions reached through those immediately adjacent to the Bridge, notably the South East. The second extension arises from the increased trade between the two regions. This could result in a diversion of supplies drawn in at the expense of a third region. If the result of the new competition is a switch to a cross-estuary source this may be at the expense of firms in other regions. Bristol firms drawing increasingly on South Wales could mean less trade from Birmingham. Conversely the new sales opportunities across the estuary may lead to a re-definition of sales areas, even to a greater emphasis on the new market than on others. The reorganisation of sales areas, especially by firms marketing nationally, may lead to changes in the opportunities open to their establishments in other parts of the country.

2.8 The hypotheses that emerge so far are as follows:—

(i) A single market is created for some goods and services within which increased competition leads to lower prices and/or improved services to consumers.

(ii) As a result those firms that engage successfully in

the new competition may emerge with increased output for despatch across the estuary linked to improved service and reduced transport costs.

(iii) Ability to engage successfully depends, in part, on knowledge of the new market areas and firms with previous knowledge through existing trade may be expected to exploit the situation more quickly.

(iv) The redistribution of shares of the market is not confined to firms in the linked regions but may extend to suppliers in other regions where sales may fall as a result of diversion of sources of supply.

(v) Reorganisation of sales areas, delivery services and administrative arrangements will follow and may extend to other regions than those immediately linked.

(vi) While these changes are more likely as between the two regions immediately linked they may also occur in the trading relations of any region which has hitherto been relatively isolated from regions to which it now has better access.

2.9 The main discussion of these hypotheses is in Chapters 6 and 7, where evidence is set out on the nature of the changes reported by firms, and in Chapter 9. This is primarily in relation to trade between South Wales and the South West. While fully comparable data has not been derived from firms in the South East — unless present as owners of depots — trade with that region has been examined. For South Wales the Bridge could be influential. For the South West it affords a useful comparison where the Bridge cannot have an effect.

Location of Industry

2.10 One assumption implicit in the argument so far is that while activities at establishments may change in scope and scale there is no change of location, whether by opening of new estblishments or closure of existing ones. This assumption has now to be reconsidered in the light of theories of the location of industry. Two important reservations have to be made at the outset. The first is that changes in location may be slow to appear because of the extent of existing commitments of resources in buildings and plant. The second is that governmental constraints and inducements may restrict and otherwise influence the selection of sites for development.

2.11 Theoretical studies of the location of activities can be examined in three stages. First, there are those studies which seek to provide a general theory of the location of activities. Second, there are those which recognise a typology of activities, each having its own particular features and constraints. Third, there are those that relate distribution and service activities to the idea of an hierarchy of urban centres and their areas of influence.

2.12 The general theories[1] assert that the choice of location is based on minimising factor costs, notably transport costs. This assumes that such costs are significant, particularly on incoming materials. Several studies have challenged this assumption in respect of most manufacturing industries and point to the increased emphasis on the market as an attraction.[2] The pulling power of the large established centre is partly a question of supporting facilities — the infrastructure of services and sub-contracting opportunities — and partly its role as a market. Relating these arguments to this study, the question arises as to whether the savings in transport costs are such as to influence the choice of location, whether in isolation or when taken with other costs as for example if production can now be concentrated in a single existing or new site to serve two regions. Clearly firms serving both regions may now find it cheaper to concentrate production in a single plant or depot. Some closures of depots may follow. Alternatively there may be specialisation of production between plants on either side with centralisation of distribution.

2.13 It is, however, questionable how far this general approach is useful and one alternative is to classify activities thereby identifying those types of business which are now likely to be affected. This approach distinguishes "extractive", "rooted", "linked", "residentiary" "footloose" industries. The "extractive" industries, such as mining and quarrying, are constrained by deposits of the particular material and by transport facilities giving access to markets. In the present study localised markets for quarry products may now be extended and the opportunity is present to benefit from the expanded local market. A second group, the "rooted" industries which process basic materials of high transport cost relative to bulk and value, are similarly placed. This type is well illustrated by the Welsh steel and tinplate plants. The Bridge does not, however, provide new alternatives for such industries and little change is likely here. The third group, "linked" industries, are those which are attracted to a particular location by the presence there of other industries which are their key markets or their sources of materials or users of similar labour and ancillary services. To examine this category some study has to be made of the linkages, particularly market linkages, of industries in the two regions including those between them before the Bridge. The emergence of a single economic region embracing Severnside and South Wales might result in new or strengthened linkages across the Severn. For this reason particular attention has to be given to trading links and the changes in them since 1966. In so far as the two economies are complementary new linkages may be unlikely but the possibility has to be explored.

2.14 There remain the "residentiary" industries and services which have to be provided close to the market represented by population however engaged, and with them the "footloose" industries, those that have no very special reasons for being in a particular place, the choice of which become questions of entrepreneurial preference, even whim, provided there is good communication for both persons and goods to main markets. The effect of the Bridge might be to create a single enlarged market for residentiary industries and services with some concentration in the largest single centre, in this case Bristol. In the absence of any planning controls the Severnside area might be regarded as very attractive to "footloose" industries, given the improved communications offered by the M.4 and M.5 motorways. The Bridge is also significant in that it makes at least the eastern edge of the South Wales industrial area much more accessible and therefore attractive to such industries.

2.15 These benefits via larger markets and reduced and more certain journey times have particular reference to the growing function of servicing complex equipment, such as computers, earth moving equipment, etc. In those cases where the firm using the equipment has insufficient load to justify its own repair staff, it must rely on outside specialists for service. The time of such specialists is costly and anything making possible more effective use of their time is a substantial economy. Still more costly is the idleness of expensive equipment as a result of breakdown and to reduce this idle time is an important saving. The tendency is for the use of such sophisticated equipment to grow and hence benefits in this field will be increasingly important. There is another aspect to the provision of these services. The creation of enlarged markets capable of being served from a single base will improve the supply of such services to a whole area and new specialisms can emerge to meet the needs of the area. By improving the infrastructure of an area in this way, that area becomes a more attractive prospect for industrialists.

2.16 This approach suggests that the Bridge may have much more marked effects on activities where market access is the dominant criterion, notably distribution, services, residentiary industries and those not involving expensive capital installations. It also suggests that a good guide to possible changes is the pre-Bridge trade pattern of each region and the linkages across the estuary before and after the completion of the Bridge. Previous studies have suggested that much of British industry is not tied to particular locations by high transport costs. Furthermore that mobility is more likely among larger firms that are less dependent on local linkages and infrastructure services[3]. Such firms can face more easily the costs of opening up branches and new sites though there is clear evidence from other research now proceeding that only a minority of firms moving have made systematic studies of either the alternative sites before making a selection or the costs of removal and of launching new units. One feature in the present study is that one of the two regions is an area of rapid growth involving a net export of employment while the other is undergoing continued structural change as its traditional industries decline and are replaced by a range of new industries. An important question is whether the Bridge has made this reconstruction easier and, in particular, to what extent the greater ease of personal movement that it permits is likely to increase the attractiveness of South Wales for firms unable to expand in the South West.

2.17 The third approach starts from a study of urban areas and the supposition that there is an hierarchy of functions among the urban areas in a region[4]. This suggests for example, that regional capitals have certain functions of a commercial or administrative nature, that they have particular roles in the distribution of goods, especially those not originating in their regions, and that areas of influence can be postulated, usually on the basis of a gravity model, subject to the physical pattern of available transport facilities. Lesser centres have their functions in an hierarchy of distribution and services, right down to the small market town. Changes in communications bring about opportunities for larger areas to be served from a given centre and for areas of influence to overlap and even coalesce. One feature is the extent to which the centre of a regional distribution system is in fact the physical mid-point of that area. Gravity model analysis suggests that centres have circular distribution areas. Clearly the Severn, if it acted as a barrier, produced a sharp differentiation of such areas for both Bristol and Cardiff. The removal of this obstacle enables both centres to expand their areas of influence but with new competition. One consequence is the emergence of a single catchment area, the ideal central point of which migth be neither city but a site close to the motorway intersection in South Gloucestershire.

2.18 Geography has dictated a further feature, namely the existence of two populated peninsulas — the South West bounded by the sea on both shores and South Wales with the sea on one side and the comparative emptiness of much of rural mid-Wales on the other. In the circumstances, instead of circular catchment areas, one has elliptical areas with the distribution centre towards the focus nearest to the original supply point. Alternatively it is suggested that this is not an accident of regional geography but a feature of distributive systems. The argument is that goods distributed from centres such as London or Birmingham are transported in bulk to a number of distribution centres. These, like the point of origin, act as regional distributors as well as being transfer points in a trunking system. It is suggested, for example, that just as the London centre will distribute to areas between London and close to Bristol, so Bristol establishments will serve most of the area between Bristol and say Exeter or Swansea. The reluctance to back-load is partly responsible for such patterns. The relevance for this approach is that it would lead one to expect that, pre-Bridge Gloucester, as the lowest bridging point on the Severn, Bristol and Cardiff might act as "centres" of such systems, whereas post-Bridge one centre, near to the M.4 and M.5 motorway intersection, would meet the needs of firms previously using two depots, one on each bank. The significance of Cardiff and Gloucester as regional distribution centres would be reduced in the long-term. The reorganisation of distribution areas would also affect the status of depots located at other points in the distribution network such as Swansea and Exeter. This emerging new pattern of distribution networks might be further changed by the completion of the motorway links M.4 to London and M.5 to Birmingham.

2.19 Given these approaches to the location of business it is now possible to put forward some hypotheses for further examination, bearing in mind the delayed reaction where investment has already occurred and the effect of governmental policies:—

(i) Changes in the location of manufacturing industry will be slow to emerge whereas changes in distribution systems such as depot locations may occur sufficiently quickly to fall within the three-year period of the present study.

(ii) The Bridge may be expected to improve the attractiveness of South Wales to industries seeking labour and sites for expansion, especially where distribution is to be direct from factory to consumers.

(iii) The Bridge may have a similar effect where firms in the South West are seeking to expand but are concerned at the need for close formal personal contact as part of managerial control.

(iv) New linkages between the two regions may emerge and existing linkages may be reinforced; similarly, between South Wales and the South East the already

strong linkages may be extended and intensified.

(v) The Bridge may reinforce the attraction of the Bristol-South Gloucestershire area as a centre for regional and sub-regional distribution with side-effects on the distributive centres of Cardiff and of lesser centres in both regions; completion of further motorways may accentuate this.

(vi) New sites away from city centres may emerge as ideal for depots in such a reconstructed distribution network and the area most likely to be favoured is that close to the motorway intersection.

Changes in Demand for Transport

2.20 A further assumption that lies behind the arguments so far advanced is that the gain from the Bridge is a shortening of distance reflected in reduced transport costs and journey times. It is now necessary to qualify this assumption by examining possible changes in the demand for transport following the technical change represented by the Bridge. Once again reservations have to be stated at the outset. The most important is the effect of the transport policies of the government and the railways. Government policy is relevant in respect of hours of work of drivers and similar constraints on vehicle utilisation. Railway policy is relevant in terms of traffic that the railways wish to discard, notably local passenger services and general merchandise in small consignments. Other reservations relate to differences in learning speeds reflected in reactions of individuals and organisations to change.

2.21 The first hypothesis is that the ending of the virtual rail monopoly of short-distance passenger transport coupled to the state of connecting rail and other services would lead to a sharp switch of business travel from rail to road and a sharp increase in business travel. This is reinforced by the arguments already advanced as to new opportunities for trade, new standards of service to customers and close administrative integration within organisations working on both sides of the Severn. Such a change would be expected to be almost entirely to private car traffic and to involve points of origin and destination over a wide area of both regions.

2.22 The second expectation would be a switch from rail to road transport of goods, such as those previously sent as sundries traffic, and that as this would be in line with railway policy there would be little likelihood of there being any rate reduction to try to retain such traffic. One line of enquiry would be a comparison of rail-road switching of traffic across the estuary with that on a route not affected by this technical change, notably South West to South East. Some switch of goods traffic was to be expected in view of other national evidence as to changes in demand for transport by industry and commerce[5]. The dominance of road transport, particularly in those classes of goods where trade and location studies suggest that change is most likely, focusses attention on a second category of change, namely between road hauliers and a firm's own vehicles.

2.23 The change in market areas already discussed brings new territories within the operating area of a firm's depot for its own vehicles. As a result two changes might be expected. The first is a switch from all forms of public carrier to a firm's own vehicles in the enlarged local area. This is all the more likely if the firm has already used its own vehicles for some cross-estuary movements and now has some "surplus" capacity. The second is a redistribution of traffic consigned by own vehicles and by hauliers leading to concentration of a firm's own vehicles on nearer destinations and regular loads. The public carrier is thus left with the longer-distance, less attractive long standing consignments and fluctuating load demand as the firm uses its own vehicles to the full. As with the rail-road switch there is a need to compare cross-estuary and other inter-regional changes.

2.24 The speed and scale of the switch in transport modes reflects the contractual obligations of consignors, the speed with which they appreciate the new possibilities and the relationship of their cross-estuary movements to their total operations. Drivers may react more quickly than planners at company headquarters. Switches in routes may therefore be more rapid not only than those in transport modes but than the firms officially acknowledge. Three questions emerge here. Is it possible to make any valid comment on this question of speed of reaction in relation to where decisions on transport and distribution are made in firms? Thus it might be expected that local managements previously aware — as motorists — of the significance of the Bridge would react more quickly than those at headquarters in some other part of the country. The next question is therefore the reaction of hauliers, especially smaller firms, to the challenge presented by a sudden shortening of journeys. This implies short-term excess capacity until new business is obtained. The rate reduction implicit in a mileage based tariff might therefore be supplemented by concessions in the search for new business. The last of the three questions concerns the reaction of drivers to the new routes. In particular one must ask to what extent has there been a switch-over on routes where the Bridge offers no obvious advantage in distance or time.

2.25 The hypotheses as regards demands in the transport industry can therefore be summarised as follows:—

(i)   A limited switch from rail to road ending an anomalous pattern of transport use and being most marked in short-distance passenger and sundries traffic between the two regions.

(ii)   A subsequent increase in the volume of road traffic as more journeys are made both on business and privately, mainly by private car.

(iii)   A switch of traffic from road hauliers to vehicles operated by manufacturers and traders as they make greater use of their own vehicles in the two regions.

(iv)   A two-stage adjustment, private car and distributive trade movements being affected first with manufacturing firms adjusting more slowly.

(v)   A reduction in road haulage rates with the shortening of journeys and a consequent competitive reduction in some rail rates.

These are discussed in later chapters.

Highway Improvement Studies

2.26 Highway improvement studies, while mainly concerned with more modest improvements, are nevertheless of especial interest in respect of more localised effects, notably on land use in and near the new motorways. They also throw some light on the possible effects

of motorways and traffic congestion on the precise location of activities in urban areas as opposed to the regional distribution of activities discussed under location of industry above.

2.27 One of the best documented effects of highway improvements is the effect on land values. Land which is in a favoured position to take advantage for any purpose of the reduced cost of movement will tend to rise in price. This may be because that land can now be used for new and more highly valued purposes, such as becoming a factory or housing site where it was formerly used for farming. The use may be unchanged but the land more profitably used for its existing purpose because a factory or shopping centre has become accessible to a wider market. The rise in price is a capitalisation of the reduced cost of journeys to and from that land over future years. The effect of improvements on land values is most clearly seen where the benefits are specific to a small area. In the context of the Bridge there is no such small area; the greater ease of movement affects a very large area, though some areas are particularly favoured.

2.28 The extent to which advantage is taken of these favours depends upon a variety of factors not least planning controls and other laws. The area to the north west of Bristol, near the junction of the London-South Wales and Birmingham-South West motorways, is such a highly favoured area, very advantageous for manufacturing where easy access to a variety of markets is particularly important or the assembly of components from a variety of origins or for warehousing or indeed large shopping facilities. Such developments may be inhibited by planning controls, but such controls will certainly be more difficult to maintain in the face of the commercial pressures that the Bridge and the associated motorways have created. Again the land to the west of the Bridge is favoured; while its improved accessibility is of advantage in its present use, mainly farming that accessibility also creates possibilities of industrial development.

2.29 As road transport becomes more efficient, reliable and economical so the importance of highway access for both firms and households increases. Since motorways constitute a considerable improvement in road transport, they stimulate industrial development and there are many studies of this aspect of improvements. The Boston circumferential highway — Route U.S. 128 — is a spectacular example. This highway skirts Boston at a distance of 10—15 miles from the centre and has stimulated rapid industrial development in a series of towns along the route as new firms have started or existing firms have moved from the city centre.

2.30 Many factors contribute to this stimulus to development. First there is the availability of land both for first development and later expansion and land that is cheap compared with city sites. Single-storey buildings can be more easily adapted as production requirements change and they also make it easier to take advantage of mechanical handling equipment, the fork lift trucks, etc. But single-storey buildings mean more land per unit of output. Higher standards of work amenities (whether as a result of legal requirements, trade union pressure or as a means to increased productivity), canteens, car parks and a variety of recreational facilities again mean more land per unit of output. Future growth in car ownership will come, to a disproportionate extent, from an increase in car ownership among manual workers and they will use them to travel to work and this means parking space. Larger lorries require more space for manoeuvring. The pollution created by some factories forces other factories onto larger sites as a defence against that pollution. One of the attractions of out of town shopping areas, restaurants and public houses is precisely that they are not on constricted sites and can provide car parking facilities.

2.31 The growth of road transport and the congestion that results in urban centres reduces the advantages of those urban centres for manufacturers. All their incoming and outgoing loads must suffer the increased costs that congestion creates. A move to an out of town location relieves all loads of these costs at least as far as the immediate factory area is concerned. Wider markets can thus be tapped as sources of supply or as sales centres for given time levels.

2.32 The ability to serve, or to be served by, a wider area leads not only to savings in transport costs; storage space required and stocks carried can be reduced for given output or sales. Also important is the greater reliability in the movement of goods and particularly of people. A person travelling from one point to another along an improved route may gain not only from the reduced time the journey takes but also from reduced precautionary time. Instead of having to depart say half an hour early in case traffic conditions are more than usually congested, the journey time can be assessed with greater accuracy and reliability and some of the half hour precautionary time saved; the same point may be reflected in making appointments more freely at all times of the day required, instead of restricting the choice of appointment time to rigorously avoid peak hours.

2.33 Reference has already been made to the increase in the ownership of cars by employees and this has important consequences for the firm in relation to its labour market. The easily accessible firm can draw on a wider area for its supply of labour as commuting distance is increased. This is not only a benefit to the firm; it applies to both parties of the labour market, with the worker having a wider selection of jobs for a given sacrifice of time spent in travelling to work.

2.34 What of those areas whose advantages as business sites are diminished to some extent as a result of highway improvements? There are two types of area in this category; first urban industrial and business sites, including city centres and second, areas by-passed by an improvement. As far as the first category is concerned, while their position as industrial sites becomes less favourable to at least some potential users, as providers of shopping, and especially business, services their net position may well be improved. American experience shows a shift in the activity of city centres away from shopping and into office activity, providing co-ordinating and other service functions to business, where face to face contact is very important. In Britain the creation of out of town shopping centres has scarcely started so that

for a long period the Bridge is likely to bring a net gain, as far as shopping is concerned, to the city centres.

2.35 It could be postulated that the building of the motorway would stimulate the long-standing tendency towards concentration of shopping, especially for such items as consumer durables and clothing, in the large city centres. Such concentration would reinforce the gains city centres have long been making at the expense of smaller urban areas; these gains are basically a result of the consumer's view that he will get the best choice at a centre supported by a large market. One question is, however, the extent to which shopping centre patterns in the study area are typical. Another is for how much longer will this contrast of American and British experience persist.

2.36 The disadvantages of industrial sites deep in urban areas are again reinforced by highway improvements such as the motorways, but the movement of industry away from down-town areas is already in being. The development of industry on the fringes of Bristol to the east was in being before the motorways were built. But again the process will be slow despite the added attraction that the motorway gives to development away from city centres. Inertia and the felt need to depreciate existing investment in works and buildings mean a slow rate of change. In so far as new industrial development outside cities reduces the demand for city sites and thus their price, the rate of change is slowed because the price realised by vacating a city site is one of the factors in the decision to relocate. The price level in this situation is itself dependent upon land-use planning and the terms of property leasing.

2.37 By-passes are frequently seen as a threat to the prosperity of small towns, especially to their retail trade, but this threat is usually, on American evidence, ill-founded. The decongestion of the streets as a result of removing through traffic is a clear gain to the pedestrian and local motor vehicle traffic in easier movement as well as reducing accidents, noise and pollution. Even for retailers there are gains; decongestion makes the town more attractive for shopping generally and as many vehicles may be drawn in from the by-pass as formerly stopped on the way through for shopping. In the United States 90 by-pass studies for a variety of sizes of town in 22 states show "almost invariably that business activity was either benefited or generally unaffected by the traffic relief route".[6] While the general picture was favourable or neutral, particular types of business were likely to suffer decreases in trade, particularly cafes and service stations.

2.38 For households, the greater freedom of movement that highway improvements bring expresses itself in a freer choice of residence and an increased use of motor cars for leisure purposes. Certainly much of the traffic using the Bridge is for leisure purposes. These benefits are incapable of precise valuation, but it is not irrelevant to refer to the long-standing, if slow, reduction in hours of work that has accompanied rising standards of material wealth: this trend is unlikely to be reversed and anything that reduces the costs to people of using that increased leisure in ways of their choice represents a clear gain. On present evidence sightseeing, holiday and visiting trips are three important ways in which people are choosing to spend their leisure time. These traffics bring trade benefits to certain favoured areas, the Wye Valley being one such area in the case of the Severn Bridge. As in the case of industry, potential expansion has implications for other aspects of life. Development of amenities for sightseers and holidaymakers may be as destructive of the environment as factory development. Highway improvements create pressures for these developments; how far the community yields to these pressures is yet to be seen.

2.39 From previous highway improvement studies the following further hypotheses emerge in addition to those already listed in paragraphs 2.19 and 2.25:—

(i)   Traffic will be diverted to the new route from others using the same transport mode, in this case the route through Gloucester, and also from other modes as discussed in paragraph 2.25 (i).

(ii)   New traffic will be generated; first along the route now improved, second by the facility itself (people travelling to see the Bridge) and third on routes from which traffic pressure has been reduced by the new facility (mainly local movements previously deterred by traffic congestion).

(iii)   The general lowering of costs through lower prices and/or vehicle operating costs will be supplemented by other savings, for goods through reduced inventories and for personal movements through the greater reliability of the new medium with its consequent cut in precautionary times on trips.

(iv)   Land values will rise in areas now favoured for development given the new facility provided physical controls on land use permit such changes in the areas concerned.

These are discussed in later chapters. The effects on users are dealt with in Chapters 3 to 7 inclusive and an attempt at quantifying the benefits forms the basis of Chapter 8. As indicated later in this chapter it has not been possible to study the changes in land values.

Organisation Studies

2.40   The outcome of the presence of the Bridge depends on the decisions of thousands of individuals. The physical planning and regional policy choices are largely matters for planning authorities and government. Yet even here the issues that have to be faced depend upon the decisions and desires of others, notably those who have responsibilities for the location of business activities of all kinds. One point of interest is therefore the way in which modern organisations as opposed to private individuals might be expected to react; hence the relevance of organisational studies.

2.41   Much of the argument has touched on the question of the behaviour of individuals and organisations, particularly in respect of how they learn about and react to changes in the environment. Modern institutions, whether in business or public service, display somewhat different features when compared to individuals, particularly the entrepreneurs of economic theory. They have institutional policies, arrived at by political processes often of considerable complexity and characterised by criteria for decision-takers within the institution that may be based on much wider objectives than profit

maximisation. Such objectives are often shared with the small business man such as the desire for a quiet life in surroundings that are satisfying to those concerned, or are concerned with longer-term changes in their situation. These have several implications for the present study.

2.42   The first is the extent to which the routine procedures adopted, notably by larger organisations, feed information to those who formulate policy, the speed with which they do so and the way in which the organisation can react. This is partly a question of how organisations learn and partly a matter of the range of alternatives that the policy decision-takers elect to consider. Thus many individuals ruled out any effect on their activities because of the Bridge and the motorways. They were therefore surprised at the outcome and now appear to have a different view of the potential of the next phase of motorway completions. But many still rule out the possibilities of changes, partly through inertia and partly through a desire to be left alone. The complaints as to new competition fall close to this category. One further point here is whether local firms have reacted more quickly than those which are based elsewhere.

2.43   The second is the extent to which reorganisation has followed the change. This would take several forms. There is the clear case of internal reorganisation — changing the functions of particular offices or depots, changing activities or combining departments. There is the external reorganisation in terms of relationships with other firms, notably in distribution. One outcome could be an additional impetus to mergers and take-overs as a means of gaining access to markets across the estuary and/or rationalising activities. Another could be the abandonment of intermediaries by the provision of a direct service to customers.

2.44   Studies of organisational behaviour therefore suggest further hypotheses:—

(i)   The extent to which firms and individuals will react to the change depends on their perception of how the change is likely to affect them, and therefore in the way in which they learn about the changing environment.

(ii)   The expectations of the value of future motorway completions will be different once firms have experience of the Bridge and its associated motorways.

(iii)   Internal reorganisation will occur with regrouping of functions and relocation of offices and depots.

(iv)   External reorganisation will follow as intermediaries are absorbed or by-passed.

(v)   Expansion across the estuary will involve mergers to gain access to markets not previously served.

Hypotheses Reconsidered

2.45   The number of hypotheses and the variety would make the project virtually unmanageable if all were to be pursued concurrently. A selection has therefore had to be made. In part this has been dictated by the availability of data. Thus all studies of land values have had to be dropped through sheer impossibility of obtaining information of any reliability. To avoid further delay in processing the data collected, some aspects have been deferred for subsequent analysis, notably that on internal organisation of firms and its relation to the nature and timing of changes. In other cases the field study conducted in 1965—66 had indicated that no change was likely and no evidence has subsequently emerged to change this view. Thus labour mobility, in particular the recruitment of labour by firms on one side from across the estuary, has not been examined in detail as the evidence suggests only modest change.[7]

2.46 The study therefore concentrates on the traffic surveys, the changes in industry, distribution and transport, a survey of householders in selected areas. The main results are set out in Chapters 3 to 7. An attempt is then made to quantify the benefits conferred in Chapter 8 and the conclusions are brought together in Chapter 9 along with the same tentative projections as to the future of the Bridge and the regions it links.

REFERENCES

1.   For a full review see H. W. Richardson "Regional Economics" Weidenfeld & Nicholson, London, 1969, especially Chapters 2—5.

2.   The first such challenge came in S. R. Dennison, Location of Industry and the Special Areas, Oxford 1938. A more recent study is that of S. L. Edwards, "Transport Cost in British Industry". Journal of Transport Economics and Policy September 1970.

3.   G. C. Cameron & R. D. Clark Industrial Movement and the Regional Problem. University of Glasgow. Social and Economic Studies. Occasional Papers No. 5 1966

4.   H. W. Richardson "Regional Economics" Weidenfeld & Nicholson, London, 1969 — Chapter 6.

5.   Industrial Demand for Transport. B. P. Bayliss and S. L. Edwards, H.M.S.O. 1970.

6.   Highways and Economic and Social Changes. U.S. Department of Commerce: Bureau of Public Roads 1964, Pp. 89.

7.   See Chapter 6 Paras. 6.24 to 6.27.

CHAPTER THREE

Volume and Composition of Severn Bridge Traffic

3.1 This chapter considers the way in which traffic using the Severn Bridge has grown over the period from its opening to the end of 1970 and the changes in the composition of that traffic. Some comparisons are made between Bridge traffic and traffic nationally.[1]

3.2 The Severn Bridge opened for normal use on 9th September, 1966. Something of the impact of this new facility can be seen by comparing the extent of movements by road between Bristol and South Wales before and after that opening. A weekday survey in August 1966 showed 1,135 light vehicles moving between those two places; a year later such traffic had grown by nearly five times the 1966 figure to 5,565. During the first year the Bridge was open 5.77 million vehicles crossed increasing by 8.7% in the second year to 6.27 million vehicles with further increases of 6.8% in the third year to 6.67 million vehicles and of 6.6% in the fourth year to 7.13 million vehicles. On a calendar year basis a comparison is possible with the national picture. Bridge traffic increased by 10.9% in 1968 compared with 1967, while the increase for the same period in vehicle miles travelled on rural trunk and classified roads was 8.6%. The Road Research Laboratory reported an increase of 14% in traffic on motorways for their 11 recording sites in operation in both 1967 and 1968. The motorway network expanded substantially in 1967

(from 444 miles to 546 miles) and some account must be taken of the time it takes people to become aware of the possibilities of alternative routes made possible by new motorways. The influence of this 'learning effect' would be more in evidence elsewhere than at the Bridge, which reduced distances on most journeys by so large an amount that most of the traffic immediately switched to using it. Further, the 1967 Bridge traffic was inflated by sightseers in a way not typical of motorways generally. Comparing 1969 with 1968, Bridge traffic increased by 5.6% and that on rural roads nationally by 2.0%: there was a further increase in 1970 in Bridge traffic of 7.1% compared with 1969.

3.3 Table 3.1 shows the total number of motor cycles, motor cars and vans, buses and heavy goods vehicles (goods vehicles which are over 30 cwts. unladen weight) using the Bridge and gives some comparative data for Great Britain. More detailed information on a monthly basis is given in Appendix 2. Motor cycles are the smallest of these components of total traffic and they show a decline with the passage of time. Given the growth of total traffic, the relative importance of motor cycles shows a sharper decline. The declining importance of motor cycles is found also in the national figures, though the decline between 1967 and 1968 is more marked in the Bridge data than in the national figures.

TABLE 3.1 Traffic crossing the Severn Bridge

Thousands/Percentages

	Motor Cycles	Cars and Vans	Lorries	Buses	Total
1966 (9th Sept.–31st Dec.)					1,551.3
1967 Calendar Year	31.8	4,701.9	996.8	90.3	5,820.8
1968 Calendar Year	26.2	5,099.9	1,245.4	81.5	6,453.0
1969 Calendar Year	24.4	5,337.0	1,384.5	70.0	6,815.9
1970 Calendar Year	22.4	5,662.4	1,551.2	70.4	7,306.4
1968 as percentage of 1967					
(i) Crossing Bridge	82.4	108.5	124.9	90.3	110.9
(ii) Vehicle miles nationally on rural trunk and classified roads	93.7	109.4	106.0	106.3	108.6
1969 as percentage of 1968					
(i) Crossing Bridge	93.1	104.6	111.2	85.9	105.6
(ii) Vehicle miles nationally on rural trunk and classified roads	88.9	102.5	100.0	101.1	102.0
1970 as percentage of 1969					
(i) Crossing Bridge	91.8	106.1	111.7	100.7	107.1

3.4   Turning to bus and coach traffic, while 1968 showed an increase over 1967 nationally, there was a decrease in the number of buses using the Bridge. In part this contrast was the result of the very heavy bus traffic at the Bridge in the summer of 1967 on sightseeing trips. This was the first summer in which the Bridge was open and the Bridge itself proved to be a very popular sight to see. By the summer of 1968 at least some of the novelty had worn off. Taking an average of 25 persons per bus, then roughly 2¼ million people crossed by bus in 1967, 2 million in 1968, 1¾ million in 1969 and the same number in 1970.

3.5   Cars and vans are the largest component of total traffic and Bridge traffic in this category grew at almost the same rate as the national figures between 1967 and 1968; increases of 8.5% and 9.4% respectively. Given that it seems reasonable to assume that it takes time for people to get to know the possibilities created by the opening of new alternative routes and to exploit those possibilities, a higher increase for light vehicle traffic at the Bridge than nationally might reasonably be expected. For much of the traffic the new route opened by the Bridge was so clearly superior to the alternatives that the learning period was much reduced. However, the opening of extensions to the motorway from the Bridge east-wards to Tormarton (December 1966) and westwards from Chepstow to Newport (March 1967) served to increase the 1967 traffic as did the attraction of the Bridge as a focus for sightseers in the summer of 1967. Also the increase in car and van registrations for the area near the Bridge, (Glamorgan, Gloucestershire, Mon-mouthshire and Somerset) was a little smaller in 1968 (compared with 1967) than nationally (4.3% against 5.0%). In contrast, for the remaining category, lorries, Bridge traffic grew much faster over the period 1967 to 1968 than national traffic; an increase of 24.9% compared with 6.0% nationally.

3.6   In 1969 the numbers of motor cycles and buses crossing the Bridge showed a further decline, with buses declining the faster of the two, a contrast with 1968. The modest recovery in buses nationally was not reflected at the Bridge. Cars and vans at the Bridge increased by 4.6% (1969 over 1968), a sharper increase than nationally. For lorries there was no increase nationally, but lorry traffic at the Bridge was still rising quite strongly, by 11.2% in 1969. The result of this pattern of growth has been to increase the relative

importance of lorries though this process still has some way to go before lorries become as important a compo-nent of Bridge traffic as they are of motorways nationally (see Table 3.3). In 1970 the small motor cycle traffic continued to decline whereas the previously declining bus traffic stabilised at the 1969 level. Cars and light vans showed a further increase of 6.1% compared with 1969. Lorries showed the strongest growth again in 1970 with a further rise of 11.7% compared with the previous year.

3.7   Table 3.2 considers the pattern of change in light and heavy vehicles in more detail, comparing the monthly total in each category in 1968, 1969 and 1970 with the same month in the previous year. Certain months are combined to minimise the effects of changes in public holidays. For lorries the decline in the rate of increase sets in very sharply after the early months of 1968. Those months had seen spectacular increases in lorry traffic. Clearly it is easier for persons to respond to the improvement in travel facilities than for the road haulier: finding new business is more difficult than it is for a family to decide to spend Saturday or Sunday on a visit to Bristol Zoo or the Wye Valley. The rapid growth of lorry traffic early in 1968 affects the 1969 figures, resulting in more modest percentage increases in early 1969 and hence a more even rate of growth through 1969. With cars and vans the fall in facility created sightseeing, traffic in 1968 is well marked; July 1968 traffic was only 98% of the 1967 figure. The rates of increase are more even for 1969 than 1968 and this relatively even growth from month to month is con-tinued in 1970 especially for lorries.

Seasonal and daily variations

3.8   Figure 3 (i) shows the seasonal variation in 1968 of traffic at the Bridge compared with the mileage travel-led nationally on rural trunk and classified roads and a seasonal index of all motorway travel. A direct motor-way comparison is inhibited by the changing mileage of motorway open, so that the index is based on the average number of miles travelled each month per mile of motorway open. The variation from low point to high point is much greater at the Bridge than on rural roads nationally and still greater than on motorways. The peak month at the Bridge has 2.3 times the traffic of the lowest month, this compares with 1.7 times for rural roads and 1.6 times for motorways. The seasonal pattern for cars, buses and motor cycles at the Bridge shows the

TABLE 3.2	Comparison of monthly traffic crossing the Severn Bridge, 1967–1970					
	1968 as % of 1967		1969 as % of 1968		1970 as % of 1969	
	Cars and Vans	Lorries	Cars and Vans	Lorries	Cars and Vans	Lorries
January	114	159	115	120	104	99
February	115	159	90	104	124	112
March & April	111	140	102	107	103	116
May & June	107	118	107	113	107	110
July	98	128	108	102	106	122
August & September	107	113	103	114	104	108
October	107	134	112	110	104	111
November	119	104	105	117	109	111
December	119	117	104	112	107	123

same movement; a strong upwards swing from the beginning of the year to a well-marked peak then a decline to winter levels again. For cars, the 1967 summer peak was more than three times the level of the winter trough and for buses over six times that level. For heavy goods vehicles, the monthly changes are less regular and the movement is within much narrower limits. In 1968 the low point (February) had, despite the shortness of that month, 84% of the vehicles in the peak month (October). This stability of goods traffic and volatility of other categories means that there are substantial changes over the year in the make-up of the traffic total. Thus, in 1968, cars and vans were 71% of total traffic in January and 85% in August. In 1968 goods vehicles accounted for 19.3% of total Bridge traffic compared with 12.6% of total mileage travelled on rural roads nationally. Full details of monthly traffic, by class, are given in Appendix 2.

3.9 The range of seasonal variation at the Bridge was somewhat reduced in 1968 compared with 1967, a feature that extended into 1969. For the four years 1967 to 1970 total traffic for January each year was 289,000; 358,000; 412,000 and 428,000. The corresponding figures for August were 779,000; 806,000; 832,000 and 892,000. The rapid growth of the fairly stable goods traffic is one element contributing to the reduced seasonal variation. A second factor is facility created traffic, that is journeys where the main purpose is to see the Bridge. This was referred to above in relation to bus traffic but it is important also in connection with cars. Thus the 1967 summer peak is lifted by the high level of facility created traffic, which does not apply as strongly in later years as the novelty effect of the existence of the Bridge wears off. This tendency for the seasonal variation to fall is helpful in administrative terms, since an even load of toll collections over time is easier to deal with. The importance of leisure traffic — sightseeing, holidays etc. — to the Bridge is brought out in the seasonal figures by the way in which a change in the date of Easter, from March in 1967 to April in 1968, affects the pattern, producing a spring sub-peak in March 1967 and April 1968. The shift of the Whitsun holiday from May to June also has a sharp effect on the monthly pattern.

3.10 The discussion above takes no account of the fact that total traffic in any month will in part depend on the precise composition of the month in terms of working days and weekends. The extent to which traffic varies from weekday to weekend and seasonal influence on this variation are shown in Figures 3 (ii) and (iii) and (iv). These figures are based on an analysis of the first week in each month that is unaffected by public holidays. Weekend traffic is subject to wider seasonal variation than weekday traffic so that weekend traffic, as a percentage of the total at the Bridge, rises from 22% in January to 37% at the August peak (an even flow of traffic over the week would give 29% of total traffic on Saturday and Sunday). The fluctuation nationally in the mileage travelled on rural trunk roads is less marked.[2] The percentage of total traffic at weekends is higher at the Bridge than nationally for eight of the twelve months, lower for two (January and February) and nearly the same for the remaining two (September and October). The importance of leisure traffic at the

Bridge is clear even before individual travel purposes are investigated. The difference between national and Bridge weekend traffic is an amalgam of two elements. Through June, July and August it is high Saturday totals that elevate total weekend Bridge traffic — an effect of holiday journeys. For the spring it is high Sunday figures that raise the Bridge total — the result of sightseeing and visiting journeys.

3.11 In 1967 a higher proportion of total Bridge traffic crossed at the weekend than in 1968. This flattening of the daily variation, similar to the seasonal variation, is further in evidence in 1969. In January 1967, 33.1% crossed at the weekend compared with 22.6% in 1968, 19.7% in 1969 and 24.6% in 1970. The respective June figures were 38.3% in 1967, 36.3% in 1968, 34.6% in 1969 and 32.6% in 1970. Since there is very little goods traffic at weekends the decline in facility created trips must contribute part of the explanation. Another factor is likely to be the better information resulting from experience about traffic delays and congestion. Of the Monday to Friday traffic, more crosses on Friday than on any other day, with Monday usually taking second place. This Monday and Friday effect consists of weekenders coming and going on visits to friends or to their homes if they are working away from home.

3.12 Some comparisons can be made between the composition of Severn Bridge traffic and that using motorways nationally in February and August 1968 on both weekdays (Monday and Friday) and at the weekend.[3] Regarding the major components of traffic, cars and vans and lorries on all days in both months, there was a higher proportion of cars and vans and a lower proportion of lorries at the Bridge than were using motorways nationally (as measured by the number of miles travelled on motorways by each type of vehicle). The 'excess' of cars was at its highest for August weekdays — for Mondays 80% of Bridge traffic were cars and vans compared with 74% nationally. Bridge traffic showed a higher proportion of motor cycles on all days (though these were never more than 0.8% of total traffic); the difference between the Bridge and the national motorway percentage was lower in August than in February. The proportion of buses was also higher at the Bridge in February, particularly on weekdays (0.7% at the Bridge and 0.4% nationally). The reverse was true in August when buses formed a slightly higher percentage of national motorway traffic than at the Bridge on all days. Table 3.3 gives the composition by vehicle class

TABLE 3.3   Composition of National Motorway and Severn Bridge Traffic, 1968

Average Week*	Motor Cycles	Cars and Vans	Lorries	Buses
February				
Motorways	0.2	71.5	27.8	0.5
Severn Bridge	0.3	75.7	23.2	0.8
August				
Motorways	0.4	81.1	17.2	1.3
Severn Bridge	0.6	86.1	12.2	1.2

* An average week taken as
2.5 x (Mon. + Fri.) + Sat. + Sun.

of national motorway and Severn Bridge traffic for average weeks in February and August 1968.

Traffic flows between areas

3.13 To amplify the overall view of traffic at the Bridge in the first three years, Tables 3.4 and 3.5 are included. They give estimates of the total flow of traffic between areas[4] for the year 1968 and the resulting pattern is discussed in detail in subsequent chapters. These tables show, in general, the expected pattern of an increase in the flow of traffic between areas as the distance from the Bridge of the areas considered decreases, with due allowance for the population of the areas concerned. Nearly half of the cars and vans were on journeys that had the Bristol area as either the origin or the destination. Similarly just over a quarter of journeys had the Cardiff area as one trip-end. When heavy goods vehicles are considered, the Bristol area is a little less important and the Cardiff area a little more important. Taking an area near the Bridge — Gloucestershire (including Bristol), Cardiff, Monmouthshire (including Newport) and Somerset — 47% of all light vehicle journeys, which involved crossing the Bridge, were between points in that area. When heavy goods vehicles are considered the dominance of the area close to the Bridge is somewhat reduced. Journeys wholly within that area were 38% of all journeys.

TABLE 3.4 Traffic Flows Between Areas* — Cars and Vans, 1968

Thousands

	Newport	Rest Mon.	West Glos.	Cardiff	Rest Glam.	Hereford & Brecon	Swansea	West Wales	Rest of Great Britain	TOTAL
Bristol & District	386	604	189	613	240	118	132	60	84	2,426
East Gloucestershire	25	37	15	65	22	14	13	5	6	202
Somerset	106	159	32	161	78	47	38	27	88	736
Wiltshire	39	45	6	63	52	17	27	17	9	275
Devon & Cornwall	22	36	17	48	40	29	31	15	80	318
Central Southern England	40	62	10	85	72	15	35	35	15	369
London & Outer London	67	62	7	189	100	11	49	41	9	535
South East Coast	20	18	1	39	32	4	18	11	6	149
Rest of Great Britain	13	10	3	30	18	2	8	3	2	89
TOTAL	718	1,033	280	1,293	654	257	351	214	299	5,099

* See Map B at end of this report

TABLE 3.5 Traffic Flows Between Areas* — Heavy Goods Vehicles, 1968

Thousands

	Newport	Rest Mon.	West Glos.	Cardiff	Rest Glam.	Hereford & Brecon	Swansea	West Wales	Rest of Great Britain	TOTAL
Bristol & District	93	74	20	160	58	27	39	30	5	506
East Gloucestershire	19	8	1	22	11	–	10	4	–	75
Somerset	17	18	3	41	13	4	5	4	1	106
Wiltshire	29	11	1	31	17	1	24	3	–	117
Devon & Cornwall	19	11	5	6	7	–	7	–	1	56
Central Southern England	40	4	2	36	18	1	9	4	–	114
London & Outer London	52	9	2	59	39	2	35	3	–	201
South East Coast	5	6	–	11	4	–	1	3	–	30
Rest of Great Britain	17	1	–	10	4	–	5	1	–	38
TOTAL	291	142	34	376	171	35	135	52	7	1,243

REFERENCES

1. National comparative figures are drawn from "Highway Statistics", Ministry of Transport and the annual 50 Point Census Results of the Road Research Laboratory.

2. Data for vehicle miles on rural trunk roads from J. B. Dunn and P. Sheppard, Road Research Laboratory Report, No. L.R.222 (1968).

3. The distribution of traffic in Great Britain through the 24 hours of the day in 1968. J. B. Dunn and I. J. Hutchings, Road Research Laboratory Report, No. L.R.295 (1970).

4. See Map B at the end of this report.

SEASONAL VARIATION

Bridge, Motorway, Rural Trunk and Classified Roads

(Each month as a percentage of average monthly traffic)

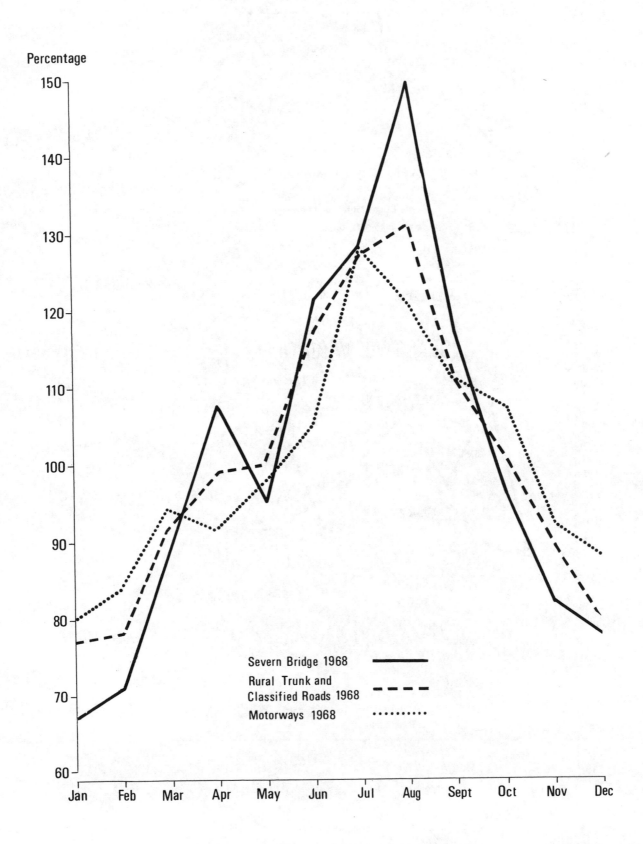

Severn Bridge 1968 ——————

Rural Trunk and
Classified Roads 1968 ------

Motorways 1968 ·············

SEASONAL VARIATION

Percentage
Average Saturday Traffic as Percentage of Average Weekly Traffic

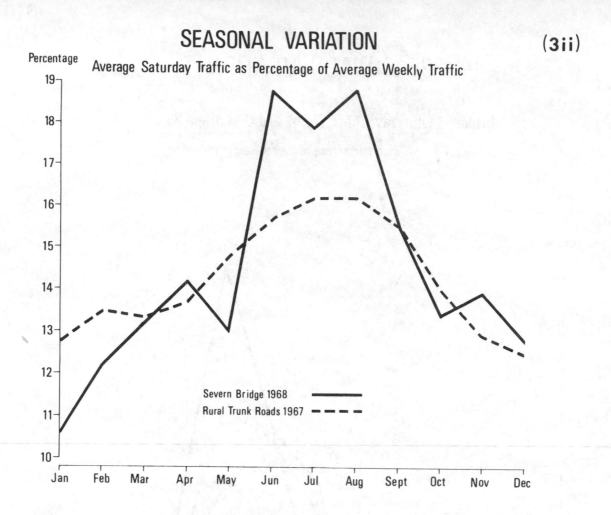

Severn Bridge 1968
Rural Trunk Roads 1967

SEASONAL VARIATION

Percentage
Average Sunday Traffic as Percentage of Average Weekly Traffic

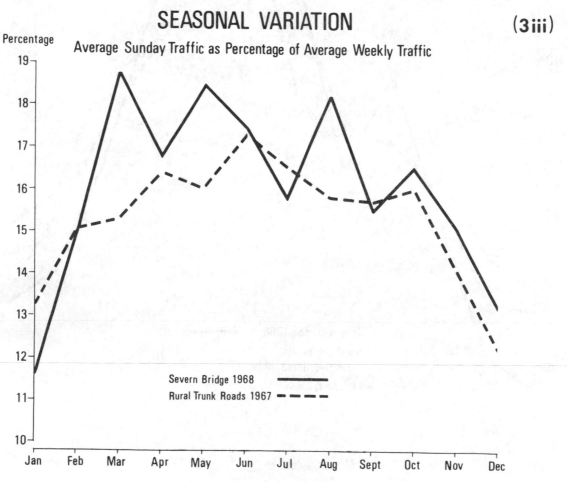

Severn Bridge 1968
Rural Trunk Roads 1967

SEASONAL VARIATION

Average Monday to Friday Traffic as Percentage of Average Weekly Traffic

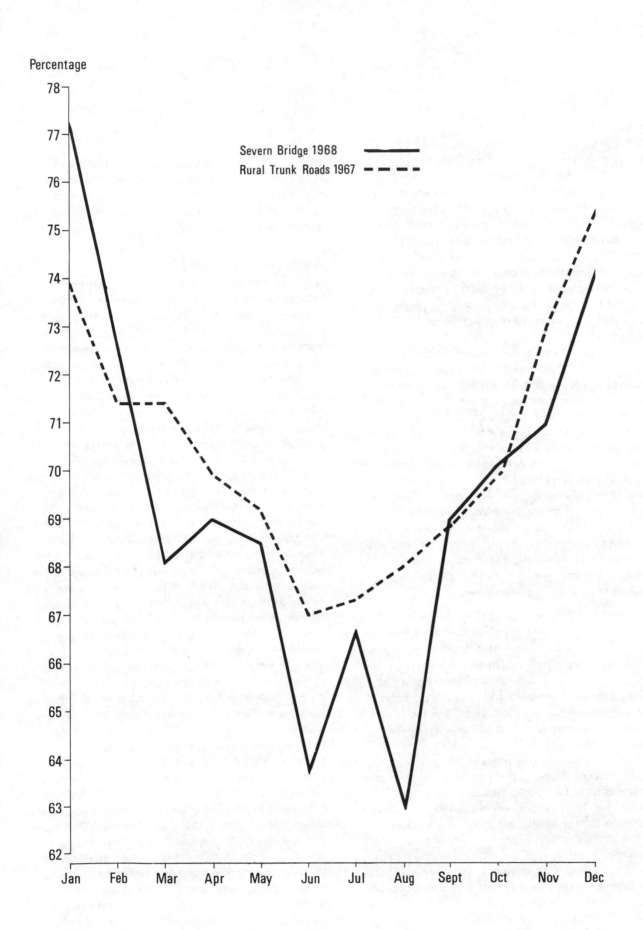

CHAPTER FOUR

The Bridge and Personal Travel

4.1 This chapter is concerned with the use people made of the Bridge for personal travel for a variety of purposes. It may be seen as an attempt to answer a series of questions about these journeys. What was their purpose? Between what points were they made? Would these journeys have been made by other routes or other means if the Bridge had not been built? What number and sort of people were crossing the Bridge and how frequently? How much money did they spend on their journeys? How far do the answers to these questions change with the passage of time and the change of seasons?

4.2 If these fairly general questions can be answered they give rise to a further set of more specific questions which cut across the first set. An example of this second set would be, how many of those travelling between, say, Bristol and Cardiff engaged on their firm's business would have made the journey if the Bridge had not been built? As the questions become more specific in time, space and purpose, their number multiplies. However, if enough of them were listed and answered, then in the course of this proceeding, answers would implicitly be given to the more general questions. The method adopted here is to consider explicitly the general questions listed above and, as the picture expands, to give at least some cross sectional detail. Further tabulations in Appendices throw light on some of the detailed questions not specifically considered here.

The nature of the data

4.3 The data used here is derived from three main sources. First, a series of sample surveys of light vehicles crossing the Bridge; second, a home interview enquiry with residents on both sides of the Severn Estuary at varying distances from the Bridge; and third, surveys of the operations of bus and coach firms. The traffic survey questions were answered by the driver although the driver was not usually the only occupant of the vehicle. Most of the discussion is in terms of the driver's (or the vehicle's) journey. Where estimates are given concerning all occupants of the vehicle it is assumed that the answers given by the driver applied also to the passengers. Some further details on business travel were obtained from the surveys of manufacturing and distributing firms.

4.4 The series of traffic surveys had the dual purpose of providing the basis for an estimate of certain characteristics of the annual flow of traffic and of giving some picture of daily and seasonal variations in these characteristics and of the growth of various sorts of journeys over time. For this second purpose the sample surveys have been grossed up to give daily or weekly flows as appropriate to the point under discussion; where a day is the unit, it represents vehicles crossing the Bridge between 6 a.m. and 10 p.m.

Journey Purposes

4.5 Information was collected on the purpose for which journeys were being made under the following categories — firm's business, where the journey was made in the course of work in the firm's time and at the firm's expense; collection and delivery of goods (usually in light vans); service and maintenance of plant, equipment etc; travel to and from work in the employee's time; shopping; holidays; visiting friends and relations; trips to places of entertainment where an admission charge is made; sightseeing; and a residual category (other and multiple purpose) where the main purpose could not be specified as one, or as only one, of the above list. Interviews were necessarily very brief and little explanation was possible. The result is that in practice the categories were not always clear cut. Thus the line between holidays and short visits to friends or relations depended on the driver's interpretation, unless he asked the interviewer for further explanation. Holidays were defined as non-business stays away from home of more than four nights. Similarly, drivers going from work on a Friday to visit friends rather than going home could reasonably regard themselves as on a work journey rather than visiting: Monday could present the same problem in the reverse direction.

4.6 An estimate of the distribution of light vehicles crossing the Bridge in 1968 by the driver's journey purpose is given in Table 4.1. The most important purposes are firm's business and visiting friends and relations each of which contributes a quarter of the total journeys. Two further purposes constitute more than a tenth of the total, holidays (14%) and sightseeing (10%). Of the remaining purposes, travel to and from work is the largest with 8% of the total. Goods delivery, shopping, travel to places of entertainment and the residual category (other and multiple) stand between 2% and 5% with a remaining 1% attributable to service and maintenance. These minor purposes are of particular interest since they represent a group of activities (with the exception of the other and multiple purpose category) where the new opportunities opened by the Bridge in respect of urban services created the possibility of substantial changes in behaviour patterns. Bristol as the

TABLE 4.1 Purpose of Light Vehicles Crossing the Severn Bridge, 1968

Thousands

Purpose	Whole Year No.	%	Monday—Friday No.	%	Saturday No.	%	Sunday No.	%
Firm's Business	1,420	28	1,336	41	59	7	25	3
Collection and Delivery	100	2	91	3	9	1	—	—
Service and Maintenance	36	1	34	1	2	—	—	—
Work	394	8	342	11	32	4	20	2
Shopping	213	4	140	4	73	9	—	—
Holidays	706	14	381	12	223	26	102	10
Visiting	1,256	25	464	15	250	29	542	54
Sightseeing	513	10	225	7	76	9	212	21
Paid Entertainment	166	3	74	2	65	8	27	3
Other and Multiple	272	5	140	4	60	7	72	7
TOTAL	5,076		3,227		849		1,000	

largest urban area, and Cardiff as the second largest, could now provide services to a much larger area and there was the possibility of heightened competition between these two centres. The data shows that while people were taking some advantage of these new opportunities, this group of purposes as a whole covered 10% of total traffic, so that, at least in the early years, there was no revolution in the pattern of these services. In the case of shopping in particular, Table 4.1 may well overstate the facts, since winter weekend traffic is heavily dependent on a late November Saturday survey when Christmas was already stimulating trade.

4.7 Table 4.1 also gives separate estimates of 1968 traffic for weekdays, Saturdays and Sundays. As expected firm's business and work are mainly a feature of weekdays, although the group of leisure purposes (which account between them for 60% of total traffic annually) are not by any means confined to the weekends. Visiting, sightseeing and holidays are all important components of weekday travel, although it is of course at the weekend that they dominate the picture.

Traffic Generation

4.8 Before tackling the question of the origins and destinations of the flows, it would be useful to examine whether the trips were ones that would not have been made had the Bridge not existed or were merely ones diverted from other routes or transport modes. Thus at three surveys in August 1967 nearly a year after the Bridge was opened, covering a Tuesday, Saturday and Sunday, drivers were asked if they would have been making their journey had the Bridge not been in existence. This 'generated' traffic was sub-divided on the basis of a further question as to whether the journey or the route choice was made specifically to see the Bridge itself; this sub-category of generated traffic is subsequently termed 'facility created'. The results for Saturday and Sunday have been combined with 5 times the Tuesday figures to give an estimate of the extent to which the traffic of an August week fell into each of the three categories, diverted, generated and facility created. Table 4.2 gives this information. Firm's business shows the smallest proportion of generated traffic followed by

TABLE 4.2 Diverted, Generated and Facility Created Traffic by Purpose: August 1967

Purpose	No. of vehicles per week				
	Diverted	Generated	Facility Created	Not Known	Total
Firm's Business	14,693	4,141	—	470	19,304
Collection and Delivery Service and Maintenance	726	727	220	21	1,694
Work	933	1,928	—	14	2,875
Shopping	655	1,941	133	—	2,729
Holidays	29,970	6,306	3,701	101	40,078
Visiting	14,090	7,650	1,253	40	23,033
Sightseeing	5,086	14,469	9,588	310	29,453
Paid Entertainment	2,038	5,832	595	—	8,465
Other and Multiple	1,882	1,124	125	—	3,131
Total	70,073	44,118	15,615	956	130,762

holidays and visiting all of which have less than 40% of generated journeys. There is a sharp break between these and the remaining purposes where generated traffic is 60% or more of the total, with sightseeing showing the highest generation at 82%. Facility created traffic accounted for 12% of all traffic and was a third of all sightseeing traffic. Generated traffic, including facility created, was 46% of total traffic, the remaining 54% was diverted. Remembering that the Bridge had already been open for a year when this data was collected, people on generated journeys who had used the Bridge a number of times, on visiting or business journeys for example, might well have accommodated to a new pattern of routes so well that they would regard their journey as so normal that they would make it even if the Bridge was not available. This would result in a lower proportion of generated journeys than was really the case. Evidence below suggests that generated traffic was higher than 46%; this alternative data, for weekdays only, suggests generated traffic was 56% of total traffic. There was, however, some modest diversion from the railways, 4% to 5% of total vehicles, and this is counted as generated traffic in the above calculation.

4.9   The results in Table 4.2 cannot be applied to the annual flow of traffic without making some further assumptions especially about facility created traffic which would be likely to decline substantially in later years. If facility created traffic is assumed to be only half as important for each purpose as it was in August 1967 and that otherwise the diverted-generated split for each purpose is the same in 1968 as for August 1967, an estimate for 1968 can be given. On these assumptions 59% of light vehicle journeys in 1968 were diverted and 41% generated, including 4% facility created journeys.

By area

4.10   In view of the importance of new, i.e. generated, traffic in total traffic using the Bridge it is of some interest to find how the, previously 'unsatisfied', demand was distributed by area. Appendix 3 gives this information for a week's traffic in August 1967. The extent of traffic generation is basically a function of time and distance saved on the new routes opened up by the Bridge compared with the pre-existing situation. Thus generated traffic is a much higher proportion of the total on routes between Bristol and Somerset on the one side of the estuary and South East Wales on the other, than on routes such as those between London and South Wales. Taking journeys between areas nearest the Bridge — Bristol, Somerset, East Gloucestershire, Cardiff, Monmouthshire, including Newport, and West Gloucestershire — 38% of them were diverted journeys and 62% generated (including 14% facility created). The corresponding percentages for all traffic are diverted 54% and generated 46%, including 12% facility created. To put the comparison in another way, journeys between these areas near the Bridge account for 32% of diverted journeys and 68% of generated journeys. The corresponding percentage for facility created traffic alone is a surprisingly low 54%; clearly the Bridge itself was an important attraction to sightseers over quite a wide area, certainly beyond the immediate area of the Bridge itself.

By Purpose

4.11   Clearly, for some journey purposes, generated traffic is all important. For example, it is double or more the diverted traffic for work, shopping, sightseeing and paid entertainment. One could therefore take total traffic movements by each of these purposes between areas (as a rough approximation to generated traffic alone), distinguishing between those areas that are origins of trips and those that are places of accomplishment. Information showing the area of origin by the area in which the journey purpose was accomplished is given in Appendices 4—10. This analysis shows that new journeys for work purposes were mainly from Newport and South Monmouthshire to Bristol, to a lesser extent from Bristol to Newport and South Monmouthshire, and thirdly, again to a lesser extent, from Bristol to Cardiff. Taking the west and east banks as a whole the flow of (mainly generated) journeys for work was roughly in balance.

4.12   As regards shopping trips, however, the flow from the west to east bank was treble that in the opposite direction, the main attraction being Bristol's shopping centre. Similarly the movements for paid entertainment, except that the imbalance was even more pronounced, resulted in four times as many people from the west bank seeking entertainment in Bristol as east bank residents seeking such diversions in South Wales — the bulk of this movement of course being 'new' traffic. For sightseeing, however, the imbalance was markedly in the opposite direction with about three times as many trips occurring westwards to the beauty spots of, mainly, Monmouthshire as eastwards to those of Gloucestershire and Somerset.

4.13   It would be enlightening to find the reasons for this pattern. The household surveys provide some answers. A wide variety of activities is included in the category sightseeing and entertainment trips and the household interviews enabled a more precise description of these trips to be given. The distribution of households according to more specific sightseeing and entertainment purposes is given in Table 4.3. While general sightseeing trips are the largest category in both directions, eastbound traffic does show the fairly strong influence of the pull of some specific entertainment facilities in Bristol. The zoo, theatre and skating and dancing all figure with some prominence in eastbound traffic, and skating and dancing all figure with some prominence in eastbound traffic, and skating and dancing have quite a high average of trips per person.

4.14   To discover why people travel over the Severn in either direction is not easy, especially in a situation where the journey is made infrequently. To ask someone "why did you travel to Somerset today?" and get the answer "for pleasure" is reasonable. If the further question "why Somerset?" is asked, then unless there has been a family discussion regarding the relative merits of say the Wye Valley and Somerset for a picnic the respondent may find it difficult to reply. These difficulties need to be borne in mind when considering Table 4.4 which gives reasons for choosing cross-Bridge areas for sightseeing and entertainment journeys.

4.15 The two main reasons given by eastbound travellers were 'for a change' and 'better facilities'. Those giving the second answer have a higher trip frequency than the first. Westbound travellers gave 'for a change' and 'out of curiosity' as the main reasons. Both of these reasons were associated with much lower trip averages than the smaller groups who gave 'cheaper', 'better facilities' or 'facility not available on this side' as the answer.

4.16 Regarding shopping trips, interviewers asked the reason for any change of shopping pattern as a result of the existence of the Bridge. These reasons are given in Table 4.5. Overall 'for a change' is the most important reason given, with 'better choice and value' as the only other substantail category of answer. The fact that so few gave 'cheaper goods' as the reason for change suggests that it is variety of choice of goods, rather than better value, that is the most important aspect of the 'better choice and value' answer. The reduced distance to Bristol is of some importance in the case of Chepstow shoppers.

TABLE 4.3 Specific Sightseeing and Entertainment Purposes

Purpose	Westbound		Eastbound	
	No. of Households	Average Trips	No. of Households	Average Trips
Country and Seaside	273	3.6	114	4.8
Theatre	7	2.0	59	3.4
Spectator Sport	22	3.4	29	7.1
Stately Homes	9	1.6	–	–
Town Sightseeing	50	1.9	–	–
Playing Sport	14	3.3	41	5.4
Zoo	–	–	106	2.1
Dancing and Skating	–	–	52	6.3
General Touring	–	–	37	1.7
Other Entertainment, Clubs and Pubs	24	2.7	–	–
Country, Seaside and other purposes	15	8.0	75	7.5

TABLE 4.4 Reasons for Sightseeing and Entertainment Trips Across the Bridge

Reason	Westbound		Eastbound	
	No. of Households	Average Trips	No. of Households	Average Trips
For a change	213	2.7	187	3.2
Cheaper	11	7.5	18	4.9
Shorter distance	37	5.8	76	9.3
Better facilities	74	6.6	186	4.3
Facility not available on home side	84	6.6	44	4.3
Curiosity	203	2.5	–	–

TABLE 4.5 Reasons for Shopping

Reason	Home Area		
	Newport	Ebbw Vale	Chepstow
		% of total	
For a change	57	68	33
Cheaper	2	2	3
Shorter Distance	1	–	7
Better Choice and Value	37	18	57
Not available on home side	–	–	–
Other	3	12	–
Number of households	198	50	125

C

4.17 Details of goods purchased were also obtained. Nearly 10% of the 438 shopping trips analysed resulted in no purchase being made: 41% were for the purchase of clothing and a further 35% for clothing combined with food or other goods. Food purchases alone were the object of 6% of trips while a further 33% purchased food and clothing or other goods. Thus clothing dominates the picture with food as the only other substantial category. Goods other than food or clothing were a more important factor in the small westbound shopping traffic than in the much larger (by a factor of nearly 6 in these interviews) eastbound traffic.

4.18 For most other journey purposes, diverted traffic is predominant in total traffic (see Table 4.2) but the origins of trips and places of accomplishment may still be examined for the useful information they provide.

4.19 Travel on firm's business is largely between the main urban centres and over half the journeys had one trip-end in Bristol and one third in Cardiff; travel between Bristol and Cardiff accounted for 20% of all firm's business journeys. The balance of this traffic is westbound, in terms of where the business is done. Of the total traffic, 63% accomplishes the purpose firm's business to the west of the Bridge against 37% to the east. For example, an estimated 26,000 trips were made from Cardiff to do business in London compared with 47,000 trips from London to do business in Cardiff. There is no reason why an even balance should be expected for any purpose or even all purposes; some activities imply much more travel than others. Clearly much depends on the industrial structure of an area. Even if all the firm's business traffic was engaged in selling, it needs fewer people to sell the output of an area if this consists of intermediate products sold in bulk for further processing than if it consists of finished consumer goods being sold to a multitude of retailers.

4.20 Some further detail on changes in travel between areas on firm's business are available from the manufacturing and distribution surveys. A substantial proportion of all light vehicle journeys were made on firm's business or on service and maintenance. In 1968 these constituted 29% of all light vehicle trips. The industrial surveys show that among all manufacturing firms, 75% had staff crossing the estuary while among all distributing firms, 61% reported such movements. Among

manufacturers a higher proportion of movements of managers were eastbound than westbound whereas the reverse was true of their sales staffs. This is to be expected. Managers move to meetings at at head offices east of the Severn and to liaise with customers. Sales staff moving westward reflect the concentration of consumer goods trades in the Bristol area as well as technical services by firms supplying capital equipment, a feature supported by the evidence on the quality of services given and received by manufacturers. Similarly among distributors, a higher proportion of sales staff moved westwards in search of trade, a reflection of the concentration of distribution firms in the Bristol area.

4.21 Two changes are of particular interest. The first is the extent to which business travel has switched from rail to road. Here two features have emerged. There has been a greater switch from rail to road in South Wales than in the South West, partly because movements in the latter were more likely to have been by road anyway. Among manufacturers employing 100 or more persons that had staff travelling across the estuary, 48% switched from rail to road in South Wales as against 30% in the South West. Among distributors 54% switched in South Wales as against 34% in the South West. Furthermore these switches were most marked in the three main urban urban areas, Bristol, Newport and Cardiff. Business travellers from other districts were already obliged to use road transport for at least part of the journey through the withdrawal of local rail services.

4.22 The second feature is the increased number of trips; 25% of manufacturers reported increases in the number of trips and so did 26% of distributors. To these must be added the firms sending staff across for the first time — 4% of manufacturers and 10% of distributors. Detailed data on the percentage increase in the number of trips shows some firms with increases of as much as 200%. Thus 20 manufacturers and 13 distributors reported increases of 100% and above, with 7 manufacturers and 6 distributors being over 200%. Some of the larger increases may have been associated with changes in organisation, such as the setting up of new units, but in others the increases arise simply from more frequent consultation.

4.23 Traffic survey data throws some further light on the switch from rail to road, as far as all travel, instead

TABLE 4.6   Light Traffic Diverted from the Railways

	Vehicles			
Purpose	No.	% of Diverted journeys for purpose	% of Total journeys for purpose	No. of People
Firm's Business	258	18	14	390
Goods Collection and Delivery	16	26	10	30
Work	20	27	8	36
Shopping	12	25	6	35
Holidays	33	2	1	89
Visiting	—	—	—	—
Sightseeing	40	10	2	128
Paid Entertainment	17	10	2	56
Other and Multiple	15	21	13	43
Total	411			807

of just business travel, is concerned. Those who stated at the August weekday interviews (Tuesday) in 1967 that they would have made the journey had the Bridge not existed, were further asked what means of transport they would have used in that case. The main interest here was in finding out how far traffic was being diverted from the railways. The resulting information is set out in Table 4.6 It is clear that those diverting from the railways form only a small proportion of total traffic. Only 5.2% of total vehicles fell into that category and only 4.0% of people. The fact that firm's business was the main purpose for which people diverted from the railways means that at other times of the year, when that purpose is more important, the proportion of rail diverted journeys would be higher.

4.24 The main routes affected were from Bristol to South Wales. Of the 411 vehicles concerned 193 were travelling between Bristol and Cardiff or Newport and 99 to Swansea or other destinations in Glamorgan. The only other substantial group was 47 vehicles travelling between Somerset and Cardiff or Newport. The picture yielded by the traffic and manufacturing industry surveys is very much the same.

4.25 The balance of the goods delivery (by cars and vans) is also from England to Wales, using those national labels somewhat inaccurately to denote the destination of eastbound and westbound traffic respectively. Van collection and delivery is only a small proportion of the total movement of goods and the main consideration of this matter is given in Chapters 5 to 7, which are concerned with heavy vehicles. Van movements are mainly short distance, with the largest traffic from Bristol to the Rest of Monmouthshire.

4.26 In contrast to the purposes considered so far, holidays give rise to relatively long journeys and places more distant from the Bridge figure more prominently. Traffic between the Rest of Great Britain (in this case the West Midlands and the North West mainly) and Devon and Cornwall provides the largest total for any cell in the holidays tables. For holiday traffic there is a greater weekday flow into Wales, 56% of the total, compared with 44% accomplishing this purpose in England.

4.27 Estimates for journeys of visits to friends and relatives are subject to two difficulties. First, the difficulty of allocating journeys for this purpose on Friday and Monday where the visit begins or ends at the place of work. Second, the difficult line for the driver to draw between an extended visit and a holiday. Given these difficulties the estimates show that the balance of visiting traffic is into Wales but the excess is very small. Visits to places in Wales account for 52% of the total, so that the traffic overall is quite well balanced.

Expenditure

4.28 Flows of vehicles or people between areas, though of some interest in themselves, become more interesting if some indication can be obtained of the cash flows these movements represent so that some idea can be obtained of the economic benefits to areas which have a net gain of flows, and the economic losses sustained by areas which are net losers.

4.29 At the weekend survey in August 1968 every fifth card distributed requested the respondent to give an address if he was willing to answer some further questions on his expenditure (and that of any passengers) on his journey. The resulting responses gave for 323 journeys detail of purchases (excluding petrol and oil) on twelve items and a residual category. The percentage of these 323 responses having each journey purpose was as follows (the percentage travelling for each purpose estimated from the main survey is given in brackets) — holidays 40 (44), visiting 27 (26), sightseeing 21 (20) and all other purposes 12 (10). Thus 88% of the responses were from motorists on holiday, visiting and sightseeing journeys and detailed analysis was restricted to these three, the number of responses for each of the other purposes being so small.

4.30 Table 4.7 gives the distribution of cars by total expenditure, excluding petrol and oil, and the average for each purpose per car and per head. Sightseeing with an average of just over £2 per car is highest, and also has the lowest proportion having no expenditure. Visiting gives the lowest average, just over £1, and much the highest proportion with no expenditure. Holidays is nearer sightseeing than visiting on both counts. Average

Expenditure per Car	Purpose			TABLE 4.7
	Holidays	Visiting	Sightseeing	
0d. —	13	25	4	
1d. — 2/6d.	5	3	3	
— 5/-	9	8	4	
— 10/-	18	14	8	
— £1	22	12	10	**Expenditure per Car and Journey Purpose,**
— £2	27	10	15	**August 1968**
— £3	14	8	8	
— £4	6	3	5	
— £5	6	1	3	
over £5	10	3	6	
	130	87	66	
Average per car (shillings)	34.8	21.0	41.5	
Average per head	9.6	7.8	12.2	

expenditure per head has the same ranking but the lower occupancy of cars on visiting journeys reduces the range of average expenditure per head.

4.31 Looking at the effect of occupancy (Table 4.8) on total expenditure the main feature is the high amount spent by those travelling alone. In general there is no stable relationship between expenditure per head and the number travelling, although for sightseeing and visiting there is a fairly continuous decrease as the number of occupants increases. This is not so with holidays.

4.32 Comparing Saturday with Sunday, there is not much variation in average expenditure per head for holidays (Saturday 9.9 shillings, Sunday 8.7). For the other two purposes the range is wider with 9.4 shillings on Saturday and 7.2 on Sunday in respect of visiting and 10.8 shillings on Saturday and 15.0 on Sunday for sightseeing. There are few marked differences between the distribution of total expenditure between items over the two days; full details are given in Appendix 11. Sunday holidaymakers bought a larger number of more expensive meals than those travelling on Saturdays; holidaymakers also spent more on groceries on Saturday while visitors spend considerably more on drinks on Sundays.

4.33 There is no simple relationship between the length of the journey and the total expenditure. The average expenditure per car was 29.9 shillings for trips up to 50 miles, 27.6 between 50 and 100 miles, 42.1 from 101 to 150 miles and 22.3 over 200 miles. Taking each purpose separately still leaves no simple relationship. The replies do not suggest that there is any significant difference between the average expenditure per car whether the place of accomplishment is east of the Bridge or west, other than those that reflect the modest differences in the purpose pattern of the traffic.

4.34 The 40 vehicles in the sample that were on other purposes had an average expenditure of 66.6 shillings. The distribution was similar to that of the three main purposes except that 11 vehicles had a total expenditure of over £5, a much higher proportion than for any of the three purposes considered above. The average expenditure per head was 24.0 shillings.

4.35 A second source of information on expenditure by those using the Bridge arises from the household interview sample. Households in Bristol, Thornbury, Chepstow and Newport were asked about their expenditure on the last trip they had made across the Bridge and the purpose of that trip. Total household expenditure was divided by the number of members making the trip to get average expenditure per head.

4.36 Of the 1311 households for which expenditure data was obtained, the last trip in the case of 865 had sightseeing as the main purpose, 300 were visiting, 105 were shopping and 41 had some other main purpose. Appendix 12 shows that in all areas except Chepstow over 30% of households did not spend anything on their last journey over the Bridge. More visitors than sightseers, and of course shoppers, spent nothing at all. Taking all areas together 8% of households spent more than £1 per head on their last trip. Shoppers show, not unexpectedly, a much larger proportion of high expenditure per head than any other purpose group.

TABLE 4.8

Mean Expenditure per Head by Occupancy

shillings

| | Occupancy | | | | | |
	1	2	3	4	5	6 & over
Holidays	24.3	8.1	10.0	9.2	10.5	4.0
Visiting	13.5	7.2	10.8	9.0	3.9	1.0
Sightseeing	77.0	17.5	15.6	7.4	8.6	11.0

4.37 Average expenditure per head was 8 shillings for sightseeing, 4 shillings for visiting and 25 shillings for shopping. The traffic survey data gave an average of 12 shillings for sightseeing and 8 shillings for visiting. It must be remembered, however, that respondents to the traffic survey were giving information within two weeks of their trips when memories were likely to be fresher than in the case of household survey respondents who could be recalling a trip made up to a year before the interview. Some items were likely to be forgotten by respondents to the household interview and the resulting figures were likely to be underestimates of actual expenditure. On the other hand those involved in the traffic survey who had made no expenditure may not have bothered to return the detailed questionnaire, resulting in some tendency for the results to overestimate average expenditure. The two sets of data differ in some other respects. Respondents to the traffic survey were necessarily car owners, some of the household respondents had made their trip by bus. All those in the traffic survey were travelling at the weekend in August, the household sample was not so restricted. Lastly the household survey was geographically restricted in a way that did not apply to the traffic survey. The particular influence of some of these factors is to be seen in the high incidence of shoppers in the household sample, especially for Chepstow where the Bridge gave readier access to a very large shopping centre than was previously the case.

4.38 Appendix 12 also shows the distribution of average expenditure per head for Bristol, Thornbury, Newport and Chepstow for sightseeing, visiting and shopping and for all purposes. The average expenditures per head were: Chepstow 16 shillings, Newport 9 shillings, Bristol 7 shillings and Thornbury 6 shillings. The high average for Chepstow is a reflection of the exceptionally high proportion of last trips which were shopping trips and shopping, as was noted above, has much the highest average expenditure.

4.39 Appendix 13 shows the distribution of expenditure as between meals and snacks, entrance fees and other purchases. Over 60% of last trips generated some expenditure on meals and snacks. A much smaller proportion of trips generated expenditure on other purchases, Chepstow with 33% being the only area with more than 18% for this type of expenditure. The distribution of expenditure on entrance fees by area reflects the fact noted in the traffic surveys that Bristol attracts many more people from west of the Severn for paid entertainment than travel to centres west of the Severn for that purpose. Appendix 13 also shows that while only 9% and 11% of the households in Bristol and Thornbury paid entrance fees on their last visit, 36% and 40% of households in Newport and Chepstow respectively incurred such expenditure.

Growth of Traffic

4.40 Appendices 14 and 15 provide a picture of the seasonal pattern of traffic by purpose and its growth over time. Each column represents a single day's traffic at the given date. The main feature of weekday traffic is the strong growth of journeys on firm's business from 1967 through 1968 as opportunities created by the Bridge were exploited. This growth, however, had largely expended itself by 1969. This rapid growth in 1968 was made against the background of a British economy growing very slowly. Regarding travel to work the figure for March 1967 is probably inflated by a number of people returning from weekend visits, classifying themselves as travelling to work. The accuracy of later figures was improved by further enquiries about home locations and frequency of travel. While a substantial proportion of work journeys was generated by the opening of the Bridge, there is evidence of further subsequent growth. Questions about frequency of travel showed that a majority of those travelling to work, up to two-thirds, were commuters making the return journey at least four times per week. Collection and delivery and service and maintenance journeys show little change between 1967 and 1968 and a decline in 1969: however, small flows of traffic are liable to substantial sampling fluctuations.

4.41 Among leisure purposes weekday holiday traffic shows strong growth whether viewed from the spring of 1967 to the spring of 1968 or between the two summers. Visiting also grows strongly over time. At the weekend, the proportion of the total contributed by the various purposes shows little change over time except for sightseeing where there is a fall — 1968 compared with 1967. The decline in facility created traffic is no doubt part of the explanation. This decline accounts in part for summer Sunday traffic being less buoyant than Saturday traffic in 1968. Sunday is the peak for sightseeing traffic. With the exception of sightseeing, travel for the various leisure purposes grows in line with total traffic, with holidays and visiting exceeding this expectation a little.

4.42 Appendix 16 gives a picture of the growth of weekday traffic by area over time; the three lines of each cell represent traffic at the surveys one week before Easter in 1967, 1968 and 1969 respectively. The data for 1967 and 1968 represents an average of Monday and Tuesday traffic and that for 1969 an average of Friday and Monday traffic. The effect of including a Friday in 1969 (instead of Tuesday) is to lift traffic by about 3%. Allowing for this there is growth of nearly one third in total traffic between 1967 and 1968 but very little growth, only 2%, between 1968 and 1969. However, all areas do not share equally in this initial growth and subsequent levelling-off of traffic.

4.43 On the English side the following areas show above-average growth (in order of the excess), East Gloucestershire, Wiltshire, London and Outer London and the South East Coast. Central Southern England shows slow growth to 1968 and a high figure for 1969. Somerset, with a very low 1969 figure, and Devon and

Cornwall have below average growth. The remaining area, the Bristol conurbation, which is one trip-end for about half the total traffic, moves closely in line with total traffic, but with marginally lower growth. On the Welsh side there is a much narrower range of variation. There is no growth after 1967 in the case of Monmouthshire, outside Newport, and the residual area (Rest); indeed in both cases a slight decline in traffic. Nearly all the other areas (Newport, Cardiff, Rest of Glamorgan, the Swansea conurbation and West Gloucestershire) have growth in traffic a little above-average. The most rapid growth occurs in the two areas least important in terms of total traffic, Hereford and Brecon and West Wales.

4.44 Traffic between areas close to the Bridge (Bristol, East Gloucestershire and Somerset in the east and Monmouthshire, including Newport, Cardiff and West Gloucestershire in the west) increased by 27%, a little less than the average, between 1967 and 1968 and fell by 7% during the following year; thus the relative importance of this area declined. In March 1967 it accounted for 52% of total traffic, falling to 49% in April 1968 and to 43% in March 1969. If attention is confined to traffic between the two largest urban areas, Bristol and Cardiff, the pattern is reversed. Traffic on this route rose from 12.8% of the total in March 1967, through 13.7% to 15.3% in March 1969.

4.45 The same pattern emerges if summer growth is viewed in terms of August weekday traffic — see Appendix 18. Again areas near the Bridge show modest declines (rather larger in the case of Bristol) while more distant areas such as Swansea, Devon and Cornwall and Central Southern England show substantial increases on their, in absolute terms, much smaller traffic.

4.46 The growth of weekend traffic by areas can be examined only over the shorter period from August 1967 to August 1968. Details are given in Appendix 17. Overall traffic increased by 8% between these two weekend surveys. The main feature is again the decline of most areas near the Bridge — Bristol, Somerset, West Gloucestershire, Cardiff and Monmouthshire (excluding Newport) all fall in this category. On the other hand the areas with the largest increases are Swansea, West Wales and Hereford and Brecon to the west and Central Southern England (with an increase by a factor 3 to 6,000 vehicles), Devon and Cornwall and the South East Coast. This contrast reflects a decline in short-distance sightseeing traffic, which may partly be the result of greater familiarity with the areas close to the Bridge, and partly the effect of the time needed for people to become aware of the practicability of longer-distance day trips, as a result of the Bridge and the associated motorways. Traffic between areas close to the Bridge fell from 40% of total traffic in August 1967 to 31% in 1968. The largest declines in traffic were on the routes Bristol—Rest of Monmouthshire, Bristol—Cardiff, Bristol—West Gloucestershire, Somerset—Rest of Monmouthshire and Somerset—West Gloucestershire. Newport and East Gloucestershire were the two near-Bridge areas running counter to the trend.

4.47 A second view of the extent of traffic generation, this time on a weekday only, is available via two enquiries made by the Gloucestershire County Surveyor's Department. On a Monday and Tuesday in mid-

August 1966 and 1967 the origins and destinations of westbound vehicles crossing a screenline covering routes into South Wales likely to be affected by the Bridge was obtained.[1] In 1967 the screenline included the Bridge instead of the Beachley-Aust ferry which was included in 1966. Table 4.9 gives the number of journeys with various origins and destinations for one August weekday in 1966 and 1967 and an index of growth. Allowing something for the normal growth of traffic (say 6%) any remaining growth will show the influence of the Bridge. The Rest of Great Britain has been excluded as both an origin and a destination; nearly all the traffic from this area into South Wales is from the West Midlands and North West on routes unaffected by the Bridge.

4.48 The screenline lay between East and West Gloucestershire and thus much local traffic out of Gloucester unaffected by the Bridge is included in the table; the same is true to a lesser extent of Herefordshire. This accounts for the low percentage increase in these areas. The difference between the very high increases of some areas to the east of the Bridge (e.g. Bristol and Somerset) and the lesser but still substantial increases to the west (e.g. Cardiff and Newport) arises because all the relevant (i.e. into South Wales) traffic from Bristol and Somerset benefited from the Bridge, while this was not true of all the relevant traffic into Cardiff and Newport. Some of this latter traffic was from origins (e.g. parts of outer London and Central Southern England) which were unaffected by the Bridge. A detailed matrix of Table 4.9 is given in Appendix 19.

4.49 The interview results in Appendix 3 show that generated, including facility created, traffic is 46% of total traffic for a week in August, 1967. In Table 4.9 traffic moving across the screenline for an August weekday gives generated traffic as 52% of total traffic crossing the Bridge on that day. Local traffic between East Gloucestershire and West Gloucestershire and Herefordshire has been excluded from the calculation as has traffic from Devon and Cornwall, Bristol and Somerset to the Rest of Great Britain. The quickest route for these latter traffics did not cross the screenline in 1966 but did in 1967, when, by using the Bridge, congested conditions in Gloucester could be avoided. Thus although it did not cross the screenline in 1966 but did use the Bridge in 1967, it is really diverted traffic. While the two estimates (46% and 52%) of generated traffic are not very far apart, the interview estimate of Appendix 3 should give a higher percentage of generated

traffic for two reasons. First, it includes the weekend when purposes with higher traffic generation (especially sightseeing) are more important. Second, since only Bridge users were interviewed routes unaffected by the Bridge, and hence routes with zero generated traffic, are excluded. For the weekday where a direct comparison is possible, some routes, a particular instance was Bristol—Cardiff, showed nearly twice as many vehicles stating that theirs was a diverted journey as had been travelling between those two cities in 1966. After the Bridge has existed for a year it is not easy to decide whether a journey would still be made had the Bridge not existed; some over-estimation of diverted traffic at the interviews is thus not unlikely.

Daily and Seasonal Variations

4.50 The seasonal pattern of purposes shows the expected picture. Firm's business and work fall off in the summer. Holidays and sightseeing show a marked summer rise. The peak is not too sharp with sightseeing, which contributes much the same proportion of May and August Saturday traffic and a decreasing proportion of Sunday traffic. The peak for holiday traffic is much sharper but even here, there is already substantial traffic in May. Holiday traffic is concentrated on Saturdays in the same way as sightseeing traffic is concentrated on Sundays. Visiting shows the smallest seasonal variation.

4.51 Appendices 16, 17 and 18 illustrate the daily and seasonal flow of traffic between areas and the pattern is the expected one. Traffic between urban centres is more important on weekdays than weekends and the reverse is true of urban-rural traffic or traffic between rural areas. Thus for the whole of 1968 traffic between Bristol and Cardiff was 14% of weekday traffic falling to 9% on Sunday and 8% on Saturday. In contrast Bristol—West Gloucestershire traffic was 3% of weekday, 4% of Saturday and 6% of Sunday traffic. The importance of holiday traffic on Saturday is reflected in journeys to and from Devon and Cornwall. These were 6% of traffic for weekdays, falling to under 4% on Sundays and rising to 10% on Saturdays.

4.52 The changing patterns of purposes influences the seasonal pattern of traffic between areas. Holiday areas such as West Wales and Devon and Cornwall show wide fluctuations between spring and summer traffic. In contrast, the Bristol—Cardiff route shows little seasonal change with the declining summer business traffic being offset by rising traffic for leisure purposes.

TABLE 4.9			Westbound Traffic for an August weekday, 1966 and 1967				
Origin	1966	1967	Index 1967 1966 = 100	Destination	1966	1967	Index 1967 1966 = 100
Bristol	1,746	5,992	343	Newport	1,088	2,245	206
East Glos.	10,032	11,021	110	Rest Mon.	1,846	3,375	183
Somerset	674	2,313	343	West Glos.	7,140	9,384	131
Wiltshire	464	993	214	Cardiff	2,157	3,786	176
Devon & Cornwall	440	1,046	238	Rest Glam.	832	1,697	204
Central Southern England	1,698	2,388	141	Hereford & Brecon	2,798	3,173	113
London & Outer London	2,648	2,512	95	Swansea	989	1,582	160
South East Coast	829	836	101	West Wales	1,411	1,859	132

Vehicle Occupancy and Frequency Rates

4.53 At each traffic survey the number of occupants in each vehicle was noted and details of the average number of occupants for each purpose at each survey are given in Appendix 20. On the basis of this information Table 4.10 estimates the total number of people crossing the Bridge in cars and vans for each purpose over the year 1968. The pattern of high and low occupancy as between particular purposes is little changed over time, but there is a tendency for average occupancy for all purposes to rise both at the weekend compared with weekdays and also during the summer. The only exception to this tendency is journeys for travel to work. Taking 1968 as a whole there is a fairly sharp break between business purposes with relatively low occupancies and leisure purposes with higher occupancies; the other and multiple purpose category being in an intermediate position. Among leisure purposes there is a further contrast between sightseeing, entertainment, holidays and shopping all of which have average occupancies of around 3 persons per vehicle; visiting has the distinctly lower figure of 2.4

4.54 At a number of surveys, drivers were asked how frequently they had crossed the Bridge during the previous 7 days. Few of those engaged on shopping, holiday and sightseeing journeys had crossed during the previous week, other than on the outward half of that particular journey of course. For visiting rather more had crossed in the previous week, about 15% of the total, and for entertainment the proportion was higher at 25%. Of those travelling on firms' business, 40% were on at least their second journey of the week and the same is true of those travelling to work, other than the commuters who had, of course, the highest frequency of previous crossings. In all cases these previous journeys were not necessarily for the same purposes as the journey which the driver was engaged on when questioned. Overall, on the basis of March and November weekdays, 65% of drivers were on their first trip across the Bridge over a period of a week, 20% made 2 or 3 round trips, 5% made 4 round trips and the remaining 10% more than 4 round trips.

4.55 Taken in conjunction with the details of average occupancy the total picture that emerges is that of a very large number of people making occasional use of the Bridge for leisure purposes and a much smaller group of people making fairly frequent use of the Bridge for business and work purposes.

Use of the Bridge by People of the Area

Factors Effecting Use

4.56 Evidence on some of the characteristics of those using the Bridge compared with non-users arises from a series of household interviews in Bristol, Chepstow, Ebbw Vale, Thornbury and Newport. Details of the survey method, the sample and response rates are given in Appendix 1. In the case of the first four towns above, the period covered by the interviews was the first 18—20 months after the opening of the Bridge. For Newport one series of interviews in two wards was carried out in the winter of 1967—68, when the Bridge had been opened about 15 months, and a second series a year later. The results in Newport are subsequently referred to separately as Newport Stage 1 and Newport Stage 2.

4.57 Appendices 21—23 compare certain characteristics of households that used the Bridge (at least one member of the household made at least one trip across the Bridge) with those not using it.

4.58 The age and sex of users and non-users in each area is given in Appendix 21. If these factors are unimportant then each age and sex group would contribute the same proportion of users and non-users. In general this is what the table shows, although there are a few exceptions. The female group over 65 years contributes a much higher proportion of non-users than users for all areas except Bristol. This group stands out particularly in relation to its neighbour, the 40—65 years old group, where for both men and women the proportion of users is higher than non-users. In both Bristol and Ebbw Vale children are somewhat under represented in the user group. Overall the age and sex variations have little influence on whether the household is in the user group or not.

4.59 Appendix 22 makes the same comparison between user and non-user households in terms of the socio-economic group of the head of the household. The user group contains a considerably higher proportion of employers, managers and professional workers than the non-user group. The reverse is true of semi-skilled and unskilled manual workers. These patterns hold for all

Purpose	Total Light Vehicles '000	Average Occupancy per Vehicle	Total People '000	TABLE 4.10
Firms' Business	1,420	1.4	1,988	
Collection and Delivery	100	1.4	140	
Service and Maintenance	36	1.3	47	**Average Occupancy of Light**
Work	394	1.7	670	**Vehicles and Total People**
Shopping	213	2.8	596	**Crossing the Bridge, 1968**
Holidays	706	2.9	2,047	
Visiting	1,256	2.4	3,014	
Sightseeing	513	3.1	1,590	
Paid Entertainment	166	2.9	481	
Other and Multiple	272	2.1	571	
Total	5,076	2.2	11,144	

the areas. If all areas are taken together then the percentage of each socio-economic group that has made some use of the Bridge falls, as follows, as one moves from group 1 (employers) to group 7 (unskilled manual workers): 99, 90, 89, 88, 80, 74, 55. The percentage for the residual groups, widows, etc. is 63. Socio-economic group is clearly associated with whether the Bridge is used or not.

4.60 The influence of home ownership is considered in Appendix 23. In the case of Bristol, Newport and Ebbw Vale the split of total households between owner occupiers and local authority and privately rented houses depends upon the particular wards included in the samples. Again if type of tenure of house is not associated with Bridge use, then each type will have the same percentage of users as non-users. The data shows a clear association. In all areas owner occupiers are a larger proportion of users than non-users and the reverse is true for local authority rented houses. Privately rented houses, which contribute only 6% to the total of households, show no clear pattern. To own a house is to increase the likelihood of the household using the Bridge.

4.61 Turning to car ownership (see Appendix 23 also), this again exercises considerable influence and a stronger influence than home ownership: the ratio of users to non-users among car owners is greater than the same ratio for home owners. The influence of car ownership is particularly strong in the case of Thornbury (which lies off the direct bus route over the Bridge) and weakest for Chepstow and Ebbw Vale. In Chepstow the influence of Bristol and, at least in relative terms, a quick and frequent bus service to it, plays down the importance of the car. For Ebbw Vale the explanation is rather different. As is revealed elsewhere special purpose organised coach trips play an important part in the pattern of life in South Wales valley towns. It is this factor which explains the relative lack of importance of car ownership in the case of Ebbw Vale.

4.62 Home and car ownership and socio-economic group are all inter-related. The extent of variation in the data, compared with the pattern as it would be if no factor exerted a special influence, was examined for the variables car ownership, home ownership, socio-economic group and age of household head. This variance analysis showed that while car ownership and

socio-economic group exerted a significant influence at the 10% and 5% level, socio-economic group alone was significant at the 1% level.

Extent of Use of the Bridge

4.63 At the more general level 90% of the households in Chepstow had at least one member who had made at least one trip across the Bridge in the first 20 months after its opening. The comparable percentages for other areas are — Newport Stage 2 (over a longer period of 27 months) 90; Thornbury 80; Newport Stage 1 79; Bristol 71; and Ebbw Vale 70. Applying the above percentages to the population of each area gives figures for the total population using the Bridge as follows — Chepstow 5,481; Newport 83,243, Thornbury 2,400; Bristol 299,438 and Ebbw Vale 19,927.

4.64 The differences between areas and between the two sides of the estuary are a reflection of two major factors. First, accessibility; the motorway leading to the Bridge is quickly reached from all parts of Newport, whereas in Bristol a trip across the Severn is relatively easy only for those living in the northern and western parts of the city; it involves a tiresome journey for a considerable number of the city's population. For Ebbw Vale households the Bridge is only accessible after a cross-country journey and 'B' roads, while by bus there is no through route without a change.

4.65 A comparison of Thornbury and Chepstow shows that accessibility is not the only factor. Chepstow is a little nearer the western end of the Bridge than Thornbury is to the eastern end. Chepstow has 10% more households using the Bridge and when frequency is considered the disparity is increased. The difference is a reflection of the relative pull of the two sides of the Bridge as trip generators especially for urban services. There is nothing on the western side to attract Thornbury traffic in the way Bristol is an attraction to traffic from Chepstow.

4.66 The household survey threw light on the frequency with which the Bridge was used, as well as on the proportion of households using it. Table 4.11 gives the pattern of trip frequency by areas. The average number of trips per household is the total number of trips made by each member summed and divided by the number of members of the household excluding infants under 1 year old. The data shows that while a large proportion of the population made some use of the Bridge, except in areas

| | **Average Trips per Household** | | | | | | **Total Households** | |
Area	0.1–1.9 %	2–5.9 %	6–10.9 %	11–20.9 %	21–50.9 %	51+ %	Users	Non-users
Bristol	36	35	15	8	5	1	693	280
Thornbury	17	37	24	10	6	6	84	21
Newport Stage 1	27	34	21	11	6	1	371	98
Newport Stage 2	11	30	20	19	16	4	378	40
Ebbw Vale	41	42	13	4	—	—	135	59
Chepstow	11	19	21	17	28	4	156	18

TABLE 4.11   **Frequency of Use of the Bridge for all Purposes***

* The period covered is 15 months for Newport Stage 1, 18–20 months for Bristol, Thornbury, Ebbw Vale and Chepstow and 27 months for Newport Stage 2.

adjacent to it, the Bridge does not play a very important part in peoples lives. Higher averages are shown for the western side of the Severn, which shows that not only do a higher proportion of households on that side use the Bridge, but also that they make more frequent use of it. In the case of Ebbw Vale the deterrent of the journey length was sufficient to ensure that the attractions of the eastern side were not strong enough to generate more than occasional cross-Bridge trips. Newport residents on the other hand, whilst not frequent travellers, found those attractions worth more than an 'inspection trip'. 'Inspection trips' were more frequent from Bristol and interviewers in that area were often met with such comments as "we only went over to see what it was like" or "we went over just to say we had been".

4.67 Appendix 24 shows the extent and frequency of travel from each area for the purposes of sightseeing and entertainment, visiting and shopping. For each area a higher proportion of the households had crossed the Bridge on sightseeing trips than on visiting or shopping trips and visiting is higher than shopping for all areas except Chepstow and Ebbw Vale. However where the Bridge is used on visiting journeys then it is used more frequently than for the other purposes. Combining the proportion of the population using the Bridge for each purpose with the influence of trip frequency, an average frequency over the whole group of households results. On this basis sightseeing and entertainment have the highest frequency (except for Thornbury) and shopping the lowest frequency (except for Chepstow).

4.68 The same purposes are considered in Appendix 25 but from the viewpoint of socio-economic group instead of area. The importance of socio-economic group in determing the proportion of Bridge-using households is clearly seen. With very few exceptions the movement from group 1 to group 7 reduces the proportion of households using the Bridge and this holds for each purpose. Among user households, however, socio-economic group is closely associated with frequency of use only in the case of sightseeing and entertainment. Among visiting households there is little variation in frequency of use. The same is true of shopping trips where groups 5, 6 and 7 have among the highest frequency of use. With regard to average trips per household (users and non-users) the higher proportion of groups 1 to 4 making some use of the Bridge does something to re-establish an overall pattern between socio-economic group and average frequency of use.

4.69 The remaining important leisure purpose, holidays, does not by its nature give rise to very frequent use of the Bridge. Holidays are defined as a non-business stay away from home over 4 nights. In practice the holidays considered here were usually the annual summer holiday. The percentage of households in each area using the Bridge on holiday journeys was as follows — Bristol 9; Thornbury 8; Newport Stage 1 32; Newport Stage 2 41; Ebbw Vale 16 and Chepstow 33. Thus one third of households west of the estuary and 9% of those to the east used the Bridge for holiday travel. Holiday areas in Wales did not attract many people from Bristol. However, two of Britain's most popular holiday areas, Devon and Cornwall and the South Coast, do not involve cross Bridge travel for those in Bristol and Thornbury whereas they do for the remaining areas considered here. This accounts for much of the difference between the two sides of the estuary.

4.70 Work as a purpose in the household survey covers trips made to or from a temporary or permanent place of work, selling trips and any other trips in connection with the employer's business. Of households to the west of the estuary 10% had made work trips while to the east 11% of those interviewed had done so. Table 4.12 gives details of the frequency of work trips by area. Work trips are not averaged over the household because of the extreme variability of the frequency; those in regular permanent employment will have very high frequencies.

4.71 As regards the socio-economic group of those travelling for work purposes, non-manual workers, a group which includes sales representatives, employers, managers and professional workers all of whom are likely to travel on their firms' business, are a high proportion of total work travellers. The other important group are the skilled and semi-skilled manual workers; carpenters, painters, building workers and steel erectors are examples of particular trades. In Bristol these groups of manual workers are 37% of all those travelling from Bristol to work whereas they form 20% in the case of Newport. This probably reflects travel to building sites and suggests that Bristol contractors have had some success in extending these operations across the Bridge.

TABLE 4.12   **Frequency of Use and Travel for Work Purposes***

Area	Average Trips per Worker					Total Households	
	0.1–1.9 %	2–5.9 %	6–10.9 %	11–20.9 %	21 plus %	Users	Non-users
Bristol	40	10	25	18	7	110	863
Thornbury	45	9	9	–	36	11	94
Newport Stage 1	47	25	11	9	7	55	414
Newport Stage 2	57	17	9	11	6	53	365
Ebbw Vale	67	33	–	–	–	6	188
Chepstow	13	25	13	19	30	16	158

* The period covered is 15 months for Newport Stage 1, 18–20 months for Bristol, Thornbury, Ebbw Vale and Chepstow and 27 months for Newport Stage 2.

Method of travel

4.72 Appendix 26 shows what method of travel was used both before and after the opening of the Bridge for sightseeing and entertainment, visiting and shopping. Shopping trips from Bristol and Thornbury are few and are not analysed. Not surprisingly cars are the most important means of travel for all purposes in the post-Bridge situation, especially for visiting. Special bus trips are more important than scheduled services for sightseeing but for visiting and shopping the reverse is true. Scheduled services are particularly important for shopping from Chepstow. The special character of Ebbw Vale is brought out in this data. Special bus trips account for 64% of sightseeing traffic from Ebbw Vale and 40% of its shopping traffic. Even in Ebbw Vale scheduled services are more important for visiting.

4.73 Regarding the pre-Bridge travel of those households that used the Bridge after its opening Appendix 26 shows how little of this there was for sightseeing and shopping except in the case of Chepstow. What little traffic there was, was dominated by the motor car; these cars used either the Beachley-Aust ferry or the route via Gloucester. Chepstow is again an exception with a much higher proportion of rail traffic. Visiting is the one purpose where the railways played a rather more significant part for all the areas.

Inter-Regional Bus and Coach Traffic

4.74 While coaches played scarcely any part in personal travel between the South West and South Wales before the opening of the Severn Bridge, its opening created substantial new opportunities to coach operators for both stage services and excursions. Destinations previously attainable, if at all, by rail or steamer were now easily reached. Day excursions became half-day excursions and new extended tours were facilitated. Any assessment of this traffic has therefore to take into account such questions as the extent to which new traffic has been generated; not only over the Bridge but in terms of total coach traffic. How much of the traffic is a diversion from other coach traffic, or from rail or steamer traffic? What areas have generated the main flows of traffic and with what implications, not only in terms of places visited but other destinations foregone? To answer some of these questions a special study of coach traffic was made.

4.75 Excursion traffic prior to September 1966 was largely limited to rail and steamer facilities. Rail services had been available throughout the year whereas steamers had been confined to the season from Easter to early October. Steamer business had been falling and was confined to sailings from Cardiff, Penarth and Barry to Weston-super-Mare and on occasions to Clevedon, Bristol and Minehead. Tidal restrictions had severely limited these operations but Weston-super-Mare and, to a much lesser extent, Minehead and Clevedon were the main destinations, the steamer fleet being based on Cardiff and not on Cardiff and Bristol as in the past. Such coach traffic as existed was insignificant. Apart from a few trips which used the Beachley-Aust ferry as a passenger ferry, and which were therefore jointly operated by companies on both sides of the estuary, the route via

Gloucester was the only one available. In the circumstances rail excursions to Bristol, notably to Clifton for Bristol Zoo to Weston-super-Mare and beyond and to Weymouth had long been a feature of South Wales rail trips. With the deliberate contraction of seasonal excursion traffic by the railways this declined and the closure of branch lines, especially in South Wales, caused a lull in excursions from the "Valleys" to the West Country. But as the "Modern Railways" wrily observed in November 1966 when reporting record traffic over the Bridge "one would never have thought there had been a tunnel for over seventy years".

4.76 The traffic surveys indicate substantial movements of buses and coaches across the Bridge. These fall into three categories — stage and express services between centres close to the Bridge, express services to and from South Wales and excursion and private hire movements; they are examined in this sequence.

Stage and Express Services

4.77 The stage and express services regularly crossing the Bridge are three in number. First there is an express service jointly operated by the Bristol Omnibus and Red and White companies of the National Bus Group. Stopping only at Westbury-on-Trym on the northern outskirts of Bristol, and at Newport, these operate every two hours throughout the day. Initially they were supplemented by local stage buses running via Filton and Chepstow on what was in effect an extension of an existing service between Chepstow and Cardiff. This service, which took 2 hours compared to 1 hour 35 minutes by the express service after the M.4 had been completed to Newport, acted as a relief to the express service especially in the first six months of operation. Thereafter the stage service was cut back to Chepstow and there is still sufficient demand, particularly at weekends, to justify the continued operation of both services to at least the end of 1970. Seasonal activities on these two services is much less than with excursion and hire traffic. Initially relief services were called for particularly at weekends but the novelty of seeing the Bridge and visiting the city across the estuary went early in 1967. The remaining stage service is less frequent and is an extension to Chepstow of an existing service from Dursley to Thornbury.

4.78 Stage and express facilities between Bristol, Newport and Cardiff represented a completely new facility and any traffic therefore represented diversions from rail or generated movements, some of it initially being facility generated. The main express route provides links at both terminals with networks of local bus services in areas where local train services have been drastically curtailed. Furthermore the rail service was not amended to provide a regular express facility until May 1967 when an hourly service linking Cardiff, Newport and Bristol was introduced. At the same time the local service from stations in North Bristol and from Pilning was largely confined to peak periods. In May 1970 the rail service was further reduced to a two-hourly basis and through services from South Wales to points reached via Bristol are now confined to one train daily to and from Portsmouth.

Express Services to and from South Wales

4.79 Prior to the Bridge, the main focal point for all regular long-distance coach services was Cheltenham, the main interchange of the Associated Motorways Network. As soon as the Bridge was opened all daytime services from South Wales to London were switched to the Bridge route offering a new facility and a shortened journey to London. At the same time several new routes were incorporated. Some were extensions into South Wales of existing routes from Bristol onwards, notably to Portsmouth. Others were experimental such as that from Aberdare to Paignton which did not call at Bristol. To enable these to serve the main originating points in South Wales — Cardiff, Treherbert, Aberdare and Swansea — a new interchange was established at Caerwent west of Chepstow. Connecting services to Cheltenham have continued for areas such as East Anglia and the North and the night services to London continue to use this route.

4.80 The main outcome has therefore been a diversion of traffic from South Wales to London, the South Coast and the South West to routes based on the Bridge, and new interchanges have come into operation for South Wales passengers at Caerwent and Bristol in place of Cheltenham. The pattern of traffic on the routes using the Bridge has now settled back in line with that on the express service network on a whole; namely that the peak of business may well have been passed and there is a growing dependence on particular social groups for whom the lack of a private motor car and the absence of local rail services make the express coach and only form of public transport to many smaller towns and to country and holiday areas. Before leaving long-distance express services note should be taken of a number of special weekend and holiday services which have either been diverted over the Bridge or inaugurated with its opening. These range from express services to Butlin's Holiday Camp at Minehead to weekend leave coaches for service personnel from South Wales stationed in the South of England.

Excursions and Private Hire Movements

4.81 For sheer volume however, excursions and private hire movements dwarf scheduled services and these have therefore been surveyed specially. In 1967 a first survey was made by postal questionnaires sent to all licensed operators in the South Wales and South Western licensing areas. A year later a second survey was made of respondents to the first survey to get comparative data for the second year of the use of the Bridge as it was felt that the novelty effect would have passed away. As a further check the largest operators were contacted again in April 1970 to check on the evolution of such traffic. The first and second surveys showed that 20 major operators carried 70% of passengers and the 1970 study was confined to these plus the 15 next largest operators. No attempt has been made to study movement originating in other regions though these are substantial.

4.82 Coach traffic, as indicated in Table 3.1 has declined after the initial novelty of the Bridge had worn off and has now settled into a more conventional pattern in the view of the principal operators with whom trends were discussed in 1970. Initially the impact was even greater than the detail in Table 3.1 indicates. From the detailed returns to the postal survey of coach operators they were heavily engaged in September/October 1966. The pattern of traffic at that time was influenced by three abnormal features — the number of "trial runs" to test the feasibility and popularity of specific destinations, the "facility generated" trips to see the Bridge and little else, and some special excursions organised by firms to induce people to come to their shops in Bristol or Cardiff. The pattern of crossings during the first year, by number of persons reported or estimated, gives 62% originating in South Wales compared to 38% originating in the South West. This is also a highly seasonal demand, one of the largest operators reporting 92% of their passengers as crossing in the period from Easter to September.

4.83 The second survey conducted in 1970 was confined to the principal territorial bus companies and the largest excursions and hire operators in the two regions. Tables 4.13 and 4.14 show the distribution by destina-

---

TABLE 4.13

Destination†	Sept. 1966–Sept. 1967*	Percentages Jan.–Dec. 1968	Jan.–Dec. 1969
West Glos. Severn Bridge	4	3	2
Bristol	37	35	25
Weston-super-Mare North Somerset	18	18	28
Bath	3	6	7
North Wilts	2	4	6
West Somerset Devon & Cornwall	9	15	15
Dorset	4	2	3
South East & London	8	16	13
Unallocated	16		
	100	100	100

Destinations of Eastbound Coach Crossings — Excursion and Private Hire by Principal Territorial and Excursion/Hire Operators

* The data for 1966–67 relates to more operators than that for 1968 and 1969.

† See Map C.

tion of coach movements originating in South Wales and the South West respectively, and it is interesting to note the changes in the popularity of destinations. This data also supports the operators' views that total business is declining, being increasingly dependent on either children or older persons, and that coach tours spread over several days are increasing absolutely and relatively in their total activity.

4.84 The principal eastbound destination is Bristol whether as the sole destination or a joint one. However, it has been declining both absolutely and relatively while the South East has become increasingly more popular partly as a destination in its own right and partly on account of continental coach tours. On the west bank the Wye Valley has been the principal destination.

4.85 The switch from destinations favoured when the Bridge was first opened is clear from Tables 4.13 and 4.14. The further exploration of the South West is seen from the increased trips to Bath, Longleat, Weston-super-Mare and North Somerset. The initiative of the tour planners is reflected in the changes. Why do people from Aberdare go to Bath while those from Port Talbot favour country houses and Weston-super-Mare? Particular operators have licences to particular destinations e.g. Minehead, Weymouth. Though total trips and carryings had increased 1968—69 nearly all operators reported significantly less traffic than when the Bridge first opened! This is true of daytrips as an increased proportion of crossings are due to longer coach tours to the South East and South West regions and to the Continent. Similarly, westwards there is a small increase in longer-distance excursions but the Wye Valley and the Newport/Caerleon areas account for 70% of all destinations.

4.86 There is also concentration of points of origin. While Bristol dominates the eastern origins if only because of its large population, Weston-super-Mare accounts for many excursions. Operators report that

middle-aged and elderly visitors take a tour a day whilst on holiday. In Cheltenham, tours are said to be a social occasion! On the Welsh side the valleys proved the main sources.

4.87 The extent to which excursions are a net addition to coach business or a diversion from other routes has been discussed with operators. In the first year there was a net increase and a diversion from other tours, but subsequently the latter have picked up while Bridge crossings have declined from their earlier peaks. Nevertheless these still represent a significant excursion movement. The net effects on sub-areas by number of persons carried is set out in Appendix 27.

4.88 The fall in rail excursion traffic and in short-distance cross-channel steamer traffic indicates a switch to road traffic whether by coach or by private car. The volume of coach business, however, is such as to indicate both a switch from other destinations and a net increase in business through traffic generated by the Bridge.

4.89 To ascertain the balance of advantage between regions or areas it is necessary to compare the expenditure in one region, i.e. fares of outgoing passengers plus expenditure by incoming travellers on meals, souvenirs etc., with that in another region. A rough guide to balance of advantage is therefore the net movement of travellers as set out in Appendix 27 and supplemented by the supposition that full-day trips are more likely to involve greater expenditure per head at the destination than half-day trips. On the other hand, where an area "sends" people a long distance the fare income per head is going to be greater there than where short distances are involved.

4.90 The evidence in net movements is clear. The South West gains overall whereas South Wales loses, especially the main industrial areas. Bristol gains whereas Cardiff does not. On this point it is perhaps appropriate to conclude with four observations, the first three of which are derived from interviews with operators and those

TABLE 4.14   Destinations of Westbound Coach Crossings — Excursion and Private Hire by Principal Territorial and Excursion/Hire Operators

		Percentages	
Destination†	Sept. 1966—Sept. 1967*	Jan.—Dec. 1968	Jan.—Dec. 1969
Wye Valley	40	61	53
Newport	2	6	17
Cardiff	8	17	10
Barry	7	1	1
North Mon.	2	2	—
Upper Valleys	1	2	2
Lower Valleys Porthcawl	7	2	2
Swansea Port Talbot	3	2	1
West Wales	1	—	—
Central Wales	4	7	12
Unallocated	26	—	—
	100	100	100

* The data for 1966—67 relates to more operators than that for 1968 and 1969.
† See Map C.

concerned with tourist traffic —

(i)   Quite apart from any question of attractiveness or interest, destinations in the South West are geared for coach traffic and South Wales destinations, with some notable exceptions, are not. Operators have stated that catering and even parking facilities are a problem in Central and West Wales. Even in Cardiff the terminus designated for excursions in the first few months turned out to be a car park from which coaches were expressly debarred.

(ii)   There is a certain ambivalence as to new traffic in such areas as the Brecon Beacons National Park which is reflected in its attitude to advertising in the South West.

(iii)   Initially a considerably greater advertising and publicity effort was directed from the South West than vice-versa.

(iv)   The bus companies in South Wales sought to develop coach excursion traffic at rates competitive with the scheduled services and sought to reinforce this by advertising. The main company east of the Bridge concentrated on developing the scheduled service as the key to the situation leaving excursion development to affiliates.

Conclusions

4.91   The overall picture that emerges is that the Bridge has generated substantial new traffic for both commercial and leisure purposes. Whilst five million cars crossing the Bridge in a year (two and a half million round trips) is a formidable total, when averaged over the population in the areas between which the Bridge has reduced distances, it is less striking. About half of the total traffic is between areas within about 30 miles of the Bridge. A further one and a half million journeys have one trip-end in this area, which implies a further third of a million round trips originating in this area near the Bridge. Allowing an average occupancy of 3, this would mean that on average each person in the area made 3 cross-Bridge trips in a year. In this area, as the household survey shows, a high proportion, about three-quarters, of all households made some use of the Bridge. However a cross-Bridge trip 3 times a year scarcely constitutes a dramatic change in the pattern of life, and of course most people make less than 3 such trips. About 1 in 15 households average 1 trip per head per month — which no doubt implies a higher frequency for at least some members of the household — so that for this not insignificant group the Bridge implies a sharper change. About 1% of households average a trip per week and for this group the Bridge implies a considerable change in patterns of life. In Chepstow for example, about 4% of households fall into this category. Further, the size of this group, where the Bridge has had a real impact, is growing over time; a comparison of the two Newport Surveys shows this.

REFERENCES

1.   The screenline interview points were, in 1966, at the A.40/A.48 junction west of Gloucester, A.449 at the approach to M.50 and the Beachley-Aust ferry. In 1967 the Severn Bridge replaced the ferry as an interview point.

CHAPTER FIVE

The Bridge and Freight Transport

5.1 This chapter is concerned with the pattern of transport in relation to the Bridge and changes that followed its opening. Data is drawn from sample surveys of vehicles crossing and from surveys of firms in the manufacturing, wholesale distribution and road haulage industries.

Traffic by Area

5.2 In 1968, 1,243,000 lorries crossed the Bridge and Table 3.5, based on traffic surveys in March, August and November 1968, estimates the extent of movements between areas. Of the annual total, 506,000 vehicles (41%) were on journeys originating or terminating in the Bristol area. East of the Bridge, London was the next most important area with 201,000 vehicles (16%) and over 100,000 vehicles had each of Wiltshire, Central Southern England or Somerset as one trip-end. Cardiff was the most important area west of the Bridge with 376,000 vehicles (30%) and Newport was a trip-end for 291,000 (23%). Three other areas also had over 100,000 vehicles — "Rest of Glamorgan" 171,000 (14%), "Rest of Monmouthshire" 142,000 (11%) and Swansea 135,000 (11%).

5.3 Something of the immediate impact of the Bridge can be inferred from the Gloucestershire County Council screenline sample surveys of west-bound vehicles in August 1966, before the Bridge opened, and a year later. These surveys included buses as well as lorries but bus traffic is too modest a proportion of the total to substantially distort the picture. The later growth of traffic can be seen by a comparison of the pattern at the pre-Easter traffic surveys at the Bridge in 1967 and 1968. Table 5.1 gives the journeys having one trip in particular areas in August 1967 as a percentage of the corresponding number in 1966 and similarly traces the change between the Spring of 1967 and 1968 (full matrices for these surveys are given in Appendix 29). For reasons discussed above in connection with light vehicles traffic journeys, Rest of Great Britain has been ignored as to both origin and destination. Generated traffic, calculated on the same basis as for light traffic, constituted 25% of the heavy vehicles crossing the Bridge in August 1967.

Area†	August 1967 as % of August 1966	Spring 1968 as % of Spring 1967	TABLE 5.1
Origins			
Bristol	184	150	
East Glos.	83	161	
Somerset	151	74	
Wiltshire	174	211	
Devon & Cornwall	101	68	**Growth of Lorry Traffic August 1966—67**
Central Southern England	89	313	**and Spring 1967—68**
London	113	199	
South East Coast	84	80	
Destinations			
Newport	164	129	
Rest Mon.	100	120	
West Glos.	96	183	
Cardiff	120	210	
Rest Glam.	175	167	
Hereford & Brecon	84	*	
Swansea	92	158	
West Wales	121	139	

* Not available: Herefore and Brecon included in
   Rest of Great Britain in Spring 1967.
† See Map B.

5.4   To the east of the Bridge the sharp impact is limited to areas nearest the Bridge — Bristol, Somerset, and Wiltshire. Subsequent growth is strongest at some points more distant — the London area and Central Southern England. Wiltshire is the one area with high growth in both periods. Something of the same pattern is found to the west of the Bridge. There is a contrast between the large initial growth at Newport and a small decline at Swansea, with subsequent stronger growth at Swansea. The Rest of Glamorgan shares Wiltshire's place with strong growth in both periods. With Cardiff, the initial impact is moderate and subsequent growth very strong; the case is similar to West Gloucestershire. The Rest of Monmouthshire shows little impact but some of its important routes (e.g. to London and parts of Central Southern England) are least changed by the Bridge. The decline in East Gloucestershire between August 1966 and August 1967 is the result of the decline in trade between East Gloucestershire and West Gloucestershire (from 1,235 vehicles to 1,051) as West Gloucestershire strengthened its Bristol connections.

The Pattern of Routes

5.5   A questionnaire sent to all members of the Road Haulage Association in the South Wales and South Western traffic areas at the end of 1966 (35% responding) gives some further detail of the pattern of road transport soon after the Bridge opened. Considering traffic between South Wales and the South West region, 30% of Welsh-based firms stated that more than one-tenth of their traffic was to or from the South West, including 13% of firms where this traffic was over one-fifth of the total and a small group of 7% where it was over three-tenths of the total. The corresponding figures for firms based in the South West were 23% of firms with over one-tenth of their traffic to South Wales, including 6% over one-fifth and 8% sending over three-tenths of their traffic to or from South Wales.

5.6   Regarding other regions, Table 5.2 gives the number of road haulage firms operating to each of the other regions with no indication of the tonnages carried. Looking at particular areas of 150 firms based in Newport, nearly all delivered in Newport, 22% in Cardiff, 35% in London and the South East

and 20% to the Midlands. Of Bristol-based firms, 17% travelled to London and 24% to the Midlands. Considering all very small firms in South Wales and the South West (1 or 2 vehicles), 14% went to London and the South East, 15% to the Midlands and 17% to the Southern Region. For the largest operators (over 16 vehicles), 36% travelled to London and the South East, 32% to the Midlands and 15% to the Southern Region. While a greater proportion of the larger firms operate over long distances there is still a considerable amount of long-distance haulage by small firms.

5.7   Further discussion of movements between areas, in relation to particular commodities, is to be found in Chapters 6 and 7.

Changes in Transport Modes

5.8   Given that the Severn acted as a major barrier to road transport, the dominant national mode, the opening of the Bridge could be expected to have three results. The first would be a switch from rail to road among those already sending goods across the estuary in line with national trends. The second would be a switch from road hauliers to a firm's own vehicles now that these could serve new areas by daily trips from existing establishments. The third would be new demands on road transport as new business is generated in areas previously inaccessible in time or distance. In examining all three it is vital to recognise that some of the changes might have occurred irrespective of the Bridge. Switches between transport modes and reorganisations could well follow from mergers and take-overs, not less than 16% of the manufacturing firms surveyed had been so involved between 1966 and 1969 nearly all having no direct connection with the opening of the Bridge.

5.9   Any switch from one mode to another has to be seen against the pre-Bridge situation as well as national trends since its opening. Appendix 30 shows the extent to which manufacturers employing 100 or more persons used particular modes pre-Bridge and at the time of the second industrial survey in 1968—69. Pre-Bridge most firms used their own vehicles in their own region particularly in South West North. For deliveries to the region across the estuary there was little difference between firms in the two regions as to use of the various modes, except for a slightly

Destinations (Regions)	Origins		Total	Percentage of all operators	TABLE 5.2
	Wales	West			
East and West Ridings	59	109	168	3.0	
North Midland	48	90	138	2.4	
Eastern	21	20	41	.7	
London and South East	322	740	1,062	18.7	**Routes Travelled by Haulage Firms**
Southern	138	875	1,013	17.9	
Midlands	420	693	1,113	19.6	
North Western	176	170	346	6.0	
Scotland	13	24	37	.7	
Northern	64	8	72	1.3	
All Regions	166	417	583	10.3	

higher use of their own vehicles by South West firms. To the rest of England and Wales there was again little difference except a greater use of British Rail from South Wales. The position in the second survey 1968–69, is that most firms continue to use their own vehicles in their home region. The percentage doing so continues to be substantially higher in the South West than in South Wales — indeed the South West percentage is higher than in the first survey while the South Wales percentage is lower. There is more use of road hauliers in both home regions and reduced use of British Rail especially in the South West. Such changes are clearly independent of the Bridge as such, and may have been due to changes in railways as well as consignors' policies. This is supported by movements from the South West to Other Regions separately set out in the second survey for London and South East and Rest of England and Wales. Here there is a sharp fall in the number and proportion of firms using British Rail and a slight increase in the number using road hauliers.

5.10 The first switch, from rail to road, is examined in three ways, the extent to which firms used rail before and after, the extent to which they expected to change and did so, and the changes reported. Table 5.3 shows the use by manufacturers of British Rail before and after the Bridge for movements between South Wales and the South West, and between both regions and Other Regions.

5.11 British Rail is little used in the region where a firm is located, rather more used across the estuary and even more to Other Regions. Among firms in both regions the proportion reporting that they used British Rail before the Bridge opened exceeds that reporting that they did so afterwards, pointing to a net movement away from rail. It is easy to link this to the availability of the Bridge but for the fact that in areas not affected by the Bridge the degree of switch away from British Rail is at least as great. Indeed, among South West firms the drop in use of rail to Other Regions is greater than to South Wales. It is hard to avoid the conclusion that cessation of use of British Rail appears to be as much a matter of an overall change as one due to the Bridge.

5.12 The extent to which manufacturers expected to switch from rail to road and the actual outcome is set out in Table 5.4 Overall, 61 firms expected to switch from rail to road, in fact 37 firms did so. Expressed as percentages of those trading across the estuary 39% expected to change and only 21% did so. Twice as many firms expected to make changes as did in fact make them. Comparing the two main survey regions, the forecasts were correct in a much higher percentage of cases in the South West than in South Wales. Whilst the questions posed to distributors in the first stage of the survey do not permit a directly comparable analysis, evidence from the second stage suggests that while very few firms switched they represented a high proportion of those that had hitherto used British Rail.

5.13 Changes were made from rail to road as set out in Table 5.5. These include "multiple switches" such as "rail to haulier and own transport" and "rail and haulier to own transport". Numerically the switch is

TABLE 5.3   Use of British Rail — Before and After Opening of Bridge*
(Manufacturers 100+ employees)

| Destination Region | Use of British Rail | Location of Firm | | | | | |
| | | South Wales | | South West | | All Firms | |
		No.	% of 1–4	No.	% of 1–4	No.	% of 1–4
South Wales	1 Before & After	31	22.6	40	24.1	71	23.4
	2 Before only	20	14.6	31	18.7	51	16.8
	3 After only	10	7.3	8	4.8	18	5.9
	4 Not used	76	55.5	87	52.4	163	53.8
	5 No trade	24	—	55	—	79	—
South West	1 Before & After	32	28.8	45	22.7	77	24.9
	2 Before only	21	18.9	31	15.7	52	16.8
	3 After only	9	8.1	9	4.6	18	5.8
	4 Not used	49	44.1	113	57.1	162	52.4
	5 No trade	50	—	18	—	68	—
Other Regions	1 Before & After	58	41.1	75	37.9	133	39.2
	2 Before only	24	17.0	39	19.7	63	18.6
	3 After only	13	9.2	12	6.1	25	7.4
	4 Not used	46	32.6	72	36.4	118	34.8
	5 No trade	19	—	19	—	38	—

* Tables based on replies by firms completing questionnaires
   in both stages of the survey

clearly more marked among manufacturers than distributors who already relied far more on road transport. It is also greater among firms in South West than South Wales. It is most marked between firms in South West North (18.4%) and South East Wales (13.6%).

5.14 Evidence from internal surveys conducted by British Rail substantiates this switch but our analysis of particular drops in traffic makes it difficult to relate them specifically to the Bridge except in so far as Newport is the point where the change has been most marked. This is further considered in Appendix 53. Clearly the Bridge has ended a special position so far as railroad competition is concerned and a more normal division of traffic between South Wales and the South West is only to be expected.

5.15 The second change, the switch from hauliers to a firm's own vehicles, can be examined in the same way. Table 5.6 shows the use of road hauliers before and after, while Table 5.7 sets out the data on use of own vehicles. These relate to manufacturers. The relevant questions were not asked in the first distribution survey.

5.16 Among manufacturers there is some increased use of road hauliers within the regions where firms are based but their main use is for longer journeys, notably to Other Regions, and especially from South Wales where 80% reported using them before and after. Table 5.6 reveals a similar pattern to that in Table 5.3 namely a greater reliance on road hauliers by South Wales firms than South West firms. However the trend between 1966 and 1969 is for more use to be made of road hauliers especially to distant regions with usage by firms in the South West rising to a similar level to that among those in South Wales.

5.17 Taking use of own vehicles by manufacturers there is a higher use of own vehicles by South West firms in their own region; there is less change in their use of their own vehicles in South Wales than in their own region. Such evidence supports the argument that South West firms used more own vehicles than South Wales before the Bridge and challenges any hypothesis that there would be a significant switch to own vehicles as a result of the Bridge. Conversely, fewer South West firms made no use of their own vehicles both before and after in their own region

---

TABLE 5.4 **Expected and Realised Changes from Rail to Road***
(Manufacturers 100+ employees)

	Location of Firm					
Change	South Wales		South West		All Firms	
	No.	% of 5 + 6	No.	% of 5 + 6	No.	% of 5 + 6
1. Expected and Achieved	6	7.0	13	15.9	19	11.3
2. Expected but not Achieved	24	27.9	18	22.0	42	25.0
3. Not Expected but Achieved	12	14.0	6	7.3	18	10.7
4. Not Expected nor Achieved	44	51.2	45	54.9	89	53.0
5. Change Occurred (1 + 3)	18	20.9	19	23.2	37	22.0
6. No Change (2 + 4)	68	79.1	63	76.8	131	78.0
7. Forecast Correct (1 + 4)	50	58.1	58	70.7	108	64.3
8. Forecast Incorrect (2 + 3)	36	41.9	24	29.3	60	35.7

* Table based on replies by firms that completed the questionnaire in both stages of the survey and includes only firms trading across the Estuary and using British Rail before the Bridge opened.

TABLE 5.5 **Changes from Rail to Road Transport for Despatches to Areas Across Severn Estuary***

	Location of Firm Despatching					
Type and Size of Firm Despatching	South Wales		South West		All Firms	
	No.	%	No.	%	No.	%
Manufacturers 100+	26	14	29	17	55	15
Manufacturers 20–99⊕	3	10	6	10	9	10
Distributors 20+	6	21	13	18	19	19

* % of firms despatching some goods by any transport mode other than their own vehicles or parcel post and excluding new firms and those not trading across the Estuary or not completing the question.
⊕ 25% sample, not weighted.

than was the case in South Wales. For movement to Other Regions there was a slight drop in the use of own vehicles. Bearing in mind the many other changes, including mergers, this slight or negative reaction to the Bridge is not surprising. Yet the evidence from other questions indicates that there has been some change attributable to the Bridge.

TABLE 5.6   Use of Road Hauliers — Before and After Opening of Bridge*
(Manufacturers 100+ employees)

Destination Region	Use of Road Hauliers	Location of Firm					
		South Wales		South West		All Firms	
		No.	% of 1 — 4	No.	% of 1 — 4	No.	% of 1 — 4
South Wales	1 Before & After	68	49.6	82	49.4	150	49.5
	2 Before only	18	13.1	19	11.5	37	12.2
	3 After only	22	16.1	23	13.9	45	14.9
	4 Not used	29	21.2	42	25.3	71	23.4
	5 No trade	24	—	55	—	79	—
South West	1 Before & After	69	62.7	99	50.3	168	54.7
	2 Before only	12	10.9	20	10.2	32	10.4
	3 After only	14	12.7	30	15.2	44	14.3
	4 Not used	15	13.6	48	24.4	63	20.5
	5 No trade	50	—	18	—	68	—
Other Regions	1 Before & After	102	72.3	133	67.2	235	69.3
	2 Before only	12	8.5	12	6.1	24	7.1
	3 After only	11	7.8	27	13.6	38	11.2
	4 Not used	16	11.4	26	13.1	42	12.4
	5 No trade	19	—	19	—	38	—

* Table based on replies by firms completing questionnaires in both stages of the survey.

TABLE 5.7   Use of Own Vehicles — Before and After Opening of Bridge*
(Manufacturers 100+ employees)

Destination Region	Use of Own Vehicles	Location of Firm					
		South Wales		South West		All Firms	
		No.	% of 1 — 4	No.	% of 1 — 4	No.	% of 1 — 4
South Wales	1 Before & After	97	70.8	104	62.7	201	66.3
	2 Before only	13	9.5	10	6.0	23	7.6
	3 After only	1	0.7	11	6.6	12	4.0
	4 Not used	26	19.0	41	24.7	67	22.1
	5 No trade	24	—	55	—	79	—
South West	1 Before & After	56	50.5	144	73.0	200	64.9
	2 Before only	13	11.7	10	5.1	23	7.5
	3 After only	12	10.8	14	7.1	26	8.4
	4 Not used	30	27.0	29	14.7	59	19.2
	5 No trade	50	—	18	—	68	—
Other Regions	1 Before & After	85	60.3	123	62.1	208	61.4
	2 Before only	15	10.6	20	10.1	35	10.3
	3 After only	10	7.1	17	8.6	27	8.0
	4 Not used	31	22.0	38	19.2	69	20.4
	5 No trade	19	—	19	—	38	—

* Table based on replies by firms completing questionnaires in both stages of the survey.

5.18 Turning to the contrast of expectations and realised changes, it is clear from Tables 5.8 and 5.9 that the forecasts as to changes within road transport were more accurate than between rail and road. The main reason is that the majority of both manufacturers and distributors did not expect a change in their use of outside hauliers. Of those that were surprised, the majority did not make the expected switch. Among manufacturers the unexpected changes were mainly in South Wales (9%). When combined with the changes that were as expected, 18.5% of South Wales firms switched from hauliers to their own vehicles compared to only 9% among South West firms where there was already a much higher proportion using their own vehicles. This is a noteworthy switch by South Wales firms.

5.19 Table 5.10 shows the changes reported. In South Wales there was a switch by a much higher proportion of manufacturers employing 100 and over than among their equivalents in the South West; conversely there was more frequent change among distributors in the South West than in South Wales.

5.20 These changes point to fewer firms using road hauliers in cross-estuary traffic but this does not mean a reduction in business offered for two reasons. The first is clearly the increased business coming from these firms — the majority — that are not making any change and amongst which increases in cross-estuary trade must have occurred. Table 5.11 shows that over a third of manufacturers in both regions and of distributors in the South West increased the number of loads despatched across the estuary. The second is the switch from rail and even own vehicles to hauliers on other routes especially long-distance ones.

TABLE 5.8   **Expected and Realised Changes from Road Haulier to Own Vehicles***
(Manufacturers 100+ employees)

			Location of Firm			
Change	**South Wales**		**South West**		**All Firms**	
	No.	% of 5 + 6	No.	% of 5 + 6	No.	% of 5 + 6
1. Expected and Achieved	11	9.2	7	6.1	18	7.7
2. Expected but not Achieved	18	15.1	21	18.3	39	16.7
3. Not Expected but Achieved	11	9.2	3	2.6	14	6.0
4. Not Expected nor Achieved	79	66.4	84	73.0	163	69.7
5. Change Occurred (1 + 3)	22	18.5	10	8.7	32	13.7
6. No Change (2 + 4)	97	81.5	105	91.3	202	86.3
7. Forecast Correct (1 + 4)	90	75.6	91	79.1	181	77.4
8. Forecast Incorrect (2 + 3)	29	24.4	24	20.9	53	22.7

* Table based on replies by firms that completed questionnaires in both stages of the survey, traded across the estuary and used hauliers before the Bridge opened.

TABLE 5.9   **Expected and Realised Changes from Road Haulier to Own Vehicles***
(Distributors)

			Location of Firm			
Change	**South Wales**		**South West**		**All Firms**	
	No.	% of 5 + 6	No.	% of 5 + 6	No.	% of 5 + 6
1. Expected and Achieved	2	16.7	7	23.3	9	21.4
2. Expected but not Achieved	1	8.3	6	20.0	7	16.7
3. Not Expected but Achieved	1	8.3	2	6.7	3	7.1
4. Not Expected nor Achieved	8	66.7	15	50.0	23	54.8
5. Change Occurred (1 + 3)	3	25.0	9	30.0	12	28.6
6. No Change (2 + 4)	9	75.0	21	70.0	30	71.4
7. Forecast Correct (1 + 4)	10	83.3	22	73.3	32	76.2
8. Forecast Incorrect (2 + 3)	2	16.7	8	26.7	10	23.8

* Table based on replies by firms that completed questionnaires in both stages of the survey, traded across the estuary and used hauliers before the Bridge opened.

Further Characteristics of Bridge Users

5.21 A second survey of road hauliers requested all firms which, at the first survey in 1966, sent more than 10% of their traffic across the Bridge to the South West or South Wales to keep complete logs for their vehicles' journeys for a given week (3rd–9th November 1968). Logs were also requested from a quarter of other firms, the remaining firms being asked to complete a less demanding questionnaire.

The response was 13% to the questionnaires and 7% to the request for logs. These surveys reveal some of the characteristics of Bridge users.

5.22 Regarding fleet size and use of the Bridge, 158 usable replies from firms receiving only the questionnaire were distributed as follows:
It can be seen that regular Bridge users tend to be the firms with larger fleets. Among regular users 63% of firms have more than five vehicles, whereas only 30% of others have this size of fleet.

TABLE 5.10   **Changes from Road Hauliers to Firms' Own Vehicles for Despatches to Areas Across Severn Estuary***

	Location of Firm Despatching					
	South Wales		South West		All Firms	
Type and Size of Firm Despatching	No.	%	No.	%	No.	%
Manufacturers 100+	27	16	13	7	40	11
Manufacturers 20–99⊕	3	10	5	8	8	9
Distributors 20+	5	17	17	24	22	22

* Percentage of firms despatching some goods by any transport mode other than their own vehicles or parcel post and excluding new firms, those not trading across the estuary or not completing the question.
⊕ 25% sample, not weighted.

TABLE 5.11   **Changes in the number of despatches per week by Road Transport across the Severn Estuary***

	Manufacturers 100+ employees						Distributors					
	South Wales		South West		Total		South Wales		South West		Total	
Changes Reported	No.	%	No.	%	No.	%	No.	%	No.	%	No.	%
No Change	73	48	79	43	152	45	31	56	56	51	87	53
Decrease in no. of loads	21	13	15	8	36	11	4	7	11	10	15	9
No traffic before now infrequent movements	7	5	22	12	29	9	13	24	4	4	17	10
Increase in despatches by road	52	34	66	37	118	35	7	13	39	35	46	28
TOTAL	153	100	182	100	335	100	55	100	110	100	165	100

* Table based on replies by firms that completed the questionnaire in both stages of the survey and also excludes firms located in the Forest of Dean and those using only the A48/A40/M50 routes to despatch goods across the estuary.

TABLE 5.12   **Fleet Size, Regular Users* and Others**

Size of Fleet	1–2	3–5	6–10	11–15	16–20	20+	Total
Regular Users	2	18	18	9	4	3	54
Others	42	31	20	6	1	4	104

* Regular use defined as at least one crossing per fortnight, or where traffic was seasonal, at least two crossings per week during the season.

5.23 Table 5.13 gives the distribution of firms by average miles travelled by their vehicles in the given week for regular Bridge users and others. While both distributions have a wide dispersion, regular users have higher mileages than the remainder. The overall average for regular users is 715 miles against 531 for the remainder. On average, 70% of the miles travelled were loaded.

Changes in Operating Conditions

5.24 At both stages of the survey of road haulage industry firms were asked whether the nature or geographical area of their operations had changed as a result of the opening of the Bridge. More than half the respondents at the first stage offered some information and in general the impact of the Bridge depended very much on the haulier's (or his customer's) initiative and competitive situation. The impact was not seen as an objective clear-cut saving applicable to all hauliers. For example, some firms replied that any saving from the Bridge was insufficient to use productively; drivers merely returned early. Others made it clear that by careful rearrangement of work and schedules, or extending the market area savings could be turned to use; in some cases by using the time available in warehousing where labour was scarce. In some cases the Bridge was seen as merely resulting in an enforced reduction in mileage and hence turnover; in others it was an increase in productivity which was passed on (in part) to the customer through reduced mileage charges and which also released men and vehicles for further work. Of large operators 20% mentioned specific savings as against 13% of small operators.

5.25 Clearly most of the savings were seen by hauliers in terms of fixed mileage savings. Few attempted to quantify this in money terms. Basically, the savings in time were seen in terms of wages, those in mileage in terms of fuel. A good many firms pointed out that their cost savings were passed on to the customer in the form of rate reductions and seemed to imply that this necessarily left no savings to the haulier himself. At the first stage of the survey, 18% of the Newport, Cardiff and Bristol firms mentioned time and distance savings whereas the figure falls to 5% of the Cornwall, Glamorgan, Carmarthen and Cardigan firms. Thus those nearer to the Bridge noticed more savings, or at least mentioned them more often.

TABLE 5.13 — Firms' Average Miles per Vehicle, Regular Users and Others

Average Miles per Vehicle (3–9/11/68)	Number of Firms	
	Regular Users	Others
0 — 300	4	36
— 500	8	22
— 700	16	18
— 1,000	17	17
— 1,500	7	9
Over 1,500	1	2
Total	53	104

5.26 At the second stage of the survey it was the major users[1] (of the firms which returned logs) which not surprisingly noted most change consequent upon the Bridge opening. Of the 31 firms in the major user group, only 4 stated that there was no change in their overall mileage. Of the rest, 15 found a proportional increase in mileage, 8 a proportional decrease in mileage and 4 gave no answer. Eight of the 22 firms in the randomly picked group found no change, 3 found an increase in mileage, 10 a decrease and 1 gave no answer.

5.27 A further question at the second stage of the survey (when more detailed questions were asked about changes in operating conditions) related to changes in the size of fleet. Only 4 firms, of the 53 which returned logs of their fleet operations, stated that the Bridge had caused them to change their size of fleet. On the general question as to whether firms had expanded their cross-Bridge trade, 15 of the major user group said that they had, 11 had not and 5 did not answer. Of the randomly picked group, 17 had expanded their cross-Bridge trade and 5 had not. This is quite an interesting distribution, though the sample is so small, since it implies that of the major users (as defined from their first stage answers) more had already a fully developed trade over the Bridge whereas for the random group the Bridge had opened up opportunities for further trade.

5.28 Of the firms which, at the second stage of the enquiry, received only questionnaires but not logs, 59 stated that a change in overall mileage had resulted from the Bridge and these 59 were distributed as follows:—

TABLE 5.14 — Changes in Overall Mileage

	Increase % of Total mileage					Decrease % of Total mileage				
	1–5	6–10	11–20	20+	Total	1–5	6–10	11–20	20+	Total
No. of firms	16	8	3	4	31	16	8	3	1	28

Of these 59 firms which experienced changed mileages, their size groups are shown in the following table:—

TABLE 5.15 Changes in Overall Mileage, Size of Firms

Size of fleet	Increased mileage	Decreased mileage
1— 2	4	4
3— 5	8	8
6—10	7	12
11—15	5	3
16—20	3	—
20+	4	1
Total	31	28

It can be seen that although the change was almost equal between firms which increased and those which decreased their mileages, there is a distinct tendency for the larger firms to be those which increased their mileages. Twelve of the increased mileage firms had 11 or more vehicles, against 4 of those which decreased mileage. It may be that larger firms are better able to exploit new opportunities.

5.29 Very few firms attempted to quantify their savings in terms of money. Those that did tended to be the larger units and this information was better obtained in interviews. Of other savings indicated, it became clear that quirks in the current licensing laws made it possible for some firms to exploit the cut in mileage, for example by using their current B licenses to get to Cardiff or Bristol where before this may have been outside their radius. Although it could be argued that this is merely a redistributive effect, in that if a firm from East Gloucestershire can now reach Cardiff as a market, so Cardiff firms can compete in East Gloucestershire, the fact is that the rural firm which suddenly gains a large industrial complex is likely to benefit somewhat more than the urban firm which can now reach a small market town. The firm in the smaller area is also more likely to retain its goodwill share of the market despite possible competition. Some firms did express fear of new competition but were outweighed by those which felt themselves to be benefiting from the opening up of new areas. In terms of the South Wales/South West distribution of trade however, it is likely that the benefits will be self-cancelling. In fact this is what seems to have happened, and the growth of heavy vehicle Bridge traffic has been more than substantial enough to fill any gap created.

5.30 A fear expressed by certain hauliers at the first stage of the survey was the danger that manufacturers would find it economic to operate a C license fleet, where before it had been more rational to use the services of a haulier. At present while there has been some switch of business to C license operation this has been offset by new business whether over the Bridge or elsewhere. This particular view was hardly mentioned during the second stage of the haulage survey. Indeed while the fate of the 1969 Transport

Act hangs in the balance it is unlikely that many manufacturers will engage in major capital investment of this kind.

5.31 The essential difference between the Severn Bridge, regarded as a highway improvement, and other motorways, is that the Severn Bridge represents a considerable saving in mileage whereas most motorways save time but little mileage. Hence whereas motorways result in a simple increase in speed and thus raise productivity (in the obvious sense) the Severn Bridge cuts mileage and, though it may also raise speeds on the reduced mileage, most of the time saving cannot be strictly regarded as a rise in productivity to the haulier whose rates are based on mileage. To the C license holder, however, who transports his own goods the reduced mileage represents a direct cut in transport costs, and to the economy as a whole the Bridge represents a cut in total transport costs since the hauliers reduced rates are a cut in costs to his customers. A further point of contrast between the Bridge and a motorway lies in the fact that whereas the motorway saving is small and liable to be kept by the haulier at least in the short-run, in the Bridge situation the saving is so dramatic as to be passed on. Where rates are based on mileage the contrast is self-evident. Ideally, one would wish to know whether the manufacturers whose transport costs are reduced pass this saving on to their customers, but in terms of calculating benefits from the Bridge it does not really matter. It seems, therefore, that the overall effect on hauliers can either be to reduce his total mileage (i.e. production) or to enable him to use the surplus capacity, which results from the Bridge savings, on other trips, which previously he had not elected to undertake. That is, given his current capital investment he previously chose to produce along the area that included the Gloucester route but excluded, for example, Brecon. He now goes over the Bridge and uses his surplus capacity to go to Brecon.

5.32 Sixty-two firms in the general questionnaire section of the second stage of the survey volunteered further information about savings. Most of those which did not give a positive answer stated that they were unable to use the Bridge because their licenses did not include that area. The very few adverse comments came from non-users and the most enthusiastic were the biggest users (and the biggest firms).

5.33 The main points made by respondents to both stages of the survey can be summarised as follows. The Bridge, by cutting mileage and time, makes it possible for drivers to cover a wider area in their permitted 11 hours driving time. This means trade can be expanded — time saved can be used for reloading for the next day's trip, or an extra trip per week (or per day) can be fitted in. Some firms mention cuts in costs and claim that this benefits customers, others just refer to improved services. All the comments made by firms returning logs of operations are to improvements and advantages and to increased opportunities whereas at the first stage of the study there were many references to disadvantages. Either the firms which completed logs are those which have best adjusted to the situation or there is genuinely a time-lag during which firms need to readjust to a new situation. Taking this survey by and large it would seem that those firms which most use the Bridge and are best able to exploit the advantages it offers are already the larger, more efficient and outward looking firms. Clearly those men with business across the estuary before the Bridge opened were best able to feel the advantages of the Bridge. But since the small haulier operating within a small radius was unlikely to be already operating across the Bridge it took him longer to feel the advantages and his fears of new competition were greater. The more glowing accounts of the Bridge's advantages tend to come from the larger firms.

Haulage Rates

5.34 The extent to which rates have fallen or have been held steady while other rates have risen can be seen from the survey of industry and distribution. Table 5.16 shows the reported experiences of firms that used road hauliers. Reductions were most frequent among manufacturers where a third of those using hauliers benefited. Among distributors the proportion is just over a quarter. In both groups the most frequent reports of reduced rates were in centres close to the Bridge, and the proportions benefiting tended to be higher in South Wales. In Newport, for example, 18 firms — nearly half the total — reported reduced rates. However, the largest number of firms benefiting was in Bristol—Severnside. These reductions are in sharp contrast to rail rates where very few rate reductions were reported — four in all!

Summary

5.35 The pattern of traffic between the two regions prior to the Bridge was abnormal because of the Severn's influence as a barrier and the nature of the trading links of both regions with one another and with the rest of the country. The changes brought about by the Bridge are therefore in two stages, an initial cut in transport costs and rates with some switch between transport modes and a subsequent development of more typical demands on the transport industry. The process of adjustment and the exploitation of new opportunities is far from complete.

TABLE 5.16						Changes in Road Haulage rates as a result of the Severn Bridge*						
	Manufacturers 100+ employees						Distributors					
Changes reported	South Wales		South West		Total		South Wales		South West		Total	
	No.	%	No.	%	No.	%	No.	%	No.	%	No.	%
Reduced	48	31	44	34	92	32	8	29	12	26	20	27
Static	29	19	17	13	46	16	8	29	9	20	17	23
Raised	79	51	70	53	149	52	12	43	25	54	37	50

* Table excludes firms not using road hauliers, new firms and firms not completing the question.

REFERENCES

1. Those in the South West are South Wales who at the 1966 survey were found to send at least 10 per cent of their traffic across the Bridge to South Wales and the South West respectively.

CHAPTER SIX

The Bridge and Industry

6.1 The creation of a new link between two regions previously separated by a major barrier to the dominant mode of transport of goods and services can be expected to have significant effects on their trade both with each other and with other regions. Where such a link also offers significant improvements in communications with the largest single market and industrial region to a region hitherto hampered in its economic reconstruction by such a barrier, the results can be expected to be even more striking. If to these is then added the possibility of a single economic region emerging with the link, then the adjustments can be expected to be not only substantial but also to continue over a longer period than two years. This is the set of challenges presented to industry by the Severn Bridge.

6.2 Such challenges can be viewed in three ways. First there is the effect on the input of resources, the organisation and location of activities and the new connections or linkages that are created. This is the ground to be covered in this chapter. Then there is the demand for transport and the changes in transport. These have been largely dealt with in Chapter 5 as regards merchandise and Chapter 4 in respect of personal movements on business. Third and last are the changes in markets and distribution arrangements which are examined in Chapter 7.

6.3 Already in Chapter 1 the pre-Bridge industrial structure of each of the two regions has been described and the conclusion reached that the majority of firms did little trade across the estuary. Organisational links between firms operating on both sides were the exception and the main interests of both regions were with the rest of the country, not with each other. In these circumstances the Bridge opened up a series of possibilities. These have been referred to in general terms in both the original terms of reference of the project and Chapter 2.

6.4 The first is that new organisational links may be set up particularly where firms are parts of wider groups having interests on both sides of the estuary. Where such links are established a second series of events may follow. It may now be possible to rationalise activities by concentrating production on one side or by specialisation of function possibly with some balancing of outputs between plants on both sides. Another consequence may be changes in administrative arrangements or a pooling of inventories.

6.5 A second set of changes could lie in the input of factors of production. This has three aspects. Clearly there is the possiblity of new sources of raw materials or of changes in such sources as a result of rationalisation by suppliers on the lines outlined above. Then there is the

TABLE 6.1

Changes in Ownership*
(Manufacturers 100+ employees)

Change	South Wales		South West		All Firms	
	No.	%	No.	%	No.	%
Respondent taken over directly	4	2.4	6	2.6	10	2.5
Respondent's parent firm taken over	18	10.7	16	6.9	34	8.5
Total taken over	22	13.1	22	9.5	44	11.0
Respondent has taken over or assumed control of branch establishment	3	1.8	10	4.3	13	3.3
Other types of change	3	1.8	5	2.2	8	2.0
Total change	28	16.7	37	16.0	65	16.3
No change	140	83.3	194	84.0	334	83.7
Total	168	100	231	100	399	100

* Table based on replies by firms that completed the questionnaire in both stages of the survey.

switching of supplies, larger intakes now coming from across the estuary and less from other sources. These could extend to services of many kinds. Lastly there is the possibility of new sources of labour

6.6 These lead on to changes in the pattern of trade and quality of service offered and received. The extent to which these arise is related to the degree of new competition that is created. One possible outcome is therefore new competition which may not always be welcomed. Some consideration has therefore to be given to additional commercial advantages and dis-advantages.

6.7 Such possible outcomes have then to be examined in relation to the evidence from traffic and other data on changes in particular industries. In this way it may be possible to form some conclusion as to the longer-term effects of these changes on the industrial structure and development of both regions.

Organisational Changes

6.8 The total population of firms has changed very little during the period of this study, only 14 new manufacturing firms being identified. Within this population there were many changes of ownership as table 6.1 indicates. These may account for many subsequent changes including some already discussed in respect of transport modes in Chapter 5. The significant point is that most of these were national, not inter-regional changes.

.9 Table 6.1 shows that 16% of the firms were in some way affected by take-overs. In most cases these were take-overs of parent companies. The heavy representation of branches of firms based in other regions in the South West accounts for this concentration, particularly in certain industries. Of the 37 changes in the South West, 13 were in the engineering industry representing 33%, tobacco (16%), textiles, clothing and footwear (16%). In South Wales, metal manufacturers

with 29% affected is associated with steel nationalisation in 1967. Engineering and Food, Drink and Tobacco show 14% affected.

6.10 The extent of changes independent of the Bridge is therefore substantial in both survey regions and is far greater than the changes in organisational links between the two regions. Table 6.2 shows the nature and extent of such links; the majority of such firms has no establishments in the region across the estuary and where firms did have more than one establishment in the survey regions this was likely to be on the same side of the estuary as the parent establishment. Even so 1 in 4 did have a unit in the region across the estuary and to this must be added the fact that many firms in South Wales had further connections across it as they were owned by firms in the South East, while many firms in the South West were in a similar position this had no implications for Bridge use.

6.11 The changes set out in Table 6.3 are so few as to confirm that there would be little or no change in the industrial location in the first few years following the opening of the Bridge, and that any changes would be likely for reasons other than that event.

6.12 One aspect of organisation that has been examined is to be more fully explored in later research. This is the location of key decisions on transport and distribution. Table 6.4 shows that despite take-overs which have increased the extent to which firms in the South West have their headquarters in the South East and in other regions, the difference between the percentage of firms having their headquarters in the region where they are located and elsewhere is very marked as between South Wales and the South West. The links to headquarters in the South East and other regions are of interest for two reasons. One is the volume of personal movements on business already discussed in Chapter 4; the other is the impact of take-over bids which is brought out in respect of distributors in Chapter 7.

TABLE 6.2
Organisation Links Between Survey Regions
(Manufacturers 100+ employees)

Nature of Organisational Link	Location of Firm					
	South Wales		South West		Total	
	No.	%	No.	%	No.	%
None; No other plants or depots in either region	111	39.5	101	34.2	212	36.8
Other plants or depots in South Wales but not in South West	95	33.8	10	3.4	105	18.2
Other plants or depots in South West but not in South Wales	19	6.8	114	38.6	133	23.1
Other plants or depots in both regions	56	19.9	70	23.7	126	21.9
Unit(s) across estuary	75	26.7	80	27.1	155	26.9
None across estuary	206	73.3	215	72.9	421	73.1
Total	281	100	295	100	576	100

Changes in Inputs – Raw Materials and Components

6.13 The first possibility is that the Bridge would offer firms the opportunity to obtain supplies of raw materials and components from new sources. The second is that there should be increased intakes from existing sources now that the Bridge offered the opportunity for lower transport costs and/or improved service. The third is that in consequence of the first two there would be reduced use of sources in other regions. All three can be examined from two aspects, the firm as a buyer of materials and services and the view taken by the firm of its own service and trade with others. Here only the former is considered.

6.14 The first possibility – new sources tackled for the first time – is not strongly supported by the evidence in Table 6.5. Among manufacturers 100+, 34 firms (5.9%) reported that they did so while among manufacturers 20–99 only 5 firms (2.9%) reported doing so. In most areas and industries it is a case of a few firms reporting such a change. Newport is an exception with 7 firms (18.9%) reporting use of new sources. On an industry basis clothing and footwear (100+) in South Wales stand out with 6 firms (24%) reporting doing so. This is, however, mainly due to rationalisation by a supplier resulting in concentrating its supply point for South West and South Wales in the Bristol area.

6.15 A different picture emerges with the second possibility – increased use of existing sources (Table 6.6). Among manufacturers employing 100+, 10% report such a change while among manufacturers employing 20-99, 15.5% do so. The largest number was in Bristol/Severnside, 10 large firms (8.8%) and 12 small firms (19%). Above-average percentages of firms were reported from Cardiff, Bridgend and Lower Valleys, North Wiltshire, Wellington-Westbury and Swansea and Port Talbot, while in the Forest of Dean 4 firms (25%) did so. The industries most frequently affected are shown in Table 6.6

TABLE 6.3
Changes in Organisational Links*
(Manufacturers 100+ employees)

Changes in Organisational Links	Location of Firm					
	South Wales		South West		Total	
	No.	%	No.	%	No.	%
Plants both sides before & after Bridge opened	30	17.9	30	13.0	60	15.1
Plant closed across estuary since Bridge opened	–	–	5	2.2	5	1.3
Plant opened across estuary since Bridge opened	5	3.0	4	1.7	9	2.3
No plants across before and after Bridge opened	133	79.2	191	83.0	324	81.4
Total	168	100	230	100	398	100

* Data based on replies by firm that completed the question in both stages of the survey. The other side of the estuary refers to the South West Region for South Wales firms.

TABLE 6.4
Location of Headquarters of Firm
(Manufacturers 100+ employees)

Ultimate Location of Company or Group Headquarters	Location of Firm					
	South Wales		South West		Total	
	No.	%	No.	%	No.	%
Same region	75	26.7	140	47.5	215	37.3
Region across Severn	9	3.2	1	0.3	10	1.7
South East	142	50.5	114	38.5	256	44.4
Other Regions	48	17.1	35	11.9	83	14.4
Overseas	7	2.5	5	1.7	12	2.1
Total	281	100	295	100	576	100

6.16 Turning to the third possibility – reduction in supplies from other regions – 58 firms (10%) of manufacturers employing 100+ and 17 firms (9.8%) of those employing 20-99 report such a change. There is a clear difference between the two survey regions in the degree to which this has occurred. It is clearly much greater in South Wales (12.5%) than in South West (7.8%) among manufacturers employing 100+ with the reverse true of manufacturers employing 20-99 – South West (10.7%) and South Wales (8.1%).

6.17 Table 6.7 shows that improved service was reported almost as frequently as transport cost savings and more frequently than better trading terms. However, in South Wales the most important factor was the decision of supplies to close their depots there with supplies to both regions being concentrated in a single depot in the South West.

TABLE 6.5   **Changes in Sources of Supplies (Manufacturers 100+ employees)**

| | Location of Firm | | | | | |
| | South Wales | | South West | | Total | |
	No.	%	No.	%	No.	%
Supplies drawn across estuary for the first time	19	7	15	5	34	6
Supplies drawn across estuary to an increasing extent	31	11	27	9	58	10
Supplies drawn across estuary for first time and to an increasing extent	50	18	42	14	92	16
Reduction in supplies from other areas	35	13	23	8	58	10

TABLE 6.6   **Industries Reporting Increased Drawing of Supplies Across Estuary (Manufacturers 100+ employees)**

| South Wales | | | South West | | |
Industry	No. of Firms	% in industry	Industry	No. of Firms	% in industry
Building Materials	5	31.3	Mining & Quarrying	5	31.3
Timber & Furniture	2	18.2	Other Metal Goods	3	25.0
Clothing & Footwear	4	16.0	Timber & Furniture	3	17.6
Engineering	8	15.7	Engineering	6	9.5
Metal Manufacture	3	7.9	Food, Drink & Tobacco	4	6.8
Total All Industries	31	11.0	Total All Industries	27	9.2

TABLE 6.7   **Main Reasons Reported for Reducing Supplies Drawn from Other Regions (Manufacturers 100+ employees)**

| | Location of Firm | | | | | |
| | South Wales | | South West | | Total | |
	No.	%	No.	%	No.	%
Saving in transport costs	12	4.3	15	5.1	27	4.7
Improved service	12	4.3	10	3.4	22	3.8
Supplier transferred depot across estuary or opened new depot or policy to supply from other side	13	4.6	5	1.7	18	3.1
Better trading terms	3	1.1	4	1.4	7	1.2
Subcontracting to other factories within group	4	1.4	3	1.0	7	1.2

Changes in Inputs — Service

6.18 The two reasons cited most often, savings in transport costs and improved service have been discussed in Chapter 5. Improved service can now be examined on a wider scale as it is not confined to those who change their intake of materials. (Table 6.8). Such improved service may take several forms, two of particular importance to this study being improved goods transport and better personal service by representatives and technical staff moving by road.

6.19 The industries showing the highest proportions of firms affected (Table 6.9) are those where existing strengths in one region are now available to firms in the cross-estuary region. Thus the services associated with the mining industry in South Wales are now available to firms in North Somerset and Wiltshire while the engineering services of Bristol are made available in South Wales.

6.20 How far had such changes been expected by firms that replied to both surveys? Questioned as to changes in areas used for supplies and raw materials 259 firms (66%) of those manufacturers employing 100+ reported that they had not expected to make any change and had not done so. A further 49 firms (12.5%) expected to change sources, but did not do so, giving 78.5% making no change. Forty firms (10%) did not expect to make changes but did so and a further 44 (11%) expected to make changes and did so, giving 21.5% making changes in areas of supplies, a slightly higher proportion than reported new sources and additional intakes. Most firms (77%) predicted correctly. The area showing the most cases of change was Bristol with 20 firms (22%) though several areas had a higher proportion expecting changes, notably Forest of Dean 50% (6 firms) and Cardiff 37% (13 firms). Industrially the groups where change was most expected were metal manufacturers (40%) and chemicals (33%) in the South West and in timber and furniture (80%), and textiles and leather (43%) in South Wales. Change occurred most often in mining and quarrying (55%) and other metal goods (50%) in the South West, and in clothing and footwear (55%) and building materials (49%) in South Wales. Forecasts were most often wrong in mining and quarrying (46%) and building materials (29%) in the South West and clothing and footwear (46%) and textiles and leather (43%) in South Wales.

6.21 The attempt to supplement this by data on changes in sub-contracting and ancillary services has been largely unsuccessful because of the paucity of replies to an admittedly complex question in the survey. For the most part the changes reported are isolated ones to which no significance can be attached. Among the few replies on sub-contracting facilities, firms on both sides of the Severn reported using facilities across the estuary for the first time and this was more frequently reported in South Wales. The same is true of plant and machinery maintenance. No evidence has emerged of changes in commercial, financial or consultancy services.

TABLE 6.8

**Firms Reporting Improved Services
from Supplier Across Estuary
(Manufacturers 100+ employees)**

	Location of Firm					
	South Wales		South West		Total	
	No.	%	No.	%	No.	%
Improved service, main supplies	91	48*	68	40*	159	44*
Improved service, ancillary services	37	20*	30	18*	67	19*

* Percentage of firms trading i.e. drawing supplies or
services from region across estuary

TABLE 6.9

**Rank Order of Main Industries Reporting Improved Services
from Suppliers across the Estuary
(Manufacturers 100+ employees)**

South Wales	No. of Firms	% in industry	South West	No. of Firms	% in industry
Building Materials	8	50	Other Metal Goods	6	50
Other Manufacturing Industries	8	50	Chemicals	6	38
Paper, Printing & Publishing	6	50	Mining & Quarrying	6	38
Engineering	23	45	Clothing & Footwear	7	32
Other Metal Goods	10	36	Vehicles	5	29
			Timber & Furniture	5	29
			Engineering	17	27
Total All Industries	91	32	Total All Industries	68	23

6.22 Table 6.10 shows the improvement in services given as reported by firms that were known to be trading across the estuary both before and after the presence of the Bridge. In addition there were firms that only traded across the estuary after the Bridge opened; these are discussed in para 7.48. The replies analysed in Table 6.10 show no difference between the two regions when all firms are considered but this conceals differences between firms in partiuclar localities and industries. By locality in the South West, Gloucester has a much lower proportion affected whereas all other areas show above-average percentages reporting better service. In South Wales the gain is concentrated in those areas along the A48 trunk road.

6.23 Table 6.11 shows the industries in which the highest percentages of firms reported improved service to cross-estuary customers. Among these the largest number in South Wales is in Engineering although the highest percentage is that for food, drink and tobacco. In the South West the corresponding industries are food, drink and tobacco and chemicals.

Changes in inputs — labour

6.24 In two respects the Bridge has had a considerable impact on labour mobility. First, marketing personnel, especially salesmen and technical representatives, can now cover both sides of the estuary from one base easily. Second, construction industry resources are highly mobile; within days of the opening of the Bridge workers and machinery were switched from the Oldbury Power Station which was nearing completion to the Newport by-pass. There is a tendency for contractors, as machinery and building techniques and buildings themselves become more complex, not to hire labour casually but to keep gangs together and provide daily transport from base to sites. Distances travelled are usually about one hour's driving distance — 25 to 40 miles and further if a motorway is available or contracts are scarce. The Bridge opened up the area between Cardiff and Bristol for competition from both sides, for contractors, plant hirers and structural engineers.

6.25 Surveys of marketing personnel and construction workers were not made and it is not possible to quantify the increases in these types of movements across the estuary although they have been considerable. The total volume of commuting across the Bridge is small. The traffic surveys showed that commuters constitute 8.5% of the total weekday traffic or between 800 and 900 vehicles out of 10,000 in 1968 and 1969. The rate of growth of commuter traffic has been the same as for light vehicles. The number of commuters by scheduled bus services is also small.

TABLE 6.10			Areas with Most Firms Reporting Improved Service to Customers across the Estuary (Manufacturers 100+ employees)		
South Wales	No. of Firms	% in area*	South West	No. of Firms	% in area*
Cardiff	27	75	Wellington/Westbury	21	66
Swansea–Port Talbot	8	62	Forest of Dean	9	64
Industrial Carmarthen	5	63	Bristol–Severnside	55	63
Newport	18	56	North Wiltshire	22	56
Total All Areas	113	56	Total All Areas	126	55

* Based on total percentages of firms trading across estuary before Bridge opened.

TABLE 6.11			Rank Order of Industries Reporting Improved Service to Customers across the Estuary (Manufacturing 100+ employees)		
South Wales	No. of Firms	% in industry*	South West	No. of Firms	% in industry*
Food, Drink & Tobacco	8	89	Chemicals	11	79
Other Manufacturing Industries	11	73	Mining & Quarrying	6	75
Timber & Furniture	7	67	Metal Manufacture	3	75
Building Materials	8	66	Food, Drink & Tobacco	29	67
Engineering	28	65	Vehicles	8	62
Total All Industries	113	56	Total All Industries	126	55

* Based on total percentages of firms trading across estuary before Bridge opened.

6.26 The reasons for the small amount and low growth of commuting lie in the urban and industrial structures of the Severnside area. On the labour supply side there are no large urban areas in the immediate vicinity of the Bridge, only Chepstow Urban and Rural Districts (23,000) on the west bank and, on the east bank, Thornbury Rural District (38,000). Job opportunities within ten miles of the Bridge are relatively few. Avonmouth chemical works, Filton-Patchway aircraft and engine works and Llanwern steel works are the nearest significant employment areas. Taking journey costs at their most marginal, petrol at 2½d. per mile for 120 miles and Bridge tolls at 5/- per day, then the minimum cost for a vehicle carrying one commuter would be £2.10.0d. per week. The nearest major population centres to the Bridge are Newport and Bristol, 25 miles apart. Minimum travelling costs between these two centres would be at least £4. 0. 0d. per week and could be double that if true costs of motoring were calculated. These travelling costs and time losses are of the order that only highly paid executives or London commuters are prepared to bear. Alternative job opportunities on the same side of the estuary are invariably cheaper to reach.

6.27 An examination of the labour demand situation showed that even if unemployment increased considerably on one side of the estuary, daily movement to the other would be unlikely to occur. The large industries on either side of the estuary are not greatly increasing their labour forces. Steel at Llanwern is expanding but there is ample trained labour from other contracting steel works within South Wales. Aircraft employment at Filton and Patchway is tending to decline until production of Concorde is actually started. Although the chemical industry is expanding on Severnside, production processes require very little manpower and absenteeism is so critical a factor as to make firms encourage shift workers to live closer to their work than the other side of the estuary to avoid unnecessary absence because of weather conditions or vehicle breakdowns.

Changes in outputs

6.28 The first stage survey examined the proportions of the output of each firm that were despatched to the region in which it was sited, the region across the estuary and the Rest of England and Wales: in particular attention was paid to the extent to which firms consigned over 50% of their output to one of those destinations. The most frequent destination to attract over 50% was the 'Rest' followed in a minority of cases by the home region and only occasionally that across the estuary. Only one trade, food, drink and tobacco, showed a majority of firms despatching over 50% to their home region. Further analysis by industry and sub-area indicated that in the great majority of trades and sub-areas the principal, if not the dominant, destinations were London and the South East and Other Regions.

6.29 The situation as revealed in the second stage survey is that for the majority of firms the relative importance to them of the region across the estuary had not changed. The great majority do no more than 10% of their trade in the region across the Bridge as Table 6.12 indicates.

6.30 Both regions have almost identical proportions with very little trade with one another. Indeed 19% of South Wales firms reported no more than 1% going to the South West and 11% of South West firms were in a similar position as regards South Wales. But a majority of South Wales firms do less than 10% in their own region, a very different situation from South West firms. In both regions the markets represented by the 'Rest' and London and South East are clearly important but this is more strongly emphasised in South Wales. In particular 10% have 70% or more of their trade with the South East and the Rest of England and Wales.

6.31 The situation is similar among smaller manufacturers employing 20-99. The overwhelming majority of firms in both regions did less than 10% of their trade with the region across the estuary and over 70% did 50% or more of their trade in their own region.

6.32 Turning to changes in inter-regional trade the only useful data relates to manufacturers employing 100 or over. First, an attempt was made to ascertain what new links had been established and also where trade had ceased. Among the firms in South West, trading with South Wales had continued with 73%, been newly established by 14% and abandoned by 2%. In the opposite direction 69% continued to trade with South

TABLE 6.12   Percentages of firms Despatching under 10%, over 50% and over 70% by Regions (Manufacturers 100+ employees)

| Destination of Despatches | Location of Firm | | | | | |
| | South Wales | | | South West | | |
	Under 10%	Over 50%	Over 70%	Under 10%	Over 50%	Over 70%
South Wales	53	26	22	83	1	1
South West	79	1	1	44	22	15
London, South East	38	17	10	26	17	4
Rest of England & Wales	35	25	10	31	20	6

West, 12% now did so for the first time and 5% had ceased such trade. The net increase in new trading links is therefore small, a point reinforced by the study of new sources of supply drawn upon for the first time. But if completely new links are few, this still leaves open the question of increased volumes of trade in existing links. An attempt has been made to measure both the magnitude and the location of changes. As to magnitude it appears that no change has been experienced experienced by 34% of South Wales firms and 35% of South West firms while the significant changes were as in Table 6.13.

6.33 Taking all gains and losses reported by firms in trading with South Wales they offset one another except in four cases. In one, Cardiff, a higher proportion of firms reported reductions in trade in South Wales than were reporting increases. Conversely in Bristol-Severnside and also in the Wellington-Westbury area a higher proportion reported gains than reported losses, notably Bristol where 10% reported trade increased by over 5% and where another 20% reported trade up by less than 5%. As for trade in the South West, three areas showed far more gains and losses, Bristol-Severnside, North Wiltshire and the Upper Valleys. If however, the position is then reconsidered on the basis of a change of 6% or more then all areas in South Wales show this degree of improvement in trade with the South West in more cases than those showing a decline of this degree. In the South West only Bristol-Severnside shows such a change: the other areas show more cases of a decrease than of an increase. Taking trade with their own regions, however, all areas in South Wales show more instances of a decline in their trade there than increases, especially Cardiff. No such clear pattern exists in the South West.

6.34 Taking trade with the South East and with the Rest of England and Wales, the pattern of changes does not appear to have much connection with the Bridge. Over the whole survey region a similar percentage of firms has experienced gains of over 5%, as has experienced losses in this trade (20%). In South Wales, gains were somewhat greater than losses, particularly in the Bridgend and Cardiff areas, where some firms reported substantial gains while the Upper Valleys and North Monmouthshire showed more losses than gains in this category as did the Forest of Dean. To the east losses were slightly higher than gains, and were both higher than in South Wales, except in North Gloucestershire. There, gains were experienced by almost twice as many firms as experienced losses and by a higher proportion of firms than elsewhere.

6.35 These changes in trade could be associated with changes in areas served. Firms were therefore asked whether there had been a diversion of deliveries from one region to another as a result of the Bridge. Nine per cent of manufacturers employing 100+ reported such changes. The industries reporting diversions above this in the two regions were as in Table 6.14.

6.36 Related to this question and that of increased trade is the extent to which firms increased output for despatch across the estuary, see Table 6.15. Among manufacturers employing 100+, 77 firms (13.4%) had increased output to areas across the estuary and of these 25 were in Bristol. Other areas in order of proportions of firms reporting increases were the Forest of Dean, Wellington/Westbury and Bridgend/Lower Valleys. Such increases were more frequent, both absolutely and relatively among firms in the South West than in South Wales. The picture was similar though more concentrated in areas near the Bridge among small firms (20-99) where 12% reported such a change.

TABLE 6.13   Proportion of Firms Reporting Changes in Trade Across Estuary*
(Manufacturers 100+ employees)

	Increase Over 5%	Decrease Over 5%
South Wales firms with South West	17.0%	7.6%
South West firms with South Wales	9.0%	9.5%

* Percentages refer to all firms trading across the estuary pre-Bridge.

TABLE 6.14   Industries Reporting Above-average Diversions of Deliveries
(Manufacturers 100+ employees)

South Wales	No. of Firms	% in area	South West	No. of Firms	% in area
Other Metal Goods	5	18	Chemicals	5	31
Textiles & Leather	2	15	Building Materials	2	22
Food, Drink & Tobacco	3	14	Metal Manufacture	1	20
Other Manufacturing Industries	2	13	Vehicles & Aircraft	2	18
Engineering	6	12	Other Metal Goods	2	17
			Other Manufacturing Industries	2	15
Total All Industries	27	10	Total All Industries	26	9

Additional Commercial Benefits

6.37 The most frequently listed benefit of the Bridge for manufacturers with over 100 employees was better vehicle utilisation. Of the 23 firms benefiting, 7 were in the food drink and tobacco industry in the South West, 5 in metal manufacturing and other metal goods in South Wales, 3 in mining and quarrying in the South West and 2 in timber and furniture in South Wales. These seem to divide into traffic requiring speed of delivery like food, and high bulk to value traffic, e.g. quarry products. Economy on mileage and cost does not have the same industrial pattern. Of the 16 cases, 5 in South Wales and 2 in the South West are in engineering. In the South West the benefits are spread over several industries; the one with the highest percentage benefiting is timber and furniture. Neither location of respondent firms nor industry really offers an explanation of the mileage saved. The nature of the product, the location of the clients, the type of service offered and the number of units in the company might explain the pattern.

6.38 Sixteen firms had benefited from quicker communication between factories and depots making management control easier. Greater ease in visiting factories and depots by customers was of beneift to 9 respondents, 5 in the South West and 4 in South Wales. It is more likely that the number and location of the units of a company rather than the location or product of the respondent firm would determine which companies would benefit.

Disadvantages

6.39 The only disadvantages of any significance were increased competition and increased congestion, congestion being more significant to larger manufacturers and especially those in Swindon and North Wiltshire. Increased competition affected mainly small manufacturers. Few large manufacturers (5%) complained of disadvantages from greater competition. The percentage among small firms was twice as high. Bristol had 12% of large firms affected and Cardiff 15%. Amongst small firms 18 had experienced increased competition — 6 in Bristol (10%), 4 in Cardiff (33%) and 6 in Gloucestershire (18%). Among larger firms (100+) 16% suffered increased road congestion. Of these 91 companies, 23 (47%) of large firms were in Swindon and North Wiltshire, 16 in Bristol, (14%) 13 in Bridgend (18%) and 11 in Upper Valleys and North Monmouth (19%) but the local percentages were not widely different from the survey average. Congestion was less important for smaller firms, 9% being affected. Some areas were not affected at all but 29% of Newport firms reported this disadvantage.

Impact on Particular Industries

6.40 Appendix 28 shows the commodities carried by 1,244,000 commercial vehicles crossing the Bridge in 1968. Seasonal variation in commodity movements are given in Table 6.16. As with traffic between areas, it represents one day's movements in April, August and November. Chemicals, paper, metal manufacture and other raw materials all have summer troughs. A summer peak is exhibited in the cases of agricultural requisites, furniture, petrol, steel and the residual group, other building materials and non-metal manufacture have autumn peaks. Road-making materials show a steady decline from spring to autumn, but this is likely to represent particular local factors. Food, drink and tobacco, wood, livestock and, surprisingly, coal show very little movement in relative importance over the year. However, even in the other cases where there is an identifiable peak or trough it is in many cases not well marked. The overal impression is again one of considerable stability. The overall total of vehicles crossing shows only a narrow movement over the three days; such a trough as there is occurs in August. However, since the November survey was westbound only this tends to underrate the relative importance of the steel traffic which is predominantly in the other direction.

TABLE 6.15   Industries Reporting Above-average Increases in Despatches Across Estuary
(Manufacturers 100+ employees)

South Wales	No. of Firms	% in industry	South West	No. of Firms	% in industry
Timber & Furniture	4	36	Building Materials	4	44
Other Manufacturing Industries	4	25	Metal Manufacture	2	40
Food, Drink & Tobacco	4	19	Food, Drink & Tobacco	15	25
Building Materials	3	19	Mining & Quarrying	4	25
Engineering	7	14	Vehicles & Aircraft	4	24
Mining & Quarrying	2	13	Other Metal Goods	2	17
Total All Industries	31	11	Total All Industries	46	16

Food, Drink & Tobacco (see Appendix 31)

6.41 The wholesale and retail distribution of food and drink dominates the commodity analysis. Appendix 31 shows the places of accomplishment of these vehicles; i.e. the places to which the vehicles distributed food. Almost 94,000 vehicles delivered to areas west of the Bridge, against 37,000 delivering to the east. Of those delivering into Wales, almost 50% came from Bristol and District. The second main origin is the London area which accounts for an estimated 12,784 vehicles. Most of the westbound vehicles delivered goods into Cardiff — 39,698 — while 15,098 went to Newport and 15,645 to Swansea.

6.42 On the other side of the Bridge, where far fewer vehicles delivered, 9,955 came from Cardiff and 7,762 from the rest of Glamorgan. Almost 50% of the total went to the Bristol District and the remainder were fairly evenly scattered in their destinations. Clearly this trade is largely dominated by the Bristol manufacturers and distributors.

6.43 This pattern was to be expected. Before the Bridge there were substantial movements from Bristol in particular and from the South West as a whole into South Wales with a smaller movement eastwards. The pre-Bridge survey found westward movements of 425 lorry-loads weekly by manufacturers and 160 by distributors, compared to 89 and 83 respectively eastwards. The combination of agriculture,and related processing industries in the South West with the food etc, manufacturing and distributing industry based on the port of Bristol had already led to this trade pattern. Among food etc., manufacturers in the South West 80% were already sending goods to Cardiff and 87% were using their own vehicles for some or all of this traffic. Conversely only 53% of the small number of food etc. manufacturers in South Wales were despatching to Bristol 67% using their own vehicles.

6.44 The benefits of the Bridge would therefore lie in reduced transport costs, improved service and delivery times and new opportunities for rationalisation of deliveries. The time element coupled to perishability and hygiene considerations meant reliance on a firm's own vehicles, often specially adapted. This is particularly pertinent to the food, drink and tobacco industry. In 1966 all the South West firms that were expecting to use the Bridge replied that they expected cost savings compared to 70% of firms in all industries. In 1968-9 54% of the firms in this industry that were trading across the estuary from both regions reported reduced haulage rates.

6.45 Increases in output to areas across the estuary were reported by 19 firms, 15 from the South West, and a further 10 firms reported diversions of deliveries to areas across the estuary. Similarly 19 firms — 13 from Bristol and 6 from Cardiff and Newport — reported increased or new trade to Cardiff-Newport and Bristol respectively.

6.46 Among manufacturers there is evidence of increased intake of supplies from across the Severn, notably Welsh livestock moving to firms in Bristol and North Wiltshire. Among distributors there is clear evidence of increased intakes from the South West in South Wales; 16 firms report such a change compared to 7 Bristol firms reporting eastward movements.

6.47 As for the quality of service given and received by firms it is interesting to note that 10 manufacturing firms in South West North reported better service from South Wales suppliers in this trade while no less than 29 (49%) claimed that they were now able to offer improved services to customers in South Wales. The pre-Bridge pattern has therefore been reinforced. The pattern of deliveries reflects the populations and relative significance of the distributive trades in Bristol, Cardiff, Swansea and Newport.

Seasonal Variation, Commodities

	April 1968		August 1968		November 1968	
	No.	%	No.	%	No.	%
Coal	226	6	198	5	196	5
Food, Drink & Tobacco	694	17	642	17	662	16
Agricultural Requisites	263	7	273	7	228	6
Chemical & Paints	256	6	201	5	292	7
Furniture	127	3	181	5	84	2
Road-making Materials	156	4	106	3	48	1
Paper	186	5	180	5	256	6
Petrol	128	3	138	4	96	2
Steel	440	11	468	12	244	6
Building Materials	228	6	291	8	356	9
Livestock	47	1	29	1	50	1
Wood	176	4	161	4	178	4
Metal Manufacture	526	13	342	9	548	14
Non-metal Manufacture	213	5	179	5	322	8
Other Raw Materials	35	1	19	—	58	1
Other	146	4	398	10	174	4
Multiple — Not Known	167	4	60	2	32	1
Scrap	N/A		N/A		206	5
TOTAL	**4,014**		**3,866**		**4,030**	

TABLE 6.16

E

Metal Manufacture (Appendix 32)

6.48 In the case of metal manufacture, the second most important commodity, the trade is also markedly in one direction. Almost 74,000 vehicles delivered into Wales while 40,606 delivered into England, i.e. nearly twice as much into Wales as into England. Of those vehicles delivering metal manufactures in Wales, 29,610 came from the Bristol District, 17,967 from the London area, 8,868 from Central Southern England, while the remainder were fairly evenly distributed. Most of these vehicles delivered to Cardiff and Newport. In the other direction, 13,698 vehicles came from Cardiff and 7,527 from the rest of Glamorgan with 16,921 going to Bristol and 5,782 to London.

6.49 The product classification used for the industrial surveys makes comment less easy here. The engineering, vehicles and aircraft, metal manufacture and other metal goods categories are all involved. A direct comparison with pre-Bridge data is difficult. However, certain changes can be noted. The first is in the direction of traffic, pre-Bridge it appeared to be much heavier from South Wales to the South West than vice-versa; now this is reversed.

6.50 The second change is in the source of supplies. Firms on both sides reported improved service from suppliers across the estuary; indeed in engineering these were the largest group in any industry to do so in both areas. In South Wales the engineering and other metal goods are the principal groups able to offer a better service and in the South West they are second only to the food trades in this respect. Given this it is no surprise that in the other metal goods trades 20% of firms on each side draw increasingly from across the estuary. In engineering and other metal goods this occurred most often in South Wales (30 firms). While such changes had been expected, there were many unexpected changes to South West suppliers, more in fact than in any other trade. One factor here was subcontracting. While this developed in both directions and within companies as well as to outside firms, the balance of sub-contracting work went to Bristol-Severnside. This was reflected in the fact that half the firms reporting new or increased business in engineering were in Bristol. To this had to be added the switching of plant and machinery maintenance leading to movements westward by Bristol firms.

6.51 The changes in transport mode and costs are notable here. Not only is it the only trade in which a few firms secured reduced rail rates — all in South Wales — but there were switches from rail to road by a number of firms. Equally, reduced haulage rates were secured and there was a further group of firms switching from hauliers to their own vehicles. Indeed there were more cases of such a switch in the engineering and other metals goods than elsewhere.

6.52 The extent to which the flow of metal manufactures is so much heavier westbound reflects not only deliveries of finished goods to consumers in South Wales, but movements of components and materials for final assembly. It is also indicative of the strength of Bristol in the engineering and metal trades which has developed in the road transport era where the Bridge was a barrier.

Steel (Appendix 33)

6.53 Steel accounted for 95,600 lorry loads with the trade predominantly eastbound: 62,745 vehicles accomplished their purpose in England against 32,855 in Wales. The bulk of the trade is from Newport to the London area and Newport (presumably Spencer works) dominates the origins (30,492 vehicles came from Newport). On the English side Bristol dominates the origins (9,702) with Central Southern England next (5,989). Newport is the main destination (10,840) followed by Cardiff (8,927) and Swansea (6,133).

6.54 As is to be expected from the industrial structure of the two regions the principal flow is eastwards. This reflects a switch from rail to road, espeically in the Newport area, and increased demands from firms east of the Bridge. Out of 34 manufacturers in the South West drawing steel, aluminium and other metals, 22 report new or increased intakes from South Wales, while among distributors and stockholders Bristol firms report increased intakes and new sales — from as far west as Carmarthen.

6.55 All the firms supplying steel report that they use the Bridge and among those in South Wales over a third report their ability to offer a better service. There is a greater use of a firm's own vehicles as opposed to rail and road hauliers though this is one product where rail movements, especially to London, remain a very substantial element.

Building Materials (Appendix 34)

6.56 The trade in building materials is fairly evenly spread (21,090 vehicles delivered into England, 32,036 vehicles into Wales). Of vehicles delivering into Wales the majority came from Central Southern England and Bristol (7,227 and 8,122 respectively). The main destination was Newport. Of the trade in the other direction the main origin was Newport and the main destination Bristol, followed by the London area and Devon and Cornwall.

6.57 The replies from firms indicate movements in both directions reflecting the variety of materials involved. These represent changes that had been expected by some firms on both sides but there have been more unexpected changes in trade among firms in the South West than in most trades. These are shown by the number (7) and proportion of firms (28%) increasing output for despatch across the estuary notably in the Wellington-Westbury area. This is the highest proportion of firms in any industry increasing output to destinations across the estuary involving 4 firms in the South West and 3 in South Wales. Improved service is reported by customer firms in South Wales while firms on both sides answered that they can now give it. All the respondent firms in the South West use the Bridge and deliver frequently whereas in South Wales just over half the firms do likewise. Haulage rates have dropped for firms on both sides.

6.58 Pre-Bridge the balance of movements was heavier from South Wales to the South West but this has now been reversed. There has been a significant change in direction as well as volume of trade in building materials. This is supported by evidence of reduced intakes from other areas in the same number of firms as report increases in cross-estuary intakes.

Coal (Appendix 35)

6.59 Coal is very much a one-way commodity. The bulk of the trade is from Glamorgan to the nearer English destinations: the Newport trade is mainly into Bristol. Bristol takes most of the coal with Central Southern England figuring surprisingly high in second place.

Agricultural Requisites (Appendix 36)

6.60 This trade is very much in a westbound direction, with Bristol alone sending almost 31,000 lorry loads across the Bridge while the whole of Wales sends only about 8,000 vehicles across. The Bristol traffic is destined mainly for the rest of Monmouthshire and West Wales. The other main origin is Somerset, though it sends less than a tenth of Bristol's traffic. Westbound, the trade is fairly well spread by destination, though Cardiff, Rest of Monmouthshire, West Wales and Hereford and Brecon dominate. However, Bristol strongly dominated the destinations on the west bank taking over 5,000 of the 8,000 lorry-loads.

6.61 This is a trade which existed pre-Bridge and is associated with the port of Bristol as an importer of supplies, a centre of agricultural feeding stuffs processing and a source of fertilisers from its expanded chemical industry. The pre-Bridge survey showed 250 lorry loads weekly moving from the South West to South Wales and only 8 loads weekly moving in the opposite direction. Given the nature of the market no change of transport mode was to be expected but here is a large flow of traffic that has been diverted over the Bridge with savings in transport costs and time.

Chemicals (Appendix 37)

6.62 Almost 40,000 lorry loads of chemicals crossed the Bridge, in fairly even spread: 17,679 were eastbound and these went mainly to Bristol (5,252) and London (3,321) while East Gloucestershire, Somerset and Wiltshire accounted for about 2,000 each. Again, the main origin was Cardiff (5,357), but Swansea also despatched a substantial share of the trade (3,686) and so did Newport (3,259). In the opposite direction, 22,220 lorry loads went to Wales. Bristol dominated the origins (9,251) but the destinations were more evenly spread, with Newport, Cardiff and Rest of Glamorgan all taking a substantial share of the trade.

6.63 The balance of movements between the South West and South Wales is westward although the overall movement is evenly spread. This inter-regional balance was to be expected. Pre-Bridge the westward movement from the South West was nearly double that in the opposite direction — 174 loads per week as against 97 per week in 1966.

6.64 Within this movement there have been noticeable switches between transport modes. Within each of the two regions there has been a switch from road haulier to own vehicles but between them there has been a marked switch to road hauliers. There are presumably contract hirers using special vehicles. The same switch of mode has occurred cross-estuary as on longer distance despatches to South East and the Rest of England and Wales.

6.65 At the same time a third of the firms in South West North (6 firms) reported diversions of deliveries to South Wales while increases in output for cross-estuary delivery were reported by firms on both sides (3 firms). All the firms in South Wales and all but one in the South West used the Bridge and the great majority made frequent deliveries across it — 19 firms (86%) in South Wales, 12 firms (75%) in the South West. Half the firms in both areas reported better service from their suppliers across the Bridge and 11 firms (69%) in the South West were able to offer better service.

6.66 The extent of movements in both directions reflects the variety of products and a measure of specialisation between plants as well as firms. It is interesting to note that this industry showed one of the highest increases in staff movements at all levels as well as notable switches from rail to road among them.

Non-metal Manufacture (Appendix 38)

6.67 Over 54,000 vehicles in 1968 carried non-metal manufactures, and these were very evenly spread (27,040 delivered into England and 27,260 into Wales). Of vehicles from England almost 50% were from Bristol to near-Bridge destinations. In the reverse direction, Cardiff dominated the trade, mainly again to Bristol.

Paper (Appendix 39)

6.68 Almost twice as much paper travels into Wales as travels into England. The bulk of the trade is from Bristol to Cardiff, and to Newport and Rest of Glamorgan. Somerset sends a sizeable proportion to Cardiff and in fact Cardiff takes approximately 40% of the total trade. In the opposite direction Bristol is seen again, this time as the main destination with Cardiff as the origin.

6.69 The concentration of paper, printing and publishing in the Bristol-Bath area explains the imbalance in the flows of traffic. Firms in South Wales report improved service (6 firms — 50%) while those east of the Severn report ability to give an improved service.

Expectations and Results

6.70 The pattern of trade revealed by the traffic data is consistent with expectations as to specialisation of the two regions before the Bridge and their reinforcement once a single market had emerged with the elimination of the barrier in time and cost of the journey via Gloucester. From the standpoint of regional trade analysis, the Bridge has created a new overlap of trading areas and extended the radius which firms on both sides can now serve while remaining competitive in costs, prices and services. Indeed the importance given to service under conditions where price competition is limited or non-existent reinforces the case presented by many firms that the Bridge has enabled them to both give and receive better service. In terms of industrial location the benefit to firms west of the Severn in this respect of better service to the South East is important. The ability to draw upon existing services and sources of supplies to a greater extent within the two regions has several facets. It leads to some switch of trade away from other regions, it is most apparent where firms were already trading across the estuary and therefore knew of probable sources, and it leads to greater competition as is clear from the fact that firms in particular industries report that they can both receive and give better service on both sides.

6.71 As regards some of the hypotheses set out in Chapter 2, it is also evident that at least in the period to the present date there has been little completely new use of cross-estuary sources and only a limited change in the orientation of most firms so far as markets are concerned. While more firms trade across the estuary and more of those doing so have increased their trade, this has not altered the basic position that, for the great majority, trade with the region across the Severn remains less important than trade with either the region in which they are sited or with other parts of the country, especially the South East. National markets remain the principal interest of those firms that are not catering to a local market.

6.72 Trade existed before the Bridge and was of a pattern that has been reinforced by its opening. Further discussion of conclusions must wait until Chapter 9 but traffic flows and transport changes discussed in earlier chapters are now seen against the reinforcement of the existing pattern of business. The argument already advanced, that this ends an anomaly in Bristol's relationships to the west, will become very evident in the study of distribution which follows in Chapter 7.

CHAPTER SEVEN

The Bridge and Distribution

7.1   Already the changes in the demands made on the transport industry discussed in Chapter 5, and in manufacturing examined in Chapter 6 have pointed to substantial changes in the distribution of goods as a consequence of the opening of the Severn Bridge. This chapter examines particular changes in distributive activities of manufacturers and distributors excluding retailers. Changes in retail distribution certain markets and the position for Bristol Channel ports are commented upon.

7.2   Such a review calls for an initial analysis of the structure of distribution so that possible outcomes can be related to the pre-Bridge situation. This involves a classification of distributive systems used by firms (paragraph 7.4). The evidence as to types of systems represented in the survey area is then examined in relation to the centres in which they are to be found and this provides a starting point for projecting possible changes.

Structure of Distributive Activities

7.3   The traditional sequence of initial producer selling via one or more wholesalers to retailers who then sell to ultimate consumers has been transformed by the by-passing of one or more stages. Forward integration has brought manufacturers into distribution; backward integration has meant that some distributors manufacture. In this survey, of 576 firms in manufacturing, 189 (33%) distributed goods made elsewhere while of 352 firms in distribution, 93 (27%) had some manufacturing excluding packaging, blending and bottling.

7.4   Whether manufacturers or distributors are involved, the type of distribution system employed is important to this study, and a classification of such systems has been adopted as follows: —

   (i) National A firm distributes throughout the country from one or at most two, depots or warehouses.

   (ii) Super-Regional Four to six depots are used to serve the entire country. One might serve a single highly populated regional such as the South East. Another might serve two or more regions such as South Wales and the South West.

   (iii) Regional The country is served from 12-15 centres, dependent on population and communications. South Wales and the South West might be treated as separate regions before the Bridge but as one after its opening.

   (iv) Sub-Regional A much smaller area is now covered from each of up to 40 depots covering the country and the survey regions might each have several.

   (v) Local Based on towns of 10,000 upwards these only serve the immediate hinterland.

7.5   The choice of system is clearly dependent on the commodity concerned, the range of which it is a part, its bulk and transport cost, the volume to be handled and the number of customers to be served. The choice of location(s) within any system is related to the population that can be served from a particular centre at a given state of transport developments.

7.6   Few national distributors are located in Severnside though it lies at one corner of the central belt bounded by London, Leeds, Liverpool and Bristol within which distribution to 90% of consumers is feasible for products suitable for national distribution. Some manufacturers have their headquarters in the survey area as do a few national distributors. Where a "binary" or two depot system is used a few firms have depots in Severnside or at Swindon. The Severn Bridge is not likely to affect such firms. The development of the motorway network, however, increases the possibilities for firms to adopt such a pattern.

7.7   Bristol and Gloucester act as super-regional centres for firms serving both South Wales and South West possibly with parts of the West Midlands and other adjacent regions. Cardiff's role as such a centre is largely confined to Welsh owned firms. The Severn Bridge makes it possible for firms to move to such a system from a regional one in which they have hitherto served South Wales and South West from separate depots.

7.8   Bristol and Cardiff act as regional centres. The pre-Bridge survey showed the extent to which Bristol was both a super-regional and a regional centre whereas Cardiff was a regional centre for South and West Wales. The Severn Bridge creates an overlap of the regions especially in respect of Monmouth and the Forest of Dean. Some adjustment of regional centres and their areas of influence is possible.

7.9   Table 7.1 shows the employment in distribution in all towns in the survey area with a population in excess of 50,000. Bristol and Cardiff stand out as regional centres with Gloucester, Newport and Swansea as sub-regional centres. Gloucester has already lost its special status as the lowest bridging point in the Severn. Swindon is a special case as it is used by some national distributors. The other towns are essentially local centres. Those that are closest to the Bridge, notably Newport, are now overlapping to a greater extent. The completion of the M.4 and M.5 motorways could have further effects. The motorway intersection favours South Gloucestershire as a potential site for regional and super-regional distribution.

7.10 Given these possible outcomes in the various distribution systems the present structure shows few changes in organisation since 1966. As with manufacturers the impact of take-overs has been considered. While the largest group of firms pre-Bridge was based in the survey regions, the next largest group was controlled from the South East. It was, therefore, thought possible that firms would seek to acquire firms across the Severn in order to obtain a ready-made distribution network. Given the higher proportion of independents in South Wales both South East and South West firms might have been tempted to do so. However, an examination of the 15% of distributors that underwent changes in ownership 1966-69 showed no such movement while the 16% of manufacturers involved in take-overs were nearly all instances of changes at national level and not changes arising from the new situation created by the Bridge. There was already substantial penetration of the South West by firms based in the South East. The majority of the establishments of distributors were owned by firms that had several depots and in nearly half the cases the owning organisation was based outside the survey regions, notably in the South East. Furthermore, of the 56 establishments in Table 7.2 which acted as regional headquarters of national companies having many depots, no less than 35 were in Bristol and only 9 in Cardiff. The absence of further take-over activity by such firms 1966-69 is an indication that distribution on both sides of the estuary was already well integrated in national systems.

TABLE 7.1   **Employment in Distributive Trades in Urban Centres Ranked by Population**

Urban Centres☆ Over 50,000 Population Ranked by Size	Total Population 1969	% of Total in Region*	% of Employment in Distributive Trades in Region*
Bristol	689,990	34.4	58.0
Cardiff	314,940	17.0	41.4
Swansea	171,320	9.2	15.9
Swindon	164,970	8.2	6.3
Newport	130,340	8.9	11.1
Gloucester	128,170	6.4	9.7
Cheltenham	118,340	5.9	4.9
Bath	103,050	5.1	2.6
Rhondda	94,300	5.1	2.0
Weston-super-Mare	85,680	4.3	1.4
Taunton	85,570	4.3	3.8
Merthyr Tydfil	56,360	3.0	2.1
Bridgwater	52,480	2.6	2.6
Port Talbot	50,970	2.7	1.9

☆ Including adjacent suburban areas
* Region is South West survey area for urban centres in South
  West and South Wales survey area for urban centres in South Wales.

TABLE 7.2   **Ownership of Distribution Establishments**

Status	South Wales firms %	South West firms %	All firms No.	All firms %
Headquarters of Multiple Depot Company	21.1	20.2	72	20.5
Independent Company with one depot	20.2	15.1	59	16.8
Regional Headquarters controlling sub-depots but parent company Headquarters elsewhere	10.5	18.5	56	15.9
Subsidiary depot	48.2	46.2	165	46.9
Total	100	100	352	100

Channels of Distribution

7.11 Already (paragraph 7.3) the role of manufacturers as distributors has been pointed out. Table 7.3 shows the distributive functions of manufacturing firms employing 100 or more. Firms in the South West are more often engaged in the distribution of goods manufactured elsewhere than those in South Wales; at the same time there is less likelihood of their use of another company to distribute than among firms in South Wales.

7.12 The 9% of South Wales firms that sent their output to another unit for despatch to customers were mostly sending to a parent company in the South East and the Midlands. One reason given was the difficulty of distributing nationally from South Wales before the Bridge was available. Interviews with new firms in South Wales indicated that they were more inclined to distribute from South Wales than would have been the case without the Bridge.

7.13 The channels of distribution used by manufacturers and distributors are set out in Table 7.4. In comparing the two regions with one another allowance has to be made for their very different products and the consequent differences in channels. When comparing cross-estuary to total despatches allowance has to be made for both products and distances; a firm may deliver directly in an adjacent region but use a distributor further afield.

Changes in Distribution — Possibilities

7.14 Having set out the main features of the structure it is next necessary to outline the possible changes that might be expected to follow from the opening of the Bridge as was done for manufacturers in Chapter 6. The first is what is virtually an organisational link, namely the channels of distribution used including such questions as the depot system, changes in sales and delivery areas and a switch to direct trade in place of the use of wholesalers. The second set, as with manufacturers,

TABLE 7.3

Distribution Activities of Manufacturers
(Manufacturers 100+ employees)

Distribution Functions	South Wales Firms %	South West Firms %	All Firms No.	All Firms %
Distribution carried out by another unit of company	9.3	3.7	37	6.4
Distribution of goods manufactured on premises only	55.5	49.8	303	52.6
Distribution of goods manufactured on premises and elsewhere including goods purchased, imported and from other factories in group	27.4	38.0	189	32.8
Packaging, blending and distributing production from elsewhere, or providing sales & service facilities	4.7	3.3	23	4.0
Mining or Quarrying Firms	3.2	5.1	24	4.2
Total	100	100	576	100

TABLE 7.4

Channels of Distribution Used, 1968–69*
(Manufacturers 100+ and Distributors)

Channel	Cross Estuary South Wales Firms Man. %	Cross Estuary South Wales Firms Dist. %	Cross Estuary South West Firms Man. %	Cross Estuary South West Firms Dist. %	All Destinations South Wales Firms Man. %	All Destinations South Wales Firms Dist. %	All Destinations South West Firms Man. %	All Destinations South West Firms Dist. %
Direct to Customer	64	24	60	42	74	43	73	62
Direct to Retail	17	20	21	35	22	51	28	55
Distributor	20	18	26	24	25	33	36	36
Contract Distributor Depots	11	6	9	4	14	7	13	8
Own Depot	20	16	15	19	30	25	27	28
Other e.g. Mail Order	9	2	10	6	10	2	14	7
No. of Firms	281	114	295	238	281	114	295	238

* Most firms use more than one channel

could lie in the input of supplies with new sources, increased use of cross-estuary sources and less use of other regions for supplies. With these changes there could be questions of service and cost. These then lead on to the pattern of trade, notably areas served, frequency of delivery and growth of competition. Last there are other advantages and disadvantages and also additional topics have been brought into this section.

Changes in Distribution Methods

7.15 Among manufacturers, the number and proportion expecting to make changes when contacted in 1966 was small. Altogether 66 firms (13%) expected to make changes, 23 (4%) involved depot locations and 15 (3%) relocation of sales or administrative offices. The 1969 survey found 49 firms reporting changes, only 8.5%. No marked differences arise between the two regions. The details are set out in Table 7.5 in which a further distinction is drawn between those firms which stated that these changes were associated with expansion and those which reported rationalisation.

7.16 A far greater change has occurred among distributors as seen from Table 7.6. This table shows only those changes reported as having occurred because of the opening of the Bridge. A considerable number of other changes in firms' distribution networks on either side of the estuary but not because of the Bridge were reported in both the first and second surveys. Analysis of these surveys showed that the trend of these other changes was the same as that due to the opening of the Bridge.

7.17 The types of changes in distribution methods made by distributing firms are listed in Table 7.6. Many firms made more than one change, the average number being 1.5 per firm. The changes in firms are listed by the one cited as of most significance. Many different types of changes have been made by firms depending on the type of distributive system operated, the location of the firm and/or its depots and whether the firm is expanding or rationalising its activities. This distinction between expansion and rationalisation is to a certain extent artificial. One category of expansion involves a considerable degree of rationalisation, namely on the opening of a new depot. Rationalisation does not infer contraction; it can be undertaken with a view to long-term expansion.

7.18 The proportion of distribution firms making changes in their distribution methods was three times that among the manufacturing firms and, at 27%,

TABLE 7.5 **Types of Changes in Distribution Methods Made by Manufacturers**
(Manufacturers 100+ employees)

Type of Change	South Wales Firms		South West Firms		All Firms	
	No.	%	No.	%	No.	%
Expansion						
1. Depot set up on other side of estuary	4	17	3	12	7	14
2. Expansions of sales office or reps. area	6	26	6	23	12	25
Total No. of Firms expanding	10	43	9	35	19	39
Rationalisation						
3. Depot closed other side	1	4	4	15	5	10
4. Changes in areas supplied from each factory	3	13	4	15	7	14
5. Rationalisation of sales offices or reps. areas	3	13	4	15	7	14
6. Switch from wholesalers to delivering direct or through depots	1	4	—	—	1	2
7. Switch from delivering through depots to delivering direct but depots not closed	3	13	2	8	5	10
8. Manufacturing on other side ceased factory used as depot	—	—	2	8	2	4
9. Miscellaneous	2	9	1	4	3	6
Total No. of Firms rationalising	13	57	17	65	30	61
Total No. of Firms changing methods	23	100	26	100	49	100
% of Total Firms in region	8		9		8.5	

sufficiently high to substantiate the hypothesis that one of the most significant short-term effects of the Severn Bridge would be on the distribution of goods.

7.19 There was a marked difference between the numbers of South Wales and South West distribution firms making changes, South Wales 22 firms (19%) South West 74 firms (31%). There were also marked differences between areas in the percentages of firms reporting changes. Firms making changes were most likely to be in either one of the major centres or a smaller centre close to the Bridge as Table 7.7 shows.

7.20 Most of the firms making changes were located in the Bristol urban area. The proportion of firms changing there was considerably greater than in Cardiff,

Gloucester and Newport. Low proportions in Swansea, Swindon and Cheltenham are probably because of distance from the Bridge together with their status as sub-regional or local centres of distribution. In the case of Bath, closer to the Bridge, it is because, being over-shadowed by Bristol, it only serves as a local centre for wholesale distribution.

7.21 Most of the changes in methods originated in the South West region. This was particularly true of firms that opened depots across the estuary or opened a depot in one region to serve both sides of the estuary. Most firms taking the latter decision chose the Bristol area as the location of their depot. Only two firms, both on the east bank of the estuary, expanded by taking over a company on the other side. This may be due to the lack

TABLE 7.6 Types of Changes in Distribution Methods Made by Distributors

Type of Change	South Wales Firms		South West Firms		All Firms	
	No.	%	No.	%	No.	%
Expansion						
1. Depot set up on other side of estuary	2	9	6	8	8	8
2. Takeover of company on other side of estuary	–	–	2	3	2	2
3. Larger depot opened to serve both sides of estuary (existing depots not closed	–	–	5	7	5	5
4. Expansion of sales office or reps. area	4	18	8	11	12	13
5. New depot opened rationalising existing system and expanding deliveries	1	5	10	13	11	11
Total No. of Firms expanding	7	32	31	42	38	39
Rationalisation						
6. Depot relocated to serve survey region	1	5	2	3	3	3
7. Depot closed other side	3	14	13	18	16	17
8. Changes in Areas supplied from depots on each side	2	9	10	13	12	13
9. Rationalisation of sales office or reps. area	1	5	3	4	4	4
10. Switch from wholesalers to delivering direct or through depots	–	–	2	3	2	2
11. Switch from delivering through depots to delivering direct but depots not closed	–	–	1	1	1	1
12. Inter-depot movements started or increased	7	32	11	15	18	19
13. Miscellaneous	1	5	1	1	2	2
Total No. of Firms rationalising	15	68	43	58	58	61
Total No. of Firms changing methods	22	100	74	100	96	100
% of Total Firms in region	19		31		27	

of suitable candidates or possibly the need for more time.

7.22 Where a firm had expanded by establishing a larger depot to serve both sides of the estuary without closing its existing depot, the South West side of the estuary was chosen for the new development. South Wales was only chosen by firms based there. Where a firm opened a depot in the area for the first time or a larger depot to serve both sides of the estuary (Categories 5 and 3 of Table 7.6) it was in most cases owned by a company based outside the two survey regions.

7.23 Most firms expanding their sales offices or sales representation across the estuary were locally owned but this may not reflect the full extent of such changes. Many of the companies operating on a national basis have separate sales and distribution organisations. A firm might have a single regional sales office with representatives and depots based on each side of the estuary. The representatives may have no contact at all with the depots but report directly to the regional sales office which again may have no control over, and little contact with, the depots. Rearrangements of the sales organisation, for example, to use one representative to cover both sides of the estuary instead of two, may proceed independently. Some managers of depots might not have been aware of changes in sales organisation arising from the opening of the Bridge.

7.24 Among firms that rationalised their existing distribution network the most frequent change was an increase, or start of inter-depot transfers. This enables stocks levels to be reduced, and by increasing the range of stock held enables a better service to be given to customers on both sides of the estuary. Inter-depot transfer of stock is not necessarily a substitute for more extensive rationalisation such as closing or relocating depots. It is most common with firms which have to maintain close physical contacts with their customers and need depots that serve local areas, such as electrical goods or motor accessories.

7.25 Where a firm has a dense network of local depots, it might have ten branches within 80 miles of Bristol; it could rationalise by setting up a stockholding and transit depot to handle inter-depot transfers and break bulk between them. This type of operation was scarcely viable before the Bridge opened because each region had too few urban areas to support a two-tiered distribution system but since the Bridge opened several such depots have been established in the Avonmouth and Chipping Sodbury areas.

7.26 The second most common type of rationalisation involved the closure of a depot on the other side of the estuary. Thirteen firms in the South West and 3 in South Wales had closed depots on the other side. Eleven of the 13 firms in the South West were located in the Bristol urban area. Nine of the depots closed by all 13 firms were in Cardiff, the remaining depots being in Newport or other towns in South East Wales. The three South Wales firms were all located in Cardiff and closed two depots in Bristol and one in Bath.

7.27 In only three cases had firms relocated depots because of the opening of the Bridge. All the cases were different in nature. In one case a firm had depots in Exeter and Cardiff. After the Bridge opened it closed both depots and opened one in Bristol to serve both the South West and South Wales. In the second a firm had depots in Glamorgan and Dorset. As a consequence of the Bridge the Glamorgan depot was relocated at Pontypool from which it was possible to give a better service to the Bristol area than had been possible from the Dorset depot. The third case is a national company with a large factory in a South Wales valley that had rationalised its national distribution network. Where similar action has been taken by firms with factories in the Bristol area the depot was usually attached to the factory. In this case it was too difficult to serve the whole estuary region from a depot located within the valleys; it was found more advantageous to site it in Bristol.

7.28 The third major type of rationalisation occurred within those firms that had depots on both sides of the estuary. Twelve firms rationalised by transferring part of the distribution area over to the depot on the other side without closing a depot, ten of them in the South West.

7.29 Although 35% of the firms used other distributors only four firms reported that they had switched from supplying customers on the other side of the estuary through wholesalers to supplying direct or through their own depots. In two cases more important changes were made such as opening a depot on Severnside to make deliveries; hence the lower figure in Table 7.6.

7.30 In the pre-Bridge survey only 23 manufacturers (4%) reported that they expected to change location of their depots as a result of the Bridge. Of the 62 firms completing both questionnaires that had depots across the estuary 56 (90%) did not expect to close their depots and did not do so. Only one firm expected to close a depot and did so. Four firms closed contrary to

	TABLE 7.7		Locations of Distribution Firms Making Changes in Methods	
	Location of Firm	No. of Firms making changes in methods	% of changes in survey region	% of Firms making changes within urban area
	Bristol Urban Area	65	68	44
	Cardiff Urban Area	14	15	26
	Gloucester Urban Area	6	6	32
	Newport Urban Area	3	3	17
	Pontypool Urban Area	3	3	50
	All other areas	5	5	5
	All Firms	96	100	27

expectation. This suggests that the effect on depots of manufacturers is slight.

7.31 Among distributors only 19 firms (10%) reported in the first stage that they expected to rationalise depot systems and almost all carried out their plans. Five South West firms that expected to open depots in South Wales did not do so. In the second stage survey 31 firms (10%) reported that they had made some change in their depot locations. The short-term forecast in the first survey was substantiated. The larger number of firms reporting changes is mainly due to a higher response rate to our second survey.

Changes in Distributive Systems of Companies on Severnside

7.32 The concentration of changes among firms in the Severnside area and the interest in the fate of the previous lowest crossing point, Gloucester, has led to a special study of companies in these areas. This has been concerned with the interaction of the firm's location, its type of distribution system and the policy changes made. Whereas elsewhere the basic unit is the "firm", an independent distribution company or a depot of a manufacturer or distributor, the duplication of data from multi-establishment firms was eliminated here and the basic unit is the "company". The company includes associates which may be legally distinct and operating under different names but which are part of the same group which has an overall marketing policy. Companies have been grouped as follows:-
(i) Gloucester-Cheltenham companies
(ii) Companies supplying only one side pre-Bridge
(iii) Companies supplying both sides from one point pre-Bridge
(iv) Companies supplying both sides from two or more points pre-Bridge.
The detailed analysis is set out in Appendices 40 and 41.

(i) Gloucester-Cheltenham Companies

7.33 Twenty-eight Companies (10%) were in this category. Of these, 29% extended their distribution area southwards either from their existing location or by opening a new depot. In 1966 a high proportion of companies expected to extend their distribution services down the estuary. Of the 21 companies, 9 (42%) reported that they expected to expand. The lower percentage reporting expansion between 1966 and 1968 may be a reflection of the view that expansion depended on the completion of the Gloucester to Bristol section of the M.5 Motorway which did not happen until 1971.

(ii) Companies supplying only one side pre-Bridge

7.34 Ninety-three companies (33%) were in this category. Of these, 22 (24%) had expanded across the estuary. The percentage of South Wales companies expanding was higher than that of South West companies (28% and 20% respectively) although if those companies that expected to expand by 1970 were included the proportions were virtually the same (36% and 34% respectively). Few companies expected to expand by opening a depot on the other side but it is noticeable that even fewer of those that expected to open depots actually did so, especially South Wales

companies in the South West. A slightly higher proportion of companies in South Wales and the South West expected to expand in 1966 than had done so in 1968-69. The fact that more South Wales than South West companies expanded is explained by the fact that a greater proportion of South West companies already served the other side of the estuary from one point before the Bridge opened.

(iii) Companies supplying both sides from one point pre-Bridge

7.35 Twenty-four per cent of companies were in this category. Fewer Welsh companies distributed in England before the Bridge opened than vice-versa. Of the 52 Welsh companies with only one depot on Severnside, 13 (25%) distributed on both sides. In contrast 54 (50%) of the South West companies distributed in South Wales. These figures are roughly comparable with the data from the 1966 survey (South Wales 29%, South West 58%). There was a marked difference between the two sides in the proportions that had further extended their delivery service across the estuary. Only 3 (23%) of Welsh companies had extended into the South West whereas 24 (44%) of the South West companies had extended into South Wales. In both regions the proportions of companies expanding was markedly less than anticipated in 1966. In 1966, 69% of South Wales firms expected to expand as did 58% of South West firms.

(iv) Companies supplying both sides from two or more points pre-Bridge

7.36 Thirty-three per cent of all companies distributed on Severnside from depots on each side of the estuary before the Bridge opened. Altogether, 45% had made some change, 15% had closed down one depot, 9% had relocated the depot to serve both sides of the estuary and 16% had transferred part of the distribution area on one side to the depot on the other. Of these cases, 85% involved a concentration on the east bank.

Changes in Inputs to Distributors

7.37 In Chapter 6 changes in inputs of supplies and labour were examined. Distribution firms are such small employers in most cases that labour inputs can be disregarded in this study. Changes in sources of supplies are set out in Table 7.8.

7.38 A significant proportion of firms made changes in their sources of supplies as a consequence of the opening of the Severn Bridge. The numbers are less than those making changes in their distribution methods, but for South Wales firms the Severn Bridge seems to have had a bigger effect on sources of supplies than on distribution areas. No less than 29% of Welsh firms increased their drawings of supplies across the estuary whilst only 19% of South West firms drew more supplies from South Wales, only half the proportion of firms extending distribution across the estuary.

7.39 More firms increased their intake of supplies than started using new sources. The firms reporting the largest increases in trade were those that already had trading connections on the other side before the Bridge opened. Market knowledge plays a considerable part in being able to react quickly to a changed environment.

7.40 An analysis by trades shows marked variations. Only 10% of wholesalers in the South West drew more supplies across the estuary compared to 26% of wholesalers in South Wales. Twenty-seven per cent of contract distributors in the South West drew more supplies from South Wales whilst no contract distributors located in South Wales drew more from the other side. This indicates that the contract distributors in the Bristol area received a double benefit from the opening of the Bridge. On the one hand they were well placed geographically to distribute goods originating in the South East region and the Midlands into South Wales and at the same time were able to obtain return loads thereby keeping their transport costs down.

7.41 The numbers of firms drawing supplies from across the estuary for the first time compared to the numbers drawing supplies before the Bridge opened, showed that a greater percentage of Welsh firms (14%) started to draw supplies across the estuary than South West firms (10%). One factor which explains the different percentages of firms changing their sources of supplies, is the transfer of depots from South Wales to the Bristol area which compels some Welsh firms to cross the estuary for supplies.

7.42 Table 7.9 shows that a wide range of commodities has been drawn across the estuary. The largest category was food, drink and tobacco. The east side of the estuary is a larger source of both fresh and manufactured produce than South Wales. Agricultural supplies and livestock is a two-way traffic. The flow of processed timber is entirely from Wales to England, a reflection of the seizure of opportunities by timber importers in South Wales when their transport costs to the West Country were reduced because of the opening of the Bridge. The recent growth of Newport as a timber importing port is a further factor.

7.43 Nearly half the firms that drew supplies from across the estuary gave reduced transport costs as the reason. Twelve per cent mentioned improved service and 9% better trading terms. The remaining changes in Table 7.10 are largely a consequence of the changes in firms' distribution networks. All the firms that had to draw supplies across the estuary because their suppliers had transferred their depots there were in South Wales.

7.44 In the case of one firm in the South West it was its supplier's policy to supply from South Wales. A further group of 5 South West firms (7%) obtained supplies as return loads. A further 7% of firms drew

---

TABLE 7.8 Changes in Sources of Supplies — Distributors

	South Wales Firms		South West Firms		All Firms	
	No.	%	No.	%	No.	%
Supplies drawn across the estuary for the first time	10	9	9	4	19	5
Supplies drawn across estuary to an increasing extent	23	20	27	11	50	14
Supplies drawn across estuary for first time and to an increasing extent	33	29	36	15	69	19
Reductions in supplies from other areas	13	11	13	5	26	7

TABLE 7.9 Commodities Drawn Across the Estuary By Distributors Because of the Opening of Severn Bridge

Commodities	South Wales No.	South West No.	All Firms No.	%
Coal	1	1	2	3
Food, Drink & Tobacco	13	6	19	28
Agricultural Supplies	2	2	4	6
Chemicals	1	1	2	3
Petrol	1	2	3	4
Steel, Non-ferrous metals and scrap metal	3	3	6	9
Building Materials	3	4	7	10
Livestock	2	2	4	6
Timber	—	4	4	6
Metal manufacturers	4	6	10	15
Non-metal manufacturers	1	2	3	4
Multiple loads or unspecified	2	3	3	4
All Firms	33	36	69	100

supplies across the estuary as a consequence of a policy decision that one depot, usually the parent company should hold stock on behalf of the group's depots. Finally two firms on each side of the estuary increased the extent to which they used ports on the other side.

7.45 Table 7.11 shows that firms' estimates as to the impact of the Bridge on the sources of their supplies or the service given to them by their suppliers were not very accurate. The exceptions were South West firms not expecting to use the Bridge for supplies. Nearly a quarter (24%) of firms in South Wales which reported in the first stage that they would not change their sources of supplies have in fact done so. Among those that expected to make changes and have not, there were

wider differences between expectation and fulfillment. Of 43 firms expecting to make changes because of the Bridge, 13 firms (30%) have not done so. There was virtually no difference in the proportions of South Wales firms and South West firms in this category.

Changes in Inputs – Service Received

7.46 Over two-thirds of the firms located in South Wales considered that they received a better service from suppliers of goods after the Bridge opened, whereas only half the firms in the South West region felt that they received a better service from South Wales — see Table 7.12. It seems, however, that suppliers

TABLE 7.10   Reasons for Changes in Sources of Supplies – Distributors

Reasons given	South Wales Firms No.	South West Firms No.	All Firms No.	%
Saving in transport costs	15	17	32	46
Improved service	5	3	8	12
More supplies in competition, better trading terms, lower prices	2	4	6	9
Supplier transferred depot across estuary	4	–	4	6
Supplies policy to supply from other side	–	1	1	1
Return loading on delivery vehicles	–	5	5	7
Bulk buying, joint stock holding	1	4	5	7
Use of ports on other side of estuary	2	2	4	6
No data given	4	–	4	6
All Firms	33	36	69	100

TABLE 7.11   The Degree to which Distributors' Expectations as to Changes in Sources of Supplies were Fulfilled

Firms expectations and changes compared	South Wales Firms No.	%	South West Firms No.	%	All Firms No.	%
Did not expect Bridge to affect supplies, has made no changes	34	59	96	79	130	72
Did not expect Bridge to affect supplies, has made changes	11	19	6	5	17	9
Expected to make changes because of Bridge opening has done so	8	14	12	10	20	11
Expected to make changes because of Bridge opening, has not done so	5	9	8	7	13	7
All Firms	58	100	122	100	180	100

on the east side of the estuary were more ready to take advantage of the opening of the Severn Bridge and to gain more business by offering a better service than South Wales firms. None of the firms in South Wales that now have to cross the estuary for supplies, reported that they received a worse service as a result of the transfer of a suppliers' depot from the west bank to the east.

7.47 Relatively few firms reported deriving any ancillary services such as market research or finance from across the estuary. Among the few firms that did so, approximately half considered that they had received a better service from their suppliers across the estuary after the Bridge was open. As with manufacturers this is hardly surprising in view of the range of such facilities available in both Cardiff and Bristol.

Changes in Outputs — Trading links

7.48 Changes in trading links are set out in Table 7.13 for manufacturing firms and in Table 7.14 for distributors. Among manufacturers more firms in each region traded with the other region after the Bridge was opened and more firms in the South West had links with South Wales both before and after than South Wales firms reported links with South West. The industrial structure of the two regions, the number of firms in each and the type of markets served account for this and it is supported by the traffic data analysed in Chapters 5 and 6.

7.49 Among distributors, nearly half those in the South West traded with South Wales both before and after. The number of firms involved was greater than that of South Wales firms trading with South West. The largest per-

TABLE 7.12

Changes in the Service Provided by Suppliers to Distributors after the Bridge opened

	Change in Service	Contract Distributors		Whole-salers		Coal, Agriculture & Builders' suppliers		Industrial suppliers		All Firms	
		No.	%	No.	%	No.	%	No.	%	No.	%
South Wales Firms	Better service received from suppliers across estuary	3	60	28	61	8	80	11	85	50	68
	No change in service received from suppliers	2	40	18	39	2	20	2	15	24	32
South West Firms	Better service received from suppliers across estuary	—	—	24	50	15	56	9	50	48	51
	No change in service received from suppliers	1	100	24	50	12	44	9	50	46	49

State of Link in relation to Bridge	South Wales with South West		South West with South Wales	
	No.	%	No.	%
Before and after	113	69	165	73
Before but not after	8	5	4	2
After only	19	12	31	14
No trade before or after	24	15	25	11
Total	164	100	225	100

TABLE 7.13

Changes in Trading Links with Regions Across Estuary (Manufacturers 100+ employees)

State of Link in relation to Bridge	South Wales with South West		South West with South Wales	
	No.	%	No.	%
Before and after	14	24	55	47
Before but not after	2	3	7	6
After only	12	20	15	13
No trade before or after	31	53	40	34
Total	59	100	117	100

TABLE 7.14

Changes in Trading Links with Regions Across Estuary — Distributors

centage increase was among South Wales firms though once allowance has been made for those ceasing to trade, the situation remains one where over twice as many firms are trading in South Wales from the Bristol side as in reverse.

7.50 The data on changes in the proportion of trade going across the estuary, Table 7.15 shows that in both regions the number and proportion of firms showing a higher percentage of their trade going to the region across the estuary after the Bridge is greater than those showing reduced percentages of trade. The higher percentages of South Wales firms showing increases in the share of their trade despatched to the South West and the lower percentages showing decreased shares have to be related to two factors — the previous importance of that market to them and its potential for growth compared to South Wales. On the former point, the evidence of the pre-Bridge survey was that the South West was less important to South Wales firms than vice-versa at a time when inter-regional trade was of very subsidiary interest to most firms in both regions. On the latter, the South West is expanding more rapidly in areas that are close to its existing distribution centres; in 1966--69 the population of the South West survey region rose by 2.9% compared with 0.4% in the South Wales survey

region though the latter still has the largest population — 1.9 million compared to 1.7 million.

7.51 The evidence of trading links does not permit easy seperation of changes due to the Bridge from those that would have occured anyway. In particular it is a fact that 25% of the manufacturers and 15% of the distributors whose replies from the main source of data were involved in take-overs during the survey. A clearer guide emerges from the examination of changes in delivery zones.

Changes in Delivery Zones — Manufacturers

7.52 The overlap of local and sub-regional areas, even the amalgamation of two parts of a regional system as a super-regional one, were made possible by the opening of the Bridge. Among manufacturers, twice as many firms changed their delivery zones as had changed their methods of distribution. Altogether 16% of manufacturers changed delivery zones because of the opening of the Bridge mainly by extending their distribution across the estuary. Such changes were most frequent among firms in Bristol-Severnside, Cardiff and Newport— 24/ of firms in each case. One other area, Wellington-Westbury, which contains a number of firms delivering nationally, showed an above-average change — 18% of firms.

TABLE 7.15
Percentages of Firms Showing Changes in Proportion of Their Trade Going to Region Across Estuary Manufacturers (100+) and Distributors

	South Wales Firms to South West		South West Firms to South Wales	
	Manufacturers	Distributors	Manufacturers	Distributors
Increase	45	29	36	31
No Change	34	61	35	46
Decrease	21	10	29	23

TABLE 7.16
Starts and Intensifications of Delivery Services Reported by South Wales Manufacturing Firms (Manufacturers 100+)

Distribution Zones†	New Zone for Deliveries	Delivery Service to Zone intensified	Total No. of Firms starting or intensifying delivery services	
	%	%	No.	%
North Gloucester	1	3	11	4
Greater Bristol	4	7	31	11
Bath	4	3	17	6
Weston-super-Mare & Mendips	2	2	11	4
North Wiltshire	3	3	16	6
Wellington-Westbury	2	3	13	5
South Somerset, South Wiltshire & Dorset	2	2	12	4
Exmoor, Devon & Cornwall	3	3	14	5
Hampshire	3	1	9	3
Berkshire & Oxfordshire	1	1	6	2
London (G.L.C.)	2	4	16	6
Rest of South East England	1	2	7	2

† See Map C

7.53 The industries most obviously affected are those highlighted in Chapter 6, namely food, drink and tobacco, building materials, mining and quarrying, timber and furniture and engineering. The food group, which stands out in the traffic data, shows changes on both sides of the estuary. The same is true of building materials to which should be added the high proportion of quarrying firms in the South West that changed zones to include South East Wales — 38%. This is in line with changes in output and traffic. The success of timber importers in South Wales is reflected in delivery zone changes by 27% and supplements the traffic analysis. In engineering 24% of firms in South Wales have changed delivery zones to include areas across the estuary.

7.54 Tables 7.16 and 7.17 show the detailed breakdown of changes, first in respect of a new zone and second in respect of more intensive services of a zone already served. Taking both changes, the area most affected was Greater Bristol where 31 Welsh firms (11%) reported them. The adjacent areas of Bath and North Wiltshire were now covered more intensively for the first time by 6% as was the Greater London area. Conversely the number of South West firms penetrating Newport and South East Monmouth and Cardiff is virtually the same as for South Wales firms in Bristol. Penetration from the South West into South and West Wales extends far west as does some South Wales penetration of Devon and Cornwall. However, it is only a small minority of firms that report changes so deep into cross-estuary regions. The only areas where 10% of firms are involved are Bristol-Newport-Cardiff.

7.55 The comparison of pre-Bridge data and that received in 1968-69 indicates that pre-Bridge trading patterns have been reinforced. Firms already trading across the estuary have stepped up their activities and only a few firms traded for the first time after the Bridge.

7.56 Table 7.18 shows the extent to which manufacturing firms' expectations as to changes in delivery zones were fulfilled. Over a third of all firms have been influenced in a way that they did not expect, and the majority of those 'surprised' have increased their delivery services. The extent to which such firms had made changes contrary to expectation confirms a conclusion of a pilot survey in 1965 which revealed that relatively few companies in Bristol had considered the impact of the Bridge on their activities.

Changes in Delivery Zones — Distributors

7.57 The pre-Bridge survey established the zones that distributors served. At least 40% distributed in the zones adjacent to their own, though usually the proportion was much higher. Beyond these zones the numbers of firms distributing fell sharply. The Severn Estuary was a definite barrier, but a substantial minority of firms on either side distributed across the estuary. For example, 32% of Newport firms distributed in the Bristol-Bath area and the same proportion from Bristol-Severnside to Newport and South East Monmouth. However, 64% of Bristol-Severnside firms delivered to North Wiltshire and 69% of Newport firms delivered to the Upper Valleys and North Monmouth. Pre-Bridge a greater proportion of firms in the Bristol-Severnside area served both near and distant areas in South Wales than South Wales firms in the South West. Welsh firms tended to restrict their activities to Wales and the border areas, whereas West Country firms distributed over wider areas, particularly in the South West peninsula and South Wales.

TABLE 7.17	Starts and Intensifications of Delivery Services Reported by South West Manufacturing Firms (Manufacturers 100+)			
Distribution Zones†	New Zone for Deliveries	Delivery Service to Zone intensified	Total No. of Firms starting or intensifying delivery services	
	%	%	No.	%
Forest of Dean	2	2	11	4
Herefordshire	1	3	8	3
Newport & South East Monmouthshire	5	7	33	12
Cardiff	5	6	30	11
Lower & Upper Valleys & North Monmouthshire	2	5	20	7
Bridgend & Porthcawl	1	4	15	5
Swansea & Port Talbot	3	4	18	7
Neath & Swansea Valleys	1	4	14	5
Brecon & Radnorshire	1	2	6	2
East Carmarthen	1	4	13	5
West Carmarthen, Pembroke & Cardigan	—	3	9	3
Rest of Wales	1	1	2	1

† See Map C

7.58 Firms were asked if they had extended or intensified their distribution service across the estuary because of the opening of the Bridge and if so to specify the areas involved. The number of firms (98 − 28%) is virtually identical to that for changes in distribution methods (96 − 27%). The firms involved were not always the same; 37% of those changing distribution zones did not change their methods.

7.59 Nearly two-thirds of all firms changing areas of distribution were located in the Bristol-Severnside area — 64 firms or 41% of all firms in that area. The rankings by proportions and areas are given in Table 7.19. The lower percentage of firms in Cardiff extending their distribution services could be due to management policy decisions. As indicated in paragraph 7.57, Welsh firms tended to restrict their activities to Wales, whereas Bristol firms tended to operate on a wider market area in all directions.

7.60 The smaller-scale reaction in Cardiff is partly related to Bristol's role as a super-regional centre, partly to the long-standing orientation of Cardiff firms inwards into Wales and partly to a feature of distribution networks. There is the tendency for deliveries from a major production centre such as London to be in bulk to a distribution centre from which they are spread out into the area beyond it but not back-tracked far into the intervening areas. Thus, goods from London would move to Cardiff and then be delivered further into Wales but not back to Gloucester which would be served from London or from an intermediate point such as Swindon. The Severn as a barrier must have strongly reinforced such a view of distribution in South Wales, and the Bridge has created a new situation by bringing South East Wales into the orbit of Bristol as the distributive centre. Hitherto, Bristol had a barrier to what would otherwise have been a natural area for it to serve.

7.61 Since the passing of the 1968 Transport Act the practicable maximum day's travelling of a goods vehicle on ordinary trunk roads has been 240 miles or 120 miles for a return journey. Westwards within this distance

TABLE 7.19

Numbers of Distributors Changing Distribution Areas

Area Ranked	No. of Firms	Percentage of Firms in Area
Bristol—Bath	64	41
Newport	6	27
Bridgend—Lower Valleys	3	23
North Gloucester	8	22
Wellington—Westbury	4	18
Cardiff	10	18
All Other Areas	3	7
All Firms	98	28

from Bristol lies most of industrial South Wales, excluding only the oil refineries around Milford Haven. There are approximately two million people living within this area. A similar distance from Cardiff takes in Gloucestershire, Somerset, Wiltshire, Dorset and East Devon in the South West region and the counties of Hampshire, Berkshire, Oxfordshire and Buckinghamshire in the South East region. This area contains approximately six million people.

7.62 A journey of 120 miles is only feasible where a lorry is making one drop. Whilst this is common for manufacturers, most distributors' delivery schedules are arranged around a large number of deliveries. For distributors it is common to take 60 miles as the radius from base within which deliveries can be made within a single day's journey. A 60 miles radius from Bristol includes Newport, Cardiff, Bridgend, the Valleys behind Cardiff and Newport and the industrialised southern edge of Breconshire. Including the Forest of Dean and Herefordshire, the area contains approximately 1.6 million people see Table 7.20. Cardiff, being 13 miles further from the Bridge than Bristol, has access to a smaller catchment area on the other side but one more densely populated. South Gloucestershire, Bristol, North Somerset and West Wiltshire contains 1.3 million. For Newport firms the catchment area within 60 miles is nearly 2 million.

TABLE 7.18 — **Degree to which Manufacturers' Expectations as to changes in Zones of Distribution Across the Estuary were fulfilled**

Firms' Expectations and Changes Compared	South Wales Firms		South West Firms		All Firms	
	No.	%	No.	%	No.	%
Did not expect Bridge to affect distribution zones, has not extended services	69	43	125	55	194	50
Did not expect Bridge to affect distribution zones, has extended delivery service	47	29	55	24	102	26
Expected to extend distribution service, has done so	21	13	32	14	53	14
Expected to extend distribution service, has not done so	24	15	14	6	38	10
Total	161	100	226	100	387	100

F

TABLE 7.20 — Population of Distribution Zones,[†] 1969

Thousands

East Side of Estuary		West Side of Estuary	
North Gloucester	414	Forest of Dean	54
Greater Bristol	690	Herefordshire	142
Bath	103	Newport & South East Monmouthshire	211
Weston-super-Mare & Mendips	120	Cardiff	405
North Wiltshire	358	Upper & Lower Valleys & North	
Wellington—Westbury	266	Monmouthshire	688
South Somerset, South Wiltshire &		Bridgend & Porthcawl	75
Dorset	452	Swansea & Port Talbot	238
Exmoor, Devon & Cornwall	1,272	Neath & Swansea Valleys	110
Hampshire	1,756	Breconshire & Radnorshire	41
Berkshire & Oxfordshire	998	East Carmarthen	128
		West Carmarthen, Pembroke & Cardigan	216
Total Population	6,429	Total Population	2,308
Total Population Within		**Total Population Within**	
One Day's Journey from Cardiff	1,268	One Day's Journey from Bristol	1,575
One Day's Journey from Newport	1,951		

[†] See Map C

7.63 In terms of market potential Bristol firms have slightly greater access to a new market in South Wales than Cardiff firms in the South West but the difference is not very significant. Because fewer Welsh firms distributed across the estuary before the Bridge opportunities for South Wales firms might be considered to be greater.

7.64 The contrast between the number and proportions of firms making changes of zones and/or intensifying deliveries is very marked. As shown in Tables 7.21 and 7.22 South Wales firms only appear in any number in Bristol and to a lesser extent in Bath and the area immediately south and west of Bristol. In contrast, Newport is now used by 61 West Country firms either for the first time or more intensively. Cardiff is additionally used by 54 firms as compared to 18 in Bristol and at least 16% of West Country — mainly Bristol — firms report new or more intensive deliveries as far west as Swansea. Even in West Wales more West Country firms report new services than do South Wales firms in Bristol. An analysis by types of distributor is set out in Appendices 42 and 43.

7.65 In assessing the impact of the Bridge and comparing it with expectations, three factors have to be borne in mind. The first is that those who replied to the surveys in 1968-69 may not have been aware of the full impact of the Bridge on their firms and still less aware of what expectations had been in 1966. Second, changes in personnel mean that policy changes are not

TABLE 7.21 — Starts and Intensifications of Delivery Services Reported by Distributors Located in South Wales

Distribution Zones[†]	New Zone for Deliveries %	Delivery Service to Zone intensified %	Total No. of Firms starting or intensifying delivery services No.	%
North Gloucester	4	4	9	8
Greater Bristol	10	6	18	16
Bath	4	5	11	10
Weston-super-Mare & Mendips	4	5	10	9
North Wiltshire	3	4	7	6
Wellington—Westbury	3	4	7	6
South Somerset, South Wiltshire & Dorset	2	3	5	4
Exmoor, Devon & Cornwall	4	1	5	4
Hampshire	—	1	1	1
Berkshire & Oxfordshire	—	1	1	1
London (G.L.C.)	1	1	2	2
Rest of South East England	1	—	1	1

[†] See Map C

TABLE 7.22 Starts and Intensifications of Delivery Services Reported by Distributors Located in South West

Distribution Zones†	New Zone for Deliveries	Delivery Service to Zone intensified	Total No. of Firms starting or intensifying delivery services	
	%	%	No.	%
Forest of Dean	5	10	35	15
Herefordshire	4	6	24	10
Newport and South East Monmouthshire	10	16	61	26
Cardiff	6	17	54	23
Lower & Upper Valleys & North Monmouthshire	7	8	37	15
Bridgend & Porthcawl	6	8	33	14
Swansea & Port Talbot	6	10	39	16
Neath & Swansea Valleys	6	6	28	12
Brecon & Radnorshire	3	5	18	8
East Carmarthen	4	4	20	8
West Carmarthen, Pembroke & Cardigan	4	5	22	9
Rest of Wales	2	4	13	6

† See Map C

recalled. Third, a radical change in the volume of cross-estuary trade may be more important than a change in areas served. Accordingly Table 7.23 includes increases in cross-estuary trade in excess of 25% with those changing areas served. This shows that a fifth of firms have been affected in a way that they did not expect, notably 26 firms (15%) that have extended their delivery services or expanded in some way. Of those that expected to extend their operations almost all in South Wales did so but over a third of those in the West Country did not. South Wales firms had fewer aspirations but they were more likely to be fulfilled.

7.66 As with manufacturers, firms reported that they were now able to give better service to customers across the estuary. Of 59 firms in South Wales 84% reported that they could do so, while of 171 firms in South West 75% reported likewise. The nature of the data on distributors does not permit a comparable analysis by trades of those offering and those receiving better service to that attempted for manufacturers.

Increased Competition Reported by Distributors

7.67 Altogether 76 (22%) firms reported that they had experienced increased competition from firms on the other side of the estuary because of the opening of the Severn Bridge. The firms were numerically divided between the two sides of the estuary as in Table 7.24 but because of the greater number in South West the percentages were very different, 33% in South Wales and 16% in the South West. Most of the firms reporting increased competition were located in major urban centres, Bristol having 25 firms, Cardiff 19, Newport 14 and Gloucester 8.

TABLE 7.23 Degree to which Distributors' Expectations as to Changes in Zones of Distribution across the Estuary were fulfilled

Firms' Expectations and Changes Compared	South Wales Firms		South West Firms		All Firms	
	No.	%	No.	%	No.	%
Did not expect Bridge to affect distribution zones, has not extended services	36	63	63	52	99	56
Did not expect Bridge to affect distribution zones, has extended delivery services	6	11	20	17	26	15
Expected to extend distribution service, has done so	14	25	28	23	42	24
Expected to extend distribution service, has not done so	1	2	10	8	11	6
Total	57	100	121	100	178	100

7.68 Table 7.24 shows that increased competition was concentrated among the coal, builders and agricultural suppliers' and industrial suppliers' trades on both sides of the estuary. Virtually no competition was experienced by contract distributors, but this is not surprising since their principals who are their main customers are generally located outside the Severnside area and competition is among them. The figure for wholesalers may be artificially low because a considerable number of firms have depots on both sides of the estuary and competition is between companies operating nationally rather than among independent firms.

7.69 Although more Welsh firms felt that they could offer a better service to firms across the estuary than English firms, more Welsh firms reported increased competition. English wholesalers who reported that

they were doing more trade across the estuary than their Welsh counterparts were correct. In two trades "coal, builders and agricultural products" and "industrial products" more firms on both sides reported increased trade and increased competition. Hence these trades can be considered as those where the most intensive competition has developed. This is particularly true of builders' merchants, steel stockholders and the timber trade.

Other Advantages and Disadvantages to Distributors

7.70 Over a third of distributors mentioned that they had received additional commercial benefits as a result of the opening of the Bridge — see Table 7.25. This is really only a guide to the types of benefits many of the firms obtained rather than the numbers of firms that have obtained them. Many of the other benefits mentioned add little information to other more direct

TABLE 7.24   Increased Competition Experienced by Different Distributive Trades

Trade	South Wales Firms — Increased competition from South West		South West Firms — Increased competition from South Wales	
	No.	%	No.	%
Contract Distributors	1	11	Nil	Nil
Wholesalers	22	30	16	12
Coal, Builders and Agricultural Suppliers	7	47	12	25
Industrial Suppliers	8	47	10	26
Total	38	33	38	16

TABLE 7.25   Additional Commercial Benefits Derived from the Opening of the Bridge

Additional Commercial Benefits	South Wales Firms		South West Firms		All Firms	
	No.	%	No.	%	No.	%
Savings in transport costs (all types)	7	6	32	14	39	11
Increased market penetration, easier access to customers, access to new markets	3	3	11	5	14	4
Customers able to visit showrooms	2	2	3	1	5	1
Expect to expand across estuary in near future	6	5	10	4	16	4
Better communications between depots, lower stocklevels held	7	6	12	5	19	5
Pre-Bridge routes less congested	–	–	6	3	6	2
Use of docks on other side of estuary	4	4	1	–	5	1
Multiplier effects (various)	–	–	4	2	4	1
Better service from suppliers	4	4	–	–	4	1
Future rationalisation of depot structure	–	–	3	1	3	1
Easier for sales staff to cover areas in holidays or emergencies	–	–	2	1	2	1
Alternative route to rail	–	–	2	1	2	1
Miscellaneous	4	4	5	2	9	3
No benefits, not completed, don't knows	77	67	147	62	224	64
Total	114	100	238	100	352	100

questions, for example, increased market penetration and the better communications between depots. Overall the replies confirm the main survey data. All the firms reporting that they received a better service from suppliers were located in South Wales and all the firms mentioning that the Bridge offered scope for future depot rationalisation were based in the South West. Benefits were most frequently reported in the large urban areas — Bristol 65 (42%), Cardiff 23 (40%), North Gloucester 16 (46%) and Lower Valleys and Bridgend 6 (46%). All the firms mentioning that pre-Bridge routes were now less congested were located in North Gloucester. Most of the firms expecting to expand in the future, reporting access to new markets, increased market penetration, better communications between depots and customers' easier access to showrooms, were located in Bristol or Cardiff.

7.71 Companies were also asked whether they had experienced any commercial disadvantage because of the opening of the Bridge. The disadvantages other than increased competition mentioned are shown in Table 7.26. Only competition and road congestion were specified. Congestion was mentioned particularly by firms in North Wiltshire (29%), Newport (24%) and Cardiff (23%). The only other disadvantage of note was the complaint that the Bridge was frequently closed because of high winds. This is of particular importance to distributors and hauliers whose drivers may not be able to return to base within the limit of their driver's hours if they have to make a detour via Gloucester. The main complaint was lack of advance warning, making contingency planning difficult.

Retail Distribution

7.72 When the first survey of wholesalers was being carried out in 1966—67 the first of two brief surveys of retailers was made. The multiple stores and co-operatives contacted did not expect the Bridge to have any effects on their trade as they were represented on both sides of the Severn and regarded the shopping hinterlands of each of their stores as being mutually exclusive. On the other hand, department stores in Bristol expected to start or increase sales to South Wales and, to stimulate demand, some extended their free delivery services to Monmouthshire. Other specialist shops that already had customers across the estuary expected to obtain increased trade from the opening of the Bridge.

7.73 At the end of 1966 stores reported that there were large numbers of sightseers from across the estuary, especially in the Bristol stores, but in the main these were "curiosity shoppers" purchasing novelty goods or food in restaurants. A second survey of ten major stores in Bristol, Bath and Cardiff in 1969 showed that the remarkable increase in the number of shoppers crossing the estuary had reached a peak in 1967 and the numbers had then declined. Purchases had made no significant impact on total sales and fluctuations in trade were due to national or seasonal trends, not cross-estuary business. Such purchases that had been noticeable apart from "novelty goods" were in speciality departments such as a Welsh store's bridal department and a Bristol store's antique trade. Stores managers agreed that shopping was not the main reason why people from South Wales visited Bristol and Bath. They combined shopping with sight-seeing or entertainment. The overall assessment by Cardiff stores was similar — the Bridge had had a negligible effect on trade and they had neither lost nor gained a significant number of customers after the Bridge opened.

7.74 The evidence from the traffic and household surveys is complementary to the findings of the survey of retailers. In 1968 shopping accounted for only 4% of all light vehicle movements across the Bridge (Table 4.1). Even on a Saturday when 33% of all shoppers travelled, the proportion of shopping traffic was only 9%. The majority of movements were from Wales to the South West (79%) and Bristol was the main destination (88% of eastward movements) (see Appendix 6). An estimated total of 304,000 people travelled across the Bridge by car and coach to shop in Bristol in 1968. It was also estimated from the household survey data that shoppers spent on average £2.10.0d. each and this gives a total sum of £760,000 spent in Bristol in 1968. This estimate must be treated with extreme caution for several reasons. First, it is based on a small number (88) of observations of expenditure of residents in Newport and Chepstow; second, the basic shopping unit is taken as an individual whereas different values might have been obtained if the unit was taken as the family where the weighting given to car travellers would have been less; third, many journeys are multiple purpose and the figures do not include purchases made by sightseers, holidaymakers and other visitors.

TABLE 7.26 **Commercial Disadvantages Reported Because of the Opening of the Bridge**

Disadvantages mentioned	South Wales Firms		South West Firms		All Firms	
	No.	%	No.	%	No.	%
Increased congestion on local roads	20	18	30	13	50	14
Severn Bridge sometimes closed by high winds	—	—	3	1	3	1
Miscellaneous	5	4	3	1	8	2
No disadvantages mentioned	89	78	262	85	291	83
All Firms	114	100	238	100	352	100

F2

7.75 In 1967, Cardiff City Planning Department, made a predictive study of the probable long-term effect of the Severn Bridge on retail shopping by applying gravity model theory to the 1961 Census of Distribution data. The values of trade reported in this exercise were increased by 20% to take account of the increase in shopping between 1961 and 1966 and this gave an estimate of £2.7 million being spent in Bristol by people from South Wales after the Bridge opened, a considerable divergence from the Severn Bridge study estimates. The discrepancy is probably larger since the Cardiff study was concerned only with consumer durables whereas the Severn Bridge data includes convenience goods, such as food, where divergence of purchases across the estuary would not be expected to be as great. The true figure is likely to be below the Cardiff estimate for two reasons. First, the diversion of trade to Bristol predicted by the Cardiff study of £2 million would be equal to 3.5% of total purchases of consumer durables in Bristol in 1966. No significant increase in trade was reported during the survey of retail stores; estimates of Welsh shoppers' expenditure in Bristol were of the order of 1%. Second, £2 million would represent 20% of the total purchases made in Bristol by non-residents according to the 1966 Census of Distribution data. This amount of trade does not seem to be consistent with the distribution of population in the hinterland of Bristol.

7.76 A previous study[1] noted Bristol's low status as a shopping centre in comparison with its population and suggested that it suffered from the restriction of its hinterland to the west. Whilst this is partly true, other factors contribute to its relatively low status as a retail centre. The existence of a large retail centre in Bath, only 13 miles from Bristol, must have reduced its shopping hinterland to the east as well. The existence across the estuary of Cardiff as a comparable centre would act as a similar counter-attraction to Bristol, the further distance offset by the provision of better facilities. The restricted hinterland for Bristol would in turn inhibit the development of the shopping facilities customarily found in centres of its size. Whether its new position as the geographical centre of Severnside and proximity to the motorway intersection can be exploited is a moot point.

Fatstock Markets

7.77 Some effects of the opening of the Bridge on the agricultural sector are implicit in the analysis of vehicle movements, for example the switch to road haulage to supply agricultural chemicals from Bristol to West Wales. A more direct effect was the possibility created for farmers to market their stock in new areas. Records kept in connection with the certification of animals under the Fatstock Price Guarantee Scheme made it possible to find out how far farmers took advantage of this possibility. For this purpose three markets were studied, Thornbury (the nearest market to the Bridge, some 4 miles to the east), Winford (6 miles south of Bristol and 17 miles from the Bridge) and Chippenham (32 miles east of the Bridge). The area of origin of all cattle, sheep and pigs certified at these markets were analysed for a 3-week period at the start of each quarter for the two years from April, 1966. The first two periods were

before the Bridge opened and the remaining six after.[2] Further information is contained in Appendices 44 to 46.

7.78 All three markets were practically isolated from supplies from west of the Severn before the Bridge opened. The only movements from this area in the two pre-Bridge periods were 15 cows and 2 sheep from Lydney entered at Thornbury! With the opening of the Bridge there were movements in all three markets. There were scarcely any movements to Winford market, but at Chippenham there was a modest movement, particularly of sheep (Appendix 44). There was no sustained pattern of growth at either market and at least some movements may well have been of an experimental nature. There is also the return load factor. Chippenham is an important market, especially for pigs, and where a farmer takes a truck to bring back an intended purchase, he may well take a few animals to sell since he has, effectively, free transport to the market for them.

7.79 At Thornbury the picture is very different. From a situation of practically zero movements before September, 1966, there is a substantial traffic after the Bridge opened (Appendix 45). Two special factors operated there. First, in the early 1960s Thornbury was a declining market, but in 1963 a new auctioneer took over the market and a strong expanding market developed before the Bridge opened. Second, following the market held on 7th October 1967 Chepstow market was closed forcing some farmers to seek a new market; for some the choice would be Thornbury. Growth was strongest and most sustained in the case of sheep, the animal most in evidence from west of the Severn. Movements of pigs are small compared with those of cattle and sheep but the absolute numbers of all three animals were increasing. While there is strong growth, there is also a sign of a seasonal influence, the proportionate importance of the area west of the Severn being greatest in the autumn and winter.

7.80 Analysis of the area of origin of animals from west of the Severn certified at Thornbury shows that, while the movement to Thornbury is strong, it is quite localised (Appendix 46). In the case of the smaller movements to Chippenham and Winford a much larger proportion of the animals moved (34%) come from farther afield.

Fruit and Vegetable Markets

7.81 Three Bristol firms and five in Cardiff completed questionnaires. All the Bristol firms were doing more business in South Wales. At a rough estimate trade across the estuary may have doubled since the opening of the Bridge although in total terms it represents only 10%—15% of the deliveries of those wholesalers using the Bridge. The areas to which deliveries are made are mainly the large urban areas along the coastal belt. The increase in deliveries is partly related to another major impact of the Severn Bridge which is on supplies. All firms reported drawing more supplies from South Wales, two firms mentioned fruit from Cardiff docks and one produce from Pembrokeshire, which is an important potato growing area.

7.82 Of the five Cardiff wholesalers only one reported trading across the estuary. This firm had had a depot in Bristol before the Bridge opened which it closed down and supplied its customers in the South West direct from Cardiff. Three of the Welsh firms reported that they were receiving faster, fresher and possibly greater supplies of fresh fruit and vegetables from Devon and Cornwall. Before the Bridge opened deliveries were mainly by rail and tended to be sporadic. Since 1966 growers have sent produce by road into Cardiff market. These deliveries are still largely marginal, in some cases growers dissatisfied with prices in Bristol. It is possible that the time-saving to be obtained when the M.5 by-passes Bristol in 1974 will give an impetus to this trade.

Imports Through the Bristol Channel Ports

7.83 This section is concerned mainly with those commodities which were handled by distributors. Raw materials, such as iron ore, which go straight to manufacturers, and manufactured goods, which are diverse in their destinations have been excluded. The commodities studied fall into four groups — foodstuffs (especially dairy produce, meat, fruit and vegetables and cereals), goods handled by agricultural suppliers (animal foods, molasses, vegetable oils and fertilisers), basic materials (timber) and petroleum products. Only those Severnside ports which dealt with such commodities were studied i.e. the ports of Bristol and Avonmouth, Gloucester, Sharpness, Newport, Cardiff, Barry and Swansea. Port Talbot, the only major port to be excluded, concentrates almost exclusively on imports for the iron and steel industry. Bridgwater, Penarth and Lydney only serve their immediate hinterlands and thus are not affected by the Bridge. In the case of Lydney, for example, all the imports are of timber which is used by local manufacturers in the Forest of Dean. The Bristol Channel ports handle roughly 8% of all imports into Britain, although they handle 12% of all foodstuffs imported. Bristol—Avonmouth is by far the largest port for imports, while Newport, Barry and Swansea are far more significant as exporters.

7.84 To study the extent to which the ports have gained or lost traffic in certain commodities during the period of the survey, 1965 was taken as the base year rather than 1966 which appeared to be anomolous. Owing to such factors as the seamen's strike, imports tended to be lower in 1966 than in 1965 or 1967. Although there was nationally an upwards trend in imports of 12%, the only ports in the Severn Estuary to increase their imports during the period were Newport and Cardiff. The latter, in fact, almost doubled the volume of goods handled, whilst Newport grew at more than double the national rate. Bristol and Swansea lost a marginal amount of business, whilst the two smallest ports, Sharpness and Barry, lost a considerable percentage of their trade. Further information is given in Appendices 47 and 48.

7.85 Taking the principal groups and starting with foodstuffs the increase in **Dairy Produce** through Newport is largely due to the development of a special shipping service to Ireland, which had no relation to the opening of the Severn Bridge.

7.86 The fall in **Fruit and Vegetables** through Bristol is chiefly due to the centralization of banana imports by Elders & Fyffes at Southampton. There has also been a decline in citrus fruit imports. This is probably because there is a tendency by the producing countries, such as Israel and South Africa, to form their own marketing organisations and in some cases to take over the shipping services. The consequent switch in shipping services has acted to the detriment of Bristol in the last few years. On the other hand the South Wales ports have benefited from such concentration because Barry has been chosen by Geest Industries as a major banana importing centre and Cardiff has been selected by the South Africa Citrus Fruit Board. Both these decisions were taken before the Bridge opened, and, as far as is known, the opening of the Bridge had no influence on the decisions. However, the opening of the Bridge obviously confers an added advantage to the South Wales ports in the future as distribution to the rest of the country has become much easier.

7.87 Most of the **Sugar** imports through Bristol are molasses which are destined for the animal feeds trade. Imports of actual sugar have fluctuated in recent years but have recently declined due to rationalisation by national importers.

7.88 For **Cereals,** the only port of major significance was Bristol for whom cereal importing was second only in importance to petroleum products. Most of this was destined for local flour mills and animal feeding stuffs' mills.

7.89 Animal Feedstuffs and Oil Seeds and Nuts constitute the third most important import into Bristol, which is the only Bristol Channel port dealing in this commodity, as is also the case with molasses and oil seeds and nuts, which are compounded into animal feedstuffs. While the Severn Bridge has conferred considerable advantages to the compounders in reducing costs of transporting the finished products from Bristol into South Wales, the fact that there was little importing of the basic raw materials into South Wales before or after the Bridge meant there was no scope for rationalisation at the importing end. Prior to the opening of the Bridge there was considerable traffic by barge of materials or semi-processed products between mills on either side of the estuary. This two-way traffic was related to the need of the mills to maintain optimum production schedules. The opening of the Bridge created opportunities for transferring some of this traffic from barge to road, especially where empty delivery vehicles could be back-loaded. However, it has not been possible to ascertain the extent to which this has occurred.

7.90 The only port in the Bristol Channel which handles **Chemical Fertilizers** is Bristol. It involves a large tonnage of goods which is mainly handled by manufacturers located in Avonmouth. The Bridge has obviously had no effect on the importing of this material. The distribution of chemical fertilizers was referred to in Chapter 6.

7.91 All ports in the Severn Estuary including Bridgwater handle **Timber.** Until recently this was a very traditional and disorganised trade, timber often being handled plank by plank. Increasingly, it is being handled by bulk loads and mechanisation has created the need for modern lay-outs and large storage areas leading to concentration in fewer ports. In the Bristol Channel all ports declined between 1965 and 1968 at a far greater rate than the national average, with the exception of Newport which expanded by 57% over this period. It is now the largest timber importing port in the Bristol Channel mainly due to the opening of a special terminal for handling Canadian timber in bulk. The decline in imports into Bristol is partly because most of the timber merchants are still located in Bristol's City Docks and only small vessels can be discharged there. Packaged timber is off-loaded at Avonmouth, but development of modern facilities has not prevented a continued decline in this trade. The Severn Bridge is not known to have affected the actual importing arrangements but the reduction in transport costs made possible by it has stimulated competition among timber distributors on both sides of the estuary, which would in turn influence tonnages moved through the ports. The figures suggest that Cardiff has benefited more than Bristol.

7.92 Petroleum accounts for over a third of all imports into the Bristol Channel ports. Most of this traffic is coastwise movements from refineries to primary distribution depots. All the ports on the Bristol Channel handle petroleum products except Lydney. The petroleum industry has expanded very rapidly in the past decade but as the Appendices show not all ports have shared equally in the growth. This is partly due to the Severn Bridge but also to other factors. Thus, the increase in imports through Cardiff is largely because several of the American oil companies attempting to get a foot-hold in the U.K. market have established depots there. The reason for choosing Cardiff as a location was not related to the opening of the Bridge but due to the cost of establishing the depot and other related port charges. The Severn Bridge has had some impact in the Upper Severn Estuary. Although Newport shows an increase in throughput, one oil company closed its depot there and divided the distribution territory between Bristol and its other Welsh depot. However, other factors have also contributed to this and to changes at Gloucester.

7.93 The main effect has been on Gloucester where petroleum traffic declined by 40% between 1965 and 1968 because two companies closed depots in Gloucester in favour of distributing from depots lower down the estuary. Even in this case the opening of the Bridge was only one factor of four causing this change. First, in rough order of importance the opening of the Merseyside — London petroleum pipeline, has enabled oil to be distributed in the Midlands from an inland depot at Kingsbury instead of from coastal locations. Second, the increasing size of road tankers made investment at

Gloucester necessary to update facilities. It was more profitable to develop such facilities at Bristol especially as the same larger tankers made road journeys over longer distances more economic. Third, increasing economies of scale in shipping has made it less economic to ship up the River Severn by barge than hitherto.

7.94 With the exception of petroleum, and to a lesser extent timber, most of the changes in imports through Bristol Channel ports in the period 1966—68 were due to other factors than the opening of the Severn Bridge. This does not mean that there are not opportunities for rationalisation in the future to the benefit of the country, if not individual ports. There are certain constraints which would delay rationalisation. One of these is that the ports on either side of the Channel appear to be very competitive with each other at the present time despite the fact that their main competitors are London, Liverpool and Southampton. A consequence of this situation is that many shipping lines call at ports on both sides of the estuary.

7.95 Other things being equal, the costs of road transport via the Bridge are less than the additional port and shipping charges incurred by accepting deliveries at two ports instead of one at the present time. Large warehouses and cold stores have been constructed at Avonmouth to serve both the South West and South Wales in 1968—69. This does not mean that future imports will all be chanelled through Avonmouth but it does increase the likelihood that, long term, ships will only call at one port in the Bristol Channel, not two.

Expectations and Results

7.96 Rapid and extensive changes in distribution have occurred and the expectations as to the general pattern of changes have been fulfilled. The arguments already set out in the final paragraphs of Chapter 6 apply with at least equal force to distribution while the concentration of this activity in the two main centres has lent further strength to the arguments as to areas of influence now that the Severn has ceased to be such a barrier.

7.97 The intensification of competition with the overlap of market areas and the changes in distributive methods and services have clearly corroborated the traffic data and in particular the pattern of light and heavy commercial traffic movements. The distributive firms were already predominantly road-based and the changes within transport are therefore less marked.

REFERENCES

1. Carruthers (Regional Studies Vol. 1 No. 1 May 1967 Pp. 74).
2. The periods were certification weeks 1—3; 14—16; 27—29 and 41—43 and roughly represent the first three weeks in April, July, October and January.

CHAPTER EIGHT

The Bridge-Costs and Benefits

8.1   The Severn Road Bridge and the length of motor-way linking it to the existing trunk road system cost over £16 million to build. If it had not been built, the money could have been put to an alternative use. The purpose of this chapter is to examine the Bridge as an investment and to ask whether the expenditure was justified by the benefits which have resulted from it.

8.2   This technique of cost-benefit analysis frequently arouses criticism when applied to any project and there are always substantial difficulties to be considered. To undertake such a study it is first necessary to measure all the costs and benefits which will result from the project. In practice, not all the effects may be known and even where they are known it may be difficult or impossible to measure them. In particular, problems occur when there are other changes taking place at the same time which also influence the variables being studied.

8.3   In the case of the Bridge, it is part of a motorway system which also saves time compared with older routes and influences the number of journeys made. Not all observed differences between the before and after situation can be attributed to the Bridge itself, and in any event information on the "before" situation is scarce, as the work of data collection did not begin on a large scale until after the Bridge had opened.

8.4   In this study, it is not claimed that all the effects of the Bridge have been accounted for and measured, since the effects of any investment of this type are widely dispersed throughout the economy, but the problem has been eased by the fact that the bulk of the immediate benefits of the Bridge accrue in the first instance to road users crossing the Bridge itself. The data gathered in the process of toll collection, together with the results of the surveys described in earlier chapters, means that a good deal of information is available on those using the Bridge. The number and type of vehicles crossing the Bridge, the origins and destinations of the trips made, the purpose for which the trips were made, the number of passengers and the type of commodity carried can all be estimated with a fair degree of accuracy.

8.5   The main difficulty occurs in estimating how many of these journeys would not have been made had the Bridge not been there and how many would have been made, but to different destinations.

8.6   Information is also only available for the present time period. The analysis requires the valuations of the benefits for the entire life of the Bridge, which itself is not known. Reliance must be placed on present trends; however, trends in car ownership and traffic growth

have presented a relatively stable pattern over time. As far as car ownership is concerned the pattern of what has been happening in Britain in recent years, closely resembles what was happening in the United States in previous years. Present United States trends can, there-fore, be used to help estimate traffic in Britain for some years to come. Beyond this, estimation becomes a much more speculative procedure. However, when approaching the 21st century the importance of costs and benefits as an influence on decision making now, declines severely as a result of applying reasonable discount rates over long periods.

8.7   Once the costs and the benefits of the Bridge have been estimated the next task is to assign them a value. In the case of the Bridge, the construction costs are known and the saving in fuel and other running costs can be determined. The main difficulties occur in valuing the time saved.

The Costs

Capital Costs

8.8   The first difficulty is deciding what proportion of the motorway, together with roundabouts, interchanges and flyovers, etc. should be regarded as an essential cost of the project. Having decided this, the next task is to isolate the costs of these from sets of accounts, some of which do not give separate figures for the sections of motorway considered. There is then the task of dis-counting these to give a single value for 1966 when payments have been spread out over several years, with accounting years differing from calendar years and some small payments remaining outstanding after the Bridge was opened.

8.9   Had no motorway been built it would have been necessary to build link roads, connecting the Bridge with the A48 on the western side and with the A38 on the eastern side. The motorway actually built was more elaborate than that needed to link with the existing road system, accepting pre-motorway congestion levels, but part of the benefit attributed to the Bridge accrues to those making the increased trips following its opening. Had there been no motorway the time saving would have been slightly smaller and the additional trips slightly fewer. Thus, part of the motorway must be included in the costs since the task of splitting the benefits between those derived from the motorway and those derived from the Bridge would seem impossible.

8.10   On the western side, the A48 runs within a mile of the Bridge and the cost of the link between the Pwllmeyric roundabout, included in the cost of the

Bridge itself, and the A48 and A466 west of Chepstow is small enough to ignore. On the eastern side, the M4 meets the A38 at Almondsbury where there is a multi-level interchange. The construction costs of the motorway between the Bridge and the interchange are known. The cost of the land is available by date of expenditure, although not by date of change of use. Separate accounts were not kept for the costs of the interchange alone; these are incorporated in the total cost of extending the motorway from Almondsbury to Tormarton. It can be argued that a much cheaper form of road junction would have been adequate for a feeder road for the Bridge alone, and that to include the total cost of the Almondsbury interchange is not justified.

8.11 Whatever methods are used to deal with the conceptual and practical problems, it will be seen later that the effect on the analysis is such that the conclusions would remain substantially unaltered.

8.12 Capital expenditure on the Bridge, including the small bridge across the Wye, was £12,218,000 and expenditure on land and the motorway to Almondsbury brings this total to £16,568,000. Charging interest on pre-1966 expenditures and discounting post-1966 expenditures at 10% gives a 1966 cost of £20,900,000.

8.13 However, assumptions have had to be made about the distribution over time of some of the capital expenditure; even where dates are known exactly, these are dates at which the funds were advanced and will differ from the dates at which the expenditure was made.

8.14 The cost of construction work, excluding that apportioned to the Bridge itself was £4,200,928, but exact records of how it was spent over time are not immediately available. It has therefore been apportioned over time on a pro rata basis. The cost of the interchange at Almondsbury for which separate records were not kept has been ignored on the assumption that the cost of a conventional road junction to link with the A38 would not have significantly affected the cost of building the motorway up to the interchange.

Maintenance Costs

8.15 As the Bridge is new, the expenditure on maintenance and upkeep has not developed any stable pattern, and it is thus very difficult to make any forecasts. Whether there will be any need for more substantial repair, and if so at what stage in the Bridge's life, is also complete guesswork. Provisions for maintenance set aside in the official accounts are not entirely helpful since they are governed by the requirements of the Severn Bridge Tolls Act and include provision for accumulating during the toll period (40 years), funds for maintenance in subsequent years. In estimating total costs provision is made at the rate of £70,000 per annum. Of this, £40.000 is for routine maintenance and £30,000 is provision for exceptional maintenance. Examination of the actual expenditure over the first 3 years suggest that a lower figure, £60,000 might be sufficient.

The Benefits

8.16 The Bridge cuts the length of journeys between the eastern and western sides of the estuary by up to 50 miles and cuts journey times by up to 2 hours or more, depending on the level of congestion that existed in pre-Bridge days.

The Problem in Theory

8.17 The task of putting a total value on the saving in travel costs is made complex by the fact that the saving on journeys itself affects the number and pattern of journeys made. Traditionally, journeys made following a transport improvement are classified into two types — diverted and generated; diverted being those trips which would have been made had the improvement not taken place and generated being the increase in trips (following the improvement) which would not have been made at the former higher cost. The benefit to diverted traffic can be taken as the number of journeys undertaken OT_1 (see Figure 8 (i) times the saving on each journey $C_1 - C_2$. The cost C_1 and the number of Trips T_1 undertaken before the improvement and the cost C_2 and number of trips T_2 undertaken after the improvement can be taken to form two points $C_1 T_1$ and $C_2 T_2$ on a demand curve showing the number of trips made as a function of the cost of a trip. The generated trips $T_1 T_2$ can then be assigned the value ABC, this being the difference for all generated trips between the cost actually incurred in making the trip and the maximum cost that the traveller would be prepared to incur rather than not make the trip at all.

8.18 In order to apply this analysis it is necessary to find the demand curve AC for every pair of origins and destinations. In the case of the Bridge abundant data is available on trips made over the Bridge after it was opened, but information on the trips made before the Bridge was opened is scarce. The only study made was a survey conducted by Gloucestershire County Council. This surveyed westbound traffic on two days in August 1966 on the major routes likely to be affected by the Bridge. The procedure was repeated on two days in August 1967, interviewing traffic on the same routes as in 1966, but with the inclusion of the Bridge itself as an interview point. Information was collected on the origins and destinations of the trip being made and whether it was for work or recreation.

8.19 As it was taken on two days only and in one direction, the data cannot be taken as representative of total traffic throughout the year, August traffic in particular having an above-average recreational content. Given the limitations of the data, what the two surveys can provide are two matrices, TB showing the number of trips between areas prior to the opening of the Bridge and TA showing the number afterwards (see Figure 8 (ii).) Two similar matrices DB and DA, showing distance before and after can also be constructed. If distance is taken to be proportional to cost, it would seem a simple enough process to compute a demand curve by regressing —

$$\frac{Ta - Tb}{Tb} \quad \text{on} \quad \frac{Db - Da}{Db}$$

8.20 In reality, however, the problem is much more complex, as the theory is only valid where the demand curve shows the number of trips that would be made at different costs, where the cost of making alternative trips remains constant. This condition does not apply in the case of the Bridge where, with the opening of the Bridge, the demand curve for most journeys probably shifted as the cost of making alternative journeys from the same origin become relatively more or less expensive.

8.21 In the case illustrated in Figure 8 (ii) a reduction in distance DB, DA, leads to an increase in trips TB, TA, but simultaneously the demand curve for this journey shifts inwards from CD to AB as other journeys from the same origin also experience cost reductions making them in some cases relatively more attractive compared with the pre-Bridge situation. In this case, fitting the regression shown above would not give the elasticity of the curve CD or AB, but that of the curve XX.

8.22 In some cases, the change in relative costs was large enough to reverse the cost differential between trips to alternative destinations open to a driver starting from a given origin. This can be illustrated as follows in Figure 8 (iii): a motorist at origin 0 can choose, amongst others, between two destinations, D_1 and D_2.

8.23 If the costs of reaching both destinations were the same he would prefer D_2 but in the pre-Bridge situation he chooses D_1 and takes the route OGD_1, since his preference for D_2 over D_1 does not exceed the additional cost of the journey D_1D_2. When the Bridge is opened, however, the costs of reaching D_1 and D_2 are reversed. D_2 is now cheaper than D_1 and by taking the route OBD_2 he obtains the benefit of both a lower trip cost and a preferred destination.

8.24 To take a specific example, the Gloucestershire County Council before and after study showed an increase in trips of 421% for light vehicles between Bristol and Cardiff. Some of these additional trips were made by people who would have stayed at home had the Bridge not been built but a proportion would have been made but to other destinations, such as Gloucester, Chepstow and Newport, which now become relatively less attractive.

8.25 The 421% increase, therefore, consists of a number of completely new trips, a number of trips attracted away from other destinations, less a number that would formerly have been made to Cardiff but have now been attracted away to other destinations. The study further illustrates this effect by showing that on routes where there has been little or no saving from the Bridge the number of trips made has declined.

8.26 A further complication is that the demand function will be a different shape for different purposes, and that the purpose structure on any route will vary throughout the year, resulting in a different aggregate demand curve in the winter to that in the summer when the before and after study was undertaken.

8.27 This problem of finding demand curves has always proved a major difficulty in studies of this type. One method of getting round the difficulty would be to try and explain the increase in trips between an origin and a destination as a function of more than one variable. If the increase in trips depends not only on the cost reduction of the route itself, but also on the cost reduction on other routes, it should be possible to isolate the two influences.

8.28 If $\triangle T$ is the change in the number of trips and $\triangle D$ is the change in the mileage of the route and $\Sigma\triangle D_n$ is the change in the mileage on all other routes from the same origin, the data from the before and after study could be used to calibrate a model

$$\triangle T = \frac{K\triangle D^a}{\Sigma\triangle D_n^b}$$

or some similar model. In the case of the Severn Bridge, the results from such an exercise are rather poor and there is the serious practical problem of deciding which other routes to select. Ideally these should be all possible alternatives but these are infinite. In practice the choice can be limited but the result is to a degree arbitrary.

8.29 Although methods using simultaneous equation systems are possible in theory the quality of pre-Bridge data imposes limitations. For the present, the best solution would appear to be to perform the calculations for the values thought to be likely. It can be seen that whatever shape of the actual curves, in aggregate, taking half of the area (trips after − trips before) x (cost before − cost afterwards) is likely to give a fair approximation.

Other Costs and Benefits

8.30 Apart from the major effects of cutting journey times and distances, other benefits and costs need to be considered. In addition to quicker journeys motorists also save time on many routes as the reduced congestion means journey times can be estimated with greater accuracy and less time needs to be allowed for unforeseen delays. Reductions in accidents for diverted journeys and accidents involving generated traffic are respectively contributions to benefits and costs whilst there are important effects on the environment both positive and negative. It is in this field that measurement problems become most acute. In this study, it has not been possible to consider these in the detail they justify. Such an investigation would involve very extensive fieldwork and probably produce highly qualified results. There are also the changes in congestion and, therefore, journey times on other routes to be considered.

8.31 The opening of the Bridge substantially reduced the volume of traffic through Gloucester and on the A48 between Gloucester and Chepstow. This has brought benefits to travellers using this and similarly affected roads even if they do not use the Bridge. At the same time there have been increases in congestion on roads leading to the Bridge resulting in losses to those who use them especially if they do not use the Bridge.

8.32 The time saved on the A.48 could be estimated fairly well, but most of the changes in journey times, due to changes in traffic density, are too small to be measured in practice. For this reason, it has been assumed that in respect of congestion the benefits are offset by the losses and that the net benefit is zero.

The Capital Cost of Vehicles

8.33 Light vehicles save only variable costs since items such as tax and insurance are independent of distance travelled and few motorists will sell their cars because journeys are shorter. There is a different situation for commercial vehicle operators since reduced distances mean the same amount of work can be completed with fewer lorries and drivers.

8.34 In valuing the savings there are two methods that could be adopted. The first would be to calculate the capital value of the fewer vehicles needed to perform the same amount of work and add to this their running costs. The second approach would be to multiply the miles saved by an operating cost per mile that included an allowance for standing costs. The results would only differ to the extent that the discounting procedure used allocated capital cost over time differently from that used to allocate the capital expenditure on vehicles and other fixed costs to a cost per mile. In this study the latter method has been adopted.

Forecasting Future Bridge Traffic

8.35 To forecast future traffic across the Bridge it was assumed that the number of trips between areas on the east and the west of the Bridge would increase in the same proportion as the number of vehicles in those areas. Forecasts of the number of vehicles in the areas concerned were made using data from several sources. Estimates of the number of vehicles per head of the population were taken from Road Research Laboratory figures, calculated in the case of light vehicles on the assumption that vehicle ownership is growing along a logistic course to reach a saturation level of 0.45 vehicles per head in the year 2010. For the period up to 1981 population estimates were obtained from the planning departments of local authorities and various official sources. For the period beyond 1981, it was assumed that the proportions of the population of England and Wales in the relevant areas considered could continue to change in the same way as they had in the estimates up to 1981. Total population after 1981 was taken from the Registrar General's forecasts for England and Wales. For the period up to 1980 forecasts were made from each year and the total numbers of trips per year by light vehicles was subdivided into ten categories according to the purpose for which the trip was made:— i.e. holidays, business, shopping, etc. The number of journeys made for each purpose was estimated as the sum of the expected trips between the 17 defined areas east and west of the Bridge. Using this method any changes in the geographical distrubution of trips are shown reflecting differences in the expected growth of vehicles in different areas. Both the purpose structure and the geographical pattern of trips were estimated from the numerous surveys of vehicles crossing the Bridge during 1967 and 1968. It was assumed that the patterns of traffic in each survey were representative of all traffic at that time of year. Thus traffic during July and August was distributed according to the pattern revealed by the August surveys, the pattern shown by the surveys in March and April was taken as representative of traffic in spring and early summer and winter traffic was represented by the November survey. The change in pattern of trips is slight as compared with the change in total volume. It reflects differences in estimated rates of population growth of regions such as South East England compared with Wales.

8.36 From an examination of Figure 8 (iv) it can be seen that the areas under the curves, which are what are required for cost-benefit calculations, would be comparatively insensitive to small changes in the curves themselves. The data in tabular form is provided in Table 8.1. As road traffic, both in Britain and abroad, has shown a fairly stable growth pattern in the past it is unlikely that estimates for the first years of the Bridge will be widely amiss. Later years, although more liable to substantial error become less significant in the calculations as the discount factors reduce their present value. Nevertheless, there are areas of uncertainty which need to be considered. It has been assumed that the number of trips per vehicle will remain constant. In recent years average milage per vehicle has been rising very slowly over time and if this trend continues, and a constant proportion of this increase is mileage on cross-Bridge trips, the figures will show a slight underestimate. Unfortunately there is little information on changes in particular types of journey over past years. All the evidence suggests that socio-economic factors are a major variable in trip generations, particularly for leisure purposes. As a high proportion of Bridge users are making trips for leisure purposes, as incomes rise over time, Bridge trips may become an increasing proportion of total trips which could be a further source of underestimation. Over-estimation could arise if an increasing proportion of the car populations become second cars, as can be expected. If this were the case, it would be a factor tending to reduce the mileage per car.

8.37 In the case of heavy vehicles the obstacles to reaching a correct forecast are probably greater. Future trips are likely to be subject to changes in government

		Thousands				
		Heavy Vehicles		Total Vehicles		
Year	Light Vehicles	Upper Forecast	Lower Forecast	Upper Forecast	Lower Forecast	TABLE 8.1 Forecasts of Future Bridge Traffic
1970	5,674	1,622	1,622	7,296	7,296	
1975	7,570	2,494	2,168	10,064	9,738	
1980	9,257	3,033	2,636	12,290	11,893	
1990	11,479	3,348	2,909	14,827	14,388	
2000	13,308	3,801	3.303	17,109	16,611	

policy such as permitted maximum lorry sizes and similar factors, many of which can only be guessed at. In the first three years of the life of the Bridge, commercial and coach traffic grew at an exceptionally rapid rate, showing little comparisons with national figures. In 1967—68 traffic rose 24%, in 1968—69 it rose 9.6% and in 1969—70 11.5%. Nationally, commercial vehicles traffic has averaged 2%—2.5% growth per annum over the last 10 years. In the second half of the 1960s, it has grown very little apart from a slight increase between 1967 and 1968. The initial rapid increase in Bridge traffic might be expected, as firms adjust to the new situations although part of the explanation may be that traffic nationally is growing at different rates in different road situations. How long this apparent adjustment process will take to work itself out cannot be known with certainty, so two separate forecasts have been made for heavy vehicles. The first assumes that traffic will decline steadily to the estimated long-term growth rate in 1980. The second forecast assumes it will reach this point by 1975. A further aspect to be considered is the effect on the volume of Bridge traffic of the extensions and eventual completions of the M.4 and M.5 motorways. The evidence suggests a net increase of 250,000 to 450,000 in 1970 terms. No account has been taken of this. Since the areas affected are relatively marginal, any benefit resulting to them from the Bridge, as opposed to the motorway, will be small and thus have little effect on the results.

Estimating the distance saved

8.38 The length of trips before and after the Bridge was opened was estimated from maps for journeys between the main centres of the 17 traffic zones used. The use of traffic zones covering small areas in regions close to the Bridge, between which Bridge traffic was greatest, and larger zones for areas further from the Bridge minimised the errors involved whilst keeping the volume of work to acceptable levels. Subtraction of the "after" matrices from the "before" matrix yields the matrices of miles saved. Multiplying each cell by the corresponding cell of the trips made gives the total saving in miles, had all the trips been made over the old route before the Bridge was opened. The trips made to or from areas outside the zones used were assumed to save the mean value of all other trips.

Estimating the time saved

8.39 The mean values of times saved were obtained by timing vehicles on the A.48 and A.38 — the main roads affected — by means of tape recordings and stop-watches. Where this method was not possible as in towns, vehicles were followed and average times determined by overtaking as many vehicles as overtook the car during the timing runs. Times on some routes away from A.38 and A.48 were calculated from average speeds supplied by the Surveyors' Department of Gloucestershire County Council. The time saved on each trip was then divided by the estimated miles saved and the average speed compared with practical experience on the route concerned as verification. The prime difficulty was estimating the time needed to drive through Gloucester prior to the Bridge as this figure varied considerably according to

traffic conditions. Gloucester was a serious bottleneck in the pre-Bridge situation and the time taken varied substantially seasonally. A summer Saturday could yield trip times of an hour and more for a distance that could be covered in 15 minutes on a winter afternoon. To avoid the risk of over-estimation the figure of 20 minutes was selected.

Valuing the time saved

8.40 The most obvious approach would be to add up the number of hours saved and multiply them by a value per hour. This method, however, conceals a number of important problems. Although it is common to talk of valuing time, time itself is not for sale since we cannot have 25 hours a day where before there were 24. The advantage of a reduction in journey time is that it enables the traveller to organise his activities differently. The value being sought is the price the individual would be willing to pay to have this opportunity. This price depends on what he thinks he would do with the wider opportunities the reduced journey time would create. It will also depend on any extra costs which he might have to incur if the enlarged opportunity is to be created for him. These would include, for example, extra petrol consumption if he decided to use the time reduction to make a different and longer journey. The value of the time saved will thus vary very widely for different people in different circumstances. An hour's reduction on a two-hour journey may have a different value from that on a ten-hour journey, and an hour in the middle of the night in a cold waiting room may have a higher or lower value than an hour in the day in a comfortable car.

8.41 A clear distinction is also frequently drawn between savings of paid work time where the wage rate is seen as giving a precise market valuation of time saved and savings of leisure time where no such valuation exists. The distinction is at least not as clear as is usually assumed as the following example shows. Suppose a person takes a job at £8 per 8-hour day which consists of 6 hours spent at some specific task which the person finds very arduous and unpleasant and 2 hours spent in travelling to perform that task. A road improvement cuts this travel time to 1 hour increasing to 7 the hours spent at the specific task. Is the value of the time saved £1? The result of the saving in travel time and increasing the time spent on the specific task may be to raise the daily rate to £8. 10. 0 because the original rate of £8 reflected an average of a high rate (say 22/6 per hour) for the specific task and a lower rate (say 12/6 per hour) for travel time. In practice a correct valuation of the travel time saved (in average terms) would be possible if his rate consisted of two stated elements, one for the specific task and one for travel time — (as in some piece work situations, forced waiting time is paid at a lower rate than the piece rate that would be earned, had the worker not been held up through no fault of his own). However, at least in the road haulage industry, the time saved is used in the same sort of work as the rest of the working time, so the wage rate provides a satisfactory valuation at least for drivers, but as one moves away from drivers to mates and on to other industries the wage rate may well become a less adequate means of valuing time saved.

8.42 A further problem arises over the significance of the size distribution of the reductions in journey time per trip. There are many constraints on the use of time, particularly in transport. It has been argued that twelve savings of only five minutes each are of less value than one saving of an hour. [1] As explained above, the immediate value of any time saved, depends not only on the amount of time saved, but also on the state of the organisation to which it accrues. An hour saved on some trips may only lead to an extra hour being spent waiting around at depots and warehouses when the immediate gain would be zero. In other cases, an hour saved may enable two trips to be completed in one day, a return journey to be made the same day avoiding an overnight stop, or some similar change in organisation resulting in a time advantage much greater than the observed time reduction on the trip in question. The problem, therefore, is how far are the observed reductions in trip times an adequate measure of the actual increase in productive working time.

8.43 This problem can be looked at by means of a simple example. If we assume that drivers can only be hired by the hour, or that a driver must have at least an hour available before he can be transferred to an additional task, and a trip takes four and a half hours, the driver must be employed for five hours, half an hour remaining unused. If a road improvement saves 10 minutes on the trip, there is no immediate saving in wages but the driver's unused time increases to 40 minutes. A saving of 30 minutes, cutting the journey time from four and a half to four hours would have cut the driver's unused time to zero and saved one hour's wages or twice the observed reductions in journey time. From this it can be seen that the immediate economic value of reductions in journey time depend on three factors; the saving on the trip, the amount of existing unused time to which that saving is added and the minimum unit of usable time. The second of these elements — existing unused time — does not depend of course, only on road improvements; a vast variety of technical and organisational changes can result, partially at least, in increasing the existing unused time.

8.44 In this study the time saving on trips is known but not the existing pool of unused time or the minimum usable time, both of which will no doubt vary between different firms or people. Since the concern is not with any particular trip or firm, it will in fact be sufficient to know, or make reasonable assumptions about, the distribution of these latter two factors as they are affected by all journeys across the Severn Bridge. Where the minimum usable time is one hour, as in the above example, and the saving is 10 minutes, then if the existing pools of unusable time were equally distributed between zero and 59 minutes, then the saving of 10 minutes would be usable in whole or in part in one-sixth of all cases. Given the vast variety of technical and organisational changes which can contribute to the existing pools of unused time, it may well be a reasonable assumption that they are equally distributed between zero and whatever is the minimum unit of usable time. It may be argued that as the unused time rises towards the minimum usable time the "waste" becomes more obvious and the organisation paying for this "waste" will vigorously search for other changes that will bring the total saving up to the minimum. Such a consideration would imply that the extent of time savings used is under-estimated in the argument that follows; It would in practice probably be offset by organisations with pools of usable time at zero or low values being less vigorous in their search for small improvements in the organisation that would, if achieved, have no immediate benefit.

8.45 Given the assumption that the existing pools of unused time are equally distributed from zero to the minimum unit of usable time, if this is an hour and the saving on each trip is 10 minutes and the total number of trips is, for example, 6000, then on 1000 of such trips the unused driver's time would be equal to or greater than 50 minutes. If a road improvement saved 1000 hours made up of 10 minutes saving per trip, the immediate realised saving would also be 1000 hours but it would be realised by only one-sixth of the vehicles who could add the 10 minutes to their existing 50 minutes or more of unused time. The remaining 5000 vehicles would add the 10 minutes to their existing unused time. In the diagram below (Table 8.2), the whole distribution would shift one class interval to the right, members of the last class interval becoming new members of the first. It is easy to see that if the 1000 hours saved was made up of 1000 vehicles saving an hour each and 5000 vehicles saving nothing, or in the case illustrated, half the vehicles saving 20 minutes and half the vehicles saving nothing, the result would be the same.

TABLE 8.2   1000 Hours of Drivers' Time Saved on 6000 Trips: An Example of Two Cases

Saving per Trip	Unused Drivers Time	minutes 0-10	11-20	21-30	31-40	41-50	51-60	Total Trips	Total Observed Saving	Total Realised Saving
10 minutes		1000	1000	1000	1000	1000	1000	6000	1000 HRS	1000 HRS
										1000 HRS
20 minutes		500	500	500	500	500	500	3000	1000 HRS	1000 HRS
0 minutes		500	500	500	500	500	500	3000	0 HRS	0 HRS
										1000 HRS

From this we could conclude that with sets of distributions similar to the above we are justified in taking the straight sum of the observed time savings, disregarding their size distribution. We are thus left with the problem of how valid this assumption is. As already argued, it could be that a more likely distribution is one where the distribution of unused time is skewed towards the lower values as hauliers adjust their operations to minimise costs. But is they are able to do this before the improvement, they can also do it afterwards and some of the initial argument on indivisibilities begins to lose weight. In the case of the Bridge, accepting a straight sum of the observed time savings would seem the best choice and, in any event, the argument over the value of very small time savings does not often arise as the bulk of the time saved is made up of trip reductions of 30 minutes or more.

8.46 For travellers in light vehicles making journeys in non-working time, the most satisfactory method of placing a value on their time saved would be to observe the choices they make when faced with trips at different speeds at different prices.

8.47 The ideal would be to observe drivers' reactions to variations in the toll. Unfortunately, the initial toll of 2/6d. is not large enough relative to the total cost of most trips to be an influencing factor.

8.48 If there is no opportunity of observing choices between time and money, we might look at choices between time and distance. The shortest route is not always the quickest. The opening of the Bridge reduced both time and miles but not in the same proportion. If we regressed the increase in trips on minutes and miles saved, the ratio of the coefficients should give us a value of time in terms of miles. Given the motorists' perceived cost per mile — if he has such a value in his head, which seems doubtful — this could be converted to money. Apart from the objections that the method is based on a whole set of assumptions about the way motorists perceive their running costs there are considerable statistical difficulties. Time and distance saved are highly correlated; (in the case of Bridge trips R = .89) and thus a straightforward regression does not yield significant coefficients due to multicollinearity. There are methods of trying to get round this using residuals but they cannot avoid the more serious former objection.

8.49 A further method, less ambitious, would be to interview drivers and ask them to give their own estimate of the value of the time saved. On two weekends in August 1967 this approach was adopted, although motorists were asked to give a total value for all savings, not just time. By adding to this figure the toll and subtracting motorists' perceived running costs, the residual could be regarded as a value of the time saved. The result of doing this produced a value of around 2/- per hour. This figure, of course, based on a whole set of assumptions, and other information from the survey showed that motorists did not give consistent replies, but it does confirm what has been found in many other studies, that the value motorists place on non-working time saved is well under half of the wage rate.

8.50 Most other studies designed specifically to find a value of non-working travel time has been route or modal choice studies of journeys to work and may not therefore be appropriate to apply to most Bridge users. They have produced values from 15% to over 80% of the wage rate. The most reliable appear to cluster around values in the 20%—30% range, or around 3/- per hour. Study of traffic generation models also suggests that the value declines with trip length so that there are good arguments for concluding that this rate, currently recommended by the Ministry of Transport, ought to be taken as the upper limit. Due to the many uncertainties discussed, an alternative set of calculations were made using values for time saved of two-thirds of those already discussed. These are included in Table 8.4 ahead.

8.51 The value of working time used was 8/9d per hour for commercial drivers and 13/- per hour for other travellers, these being based on the estimates produced by the Road Research Laboratory which in turn are based on current earnings.

8.52 The figure of 13/- is clearly below the hourly earnings of many businessmen, but no direct information was available. However, referring to the conceptual problem mentioned earlier, if commercial travellers for example are attracted to their job because they find travelling relatively attractive, even a wage rate determined in a perfect market could overvalue the time saved.

Vehicle Running Costs

8.53 Running costs per mile for light vehicles were taken as 5d per mile based on Road Research Laboratory estimates. These are based on the assumption that 40% of depreciation is due to use. There are a number of conceptual problems which arise when one tries to find the true incidence of depreciation costs and there are other arguments for thinking that this figure may be on the high side. Travellers deciding to make new journeys as a result of the Bridge will also make their decision in the light of what they perceive to be the cost which may be different from the actual cost. If asked, they would probably quote the petrol cost at a price inclusive of tax and little else.

8.54 For these reasons two additional sets of calculations have been made. The first in which only miles saved by diverted vehicles were valued at 5d per mile, the remainder being valued at 3d. The second where all estimated miles saved by light vehicles were valued at 3d per mile.

8.55 Costs per mile for heavy vehicles were estimated from the work of Edwards and Bayliss.[2] These averaged just over 16d per mile which is slightly higher than that for a representative vehicle, due to the above-average size of heavy vehicles using the Bridge.

Accident Costs

8.56 By cutting distances the Bridge reduces road accidents, but at the same time it has generated new trips during which extra accidents take place.

8.57 The cost of road accidents has been studied by R. F. F. Dawson[3] The difficulty, of course, arises over putting a value on death, pain and suffering, but accepting Dawson's subjective values of £5000 per fatality and £200 per serious injury it is possible to work out an accident cost per vehicle mile by combining his accident cost figures with those of accident rates per mile calculated by H. D. Johnson.[4] For rural roads in 1966 this gives a cost of £2.400 per million vehicle miles although this figure is not consistent over time. Two years later, in 1968, the accident rate per mile for rural roads had declined by over 20%.

8.58 For every mile saved by vehicles thought to be on trips which they would have made had the Bridge not been built, 1.15 miles were covered by vehicles not so identified. Applying the 1966 estimate of accident cost per mile, at a 10% discount factor to the year 2050, this would give an increase in accident costs resulting from the Bridge of £720,000.

8.59 This figure, however, assumes that those travellers on journeys not identified as being diverted would have incurred no accident costs at all. Apart from the general difficulty of deciding what people would have been doing had they not been doing what they were doing, an inability to isolate net generation with any great precision suggests that the above figure ought to be taken only as an upper limit.

8.60 Although valuable as an indication of the general magnitude of the figures involved, in addition to the subjective element of part of the cost, the amount of uncertainty is considerable. It is probably wisest to conclude that not enough information is available to put a meaningful monetary value on net accident costs, although what evidence is available suggests that it is small relative to the other figures involved.

Results

8.61 Before any figures can be produced it is necessary to make an estimate of the life of the Bridge. The following calculations have been produced for the period 1966 to 2050. Eighty four years is quite a short life by most standards but benefits accuring in the second half of the next century have such little value given most peoples scale of time preference, thus assuming it will last longer would make little difference to the results.

8.62 It is also necessary to estimate the maximum capacity of the Bridge. This will clearly depend on the response of both motorists themselves and the Bridge management to congestion at peak periods, and the possible development of alternative methods of crossing

— e.g. another Bridge or Barrage. In the sums that follow it has been assumed that traffic will expand to a maximum of around 17 million vehicles in the year 2000 and then remain constant. Our ability to forecast traffic in the next century with any accuracy in any event is open to question. The proportion of traffic taken as generated was as follows:—

TABLE 8.3 Generated Proportion of Traffic

Type	Percentage
Light vehicles by Purpose:	
Firm's Business	25
Goods Collection and Delivery	69
Service and Maintenance	69
Work	82
Shopping	86
Holidays	34
Visiting	49
Sightseeing	89
Paid Entertainment	86
Other and Multiple	53
Total	47
Heavy Vehicles	30

8.63 The estimated costs and benefits in 1966 at three different discount factors are shown in Tables 8.4, 8.5 and 8.6. The benefits to travellers in light vehicles are according to the purpose structure estimated in 1968. The figures for heavy vehicles are shown for the two alternative forecasts. The figures for net benefits are also shown using the alternative values for time and running costs saved. The results must be interpreted with considerable care. Tables 8.4, 8.5 and 8.6 are attempts to estimate the benefit attributed to the Bridge itself and only that portion of the motorway necessary to link it with the existing road system. There are hazards in trying to do this since some of the generated traffic will be the result of savings in journey time on other parts of the motorway network. Nevertheless, the savings on trips of this type will be small compared with the benefits attributed to the Bridge alone.

REFERENCES

1. e.g. D. G. Tipping — "Time Savings in Transport" **Economic Journal** Vol. 78 (1968)

2. S. L. Edwards & B. T. Bayliss, **Road Freight Operators' Costs.** Department of Environment (1971)

3. R. F. F. Dawson, **Cost of Road Accidents in Great Britain.** Department of Environment LR79 (1967)

4. H. D. Johnson, **Road Accident and Casualty Rates in 1968.** Road Research Laboratory LR 348 (1970)

TABLE 8.4

Estimated Costs and Benefits, discounted to 1966 values

£ million

| | 5% Discount Factor | | |
	Miles	Time	Total
Estimated Gross Benefits			
Light Vehicles			
Firm's Business	39.7	30.8	70.6
Goods Collection and			
Delivery	1.5	1.1	2.6
Service and Maintenance	0.6	0.5	1.1
Work	5.3	4.2	9.5
Shopping	1.9	1.5	3.4
Holidays	11.0	8.5	19.5
Visiting	20.4	15.8	36.2
Sightseeing	6.0	4.7	10.6
Paid Entertainment	2.4	1.9	4.3
Other & Multiple	3.2	2.5	5.7
Total	92.1	71.5	163.6
Heavy Vehicles			
Upper Traffic forecast	105.3	23.8	129.1
Lower Traffic forecast	95.8	21.6	117.4
Totals			
Upper Heavy Traffic			
forecast	197.4	95.2	292.7
Lower Heavy Traffic			
forecast	187.9	93.1	281.0
Estimated Costs			
Capital Costs			18.5
Maintenance			1.2
Total			19.7
Estimated Net Benefit			
Upper Traffic forecast			273.0
Lower Traffic forecast			261.3
Upper Traffic forecast			241.2
Lower Traffic forecast			230.3
Upper Traffic forecast			255.7
Lower Traffic forecast			244.0
Upper Traffic forecast			236.2
Lower Traffic forecast			224.5

Lower time value

Upper light vehicles running costs value for diverting trips only

Lower light vehicle running cost value for all light vehicle trips

G

TABLE 8.5

Estimated Costs and Benefits, discounted to 1966 values

£ million

8% Discount Factor

	Miles	Time	Total	
Estimated Gross Benefits				
Light Vehicles				
Firm's Business	24.9	19.3	44.2	
Goods Collection and				
Delivery	0.9	0.7	1.6	
Service and Maintenance	0.4	0.3	0.7	
Work	3.3	2.6	5.9	
Shopping	1.2	0.9	2.2	
Holidays	6.9	5.3	12.2	
Visiting	12.8	9.9	22.7	
Sightseeing	3.8	2.9	6.7	
Paid Entertainment	1.5	1.2	2.7	
Other & Multiple	2.0	1.6	3.6	
Total	57.7	44.8	102.4	
Heavy Vehicles				
Upper Traffic forecast	65.9	14.9	80.8	
Lower Traffic forecast	60.0	13.5	73.5	
Totals				
Upper Heavy Traffic				
forecast	123.6	59.6	183.2	
Lower Heavy Traffic				
forecast	117.6	58.3	175.9	
Estimated Costs				
Capital costs			19.9	
Maintenance			0.7	
Total			20.6	
Estimated Net Benefit				
Upper Traffic forecast			162.6	
Lower Traffic forecast			155.3	
Upper Traffic forecast			142.7	Lower time value
Lower Traffic forecast			135.9	
Upper Traffic forecast			151.8	Upper light vehicles running
Lower Traffic forecast			144.5	costs value for diverted
				trips only
Upper Traffic forecast			139.5	Lower light vehicle running
Lower Traffic Forecast			132.2	cost value for all light
				vehicle trips

TABLE 8.6

Estimated Costs and Benefits, discounted to 1966 values

£ million

10% Discount Factor

	Miles	Time	Total	
Estimated Gross Benefits				
Light Vehicles				
Firm's Business	19.7	15.3	35.1	
Goods Collection and Delivery	0.7	0.6	1.3	
Service and Maintenance	0.3	0.2	0.6	
Work	2.7	2.1	4.7	
Shopping	1.0	0.7	1.7	
Holidays	5.5	4.2	9.7	
Visiting	10.1	7.9	18.0	
Sightseeing	3.0	2.3	5.3	
Paid Entertainment	1.2	0.9	2.1	
Other & Multiple	1.6	1.2	2.8	
Total	45.8	35.5	81.3	
Heavy Vehicles				
Upper Traffic forecast	52.3	11.8	64.1	
Lower Traffic forecast	47.6	10.7	58.3	
Totals				
Upper Heavy Traffic forecast	98.1	47.3	145.4	
Lower Heavy Traffic forecast	93.4	46.3	139.6	
Estimated Costs				
Capital Costs			20.9	
Maintenance			0.6	
Total			21.5	
Estimated Net Benefit				
Upper Traffic forecast			123.9	
Lower Traffic forecast			118.1	
Upper Traffic forecast			108.1	
Lower Traffic forecast			102.7	Lower time value
Upper Traffic forecast			115.3	Upper light vehicles running costs value for diverted trips only
Lower Traffic forecast			109.5	
Upper Traffic forecast			105.6	Lower light vehicles running cost value for all light vehicle trips
Lower Traffic forecast			99.8	

Fig. 8(i)   The Demand Curve for Trips

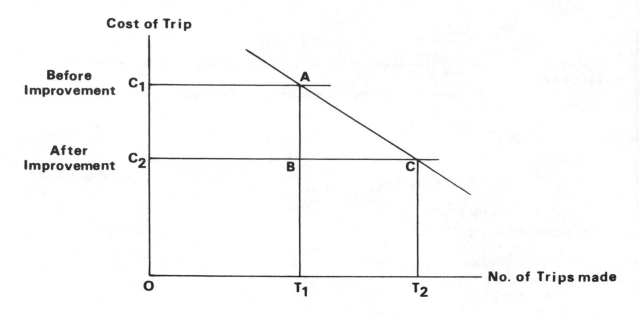

Fig. 8(ii)   Distance Saved and Number of Trips

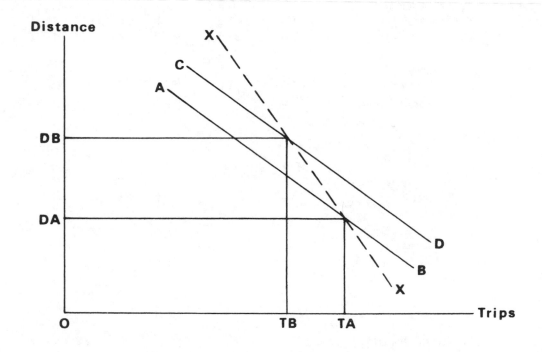

Fig. 8(iii) Alternative Trips

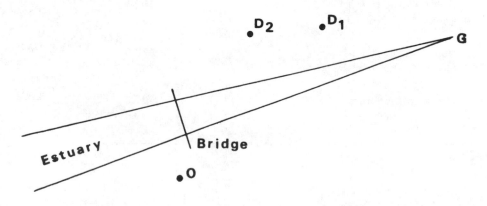

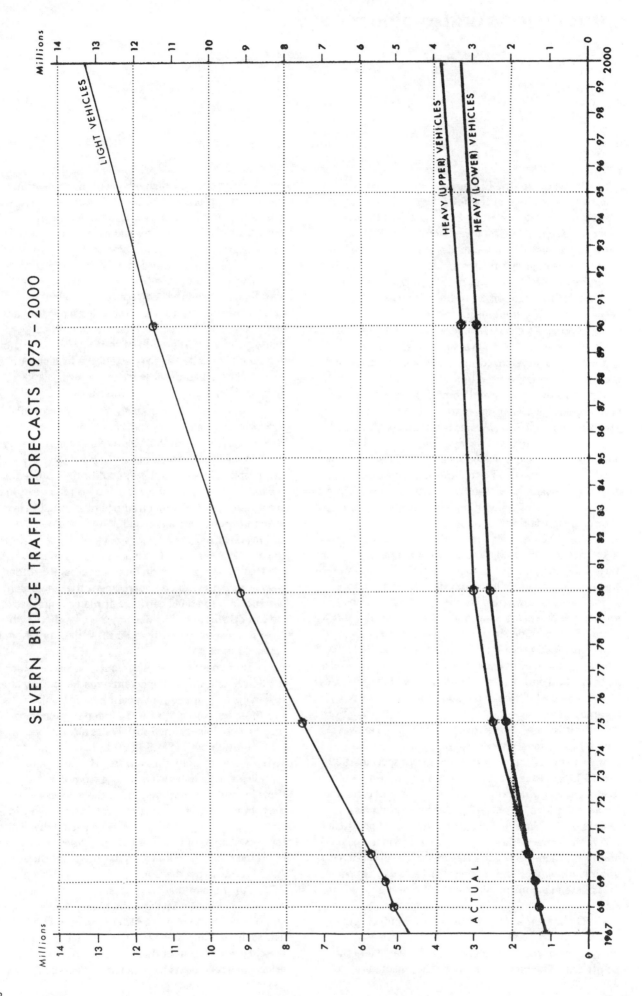

Fig. 8(iv)

SEVERN BRIDGE TRAFFIC FORECASTS 1975 – 2000

G2

CHAPTER NINE

Conclusions and Projections

9.1 At the outset the Bridge has to be viewed in an historical perspective of the fortunes of not only South Wales and the South West of England but of the national economy as a whole. The investment in the Bridge is a national one and its consequences are, therefore, of interest in evaluating other comparable investments by government. Similarly those consequences have to be seen against the state of the national economy in the period covered by this study.

9.2 Chapter 1 set out the history of the Bridge, the earlier projects for a road crossing and the relationship of the transport system to the economic structures of the two regions connected by it. Up to 1914 the foundations of industry and commerce were such that both regions were well served as to power and transport. The prosperity of South Wales based on coal, iron and steel and related industries was exemplified by such bold initiatives as the Barry Dock and the Severn Tunnel itself. Bristol's traditional role as a port and a centre of distribution was well served by coastal shipping and railways while local mining provided power for manufacturing in the Bristol region.

9.3 The dramatic new mobility given to industry by electricity which could be generated increasingly further away from the point of consumption coupled to the challenge to the established discriminating monopoly of the railways, presented by the road haulier, transformed the prospects of whole regions. Added to this there was a coincidence of structural decline of the traditional industries of regions such as South Wales with an upsurge of new manufacturing industries primarily in the Midlands and the South East and the adequacy of the transport system, especially for South Wales, became questionable.

9.4 Neither the competitive reaction of the railways, notably in passenger services, nor the attempts to protect them by restrictions on road transport in 1930 and 1933, could prevent a large upsurge of demand for road transport of all kinds leading to renewed pressure for a road bridge in 1934—36. Yet looking at press reports of the plans in 1935, the estimates of peak daily traffic then regarded as so large are less than the peak hourly rate achieved soon after the Bridge opened! That upsurge of demand in the inter-war years was but the first phase in a continuing growth of road traffic of all kinds.

9.5 The industrial reconstruction of South Wales which began in 1934—35 was to demonstrate the importance of road transport to the Midlands and the South East. The new industrial development in Bristol and Gloucestershire which increased in momentum as the nation approached the Second World War created similar pressures on the road system. Although the railways reacted with new rates and bases of charging[1], the pressure on the A.38 was already leading to its adaptation to the then new idea of a 3-lane single carriageway. The growth of road transport with heavy traffic via Gloucester and the A.40 route to London had diverted much long-distance traffic from rail to road years before the Bridge again became a political possibility. Similarly the growth of traffic between Bristol and South Wales had already established a distributive pattern that defied the absence of the Bridge and ignored the presence of the railway tunnel.

9.6 Yet the very success of the re-distribution of industry, especially from 1943 onwards, by bringing new prosperity to South Wales as well as that already developing on Severnside made the need for a Bridge all the greater. The savings that it could offer coupled to the enhanced opportunities that would follow became even more apparent when trading links of industries in both regions were examined. While the South East and regions from the Midlands northwards constituted the main markets for most manufacturers in both regions, the trading and production linkages across the estuary were such as to weaken the argument that the Severn was such a formidable barrier. For many firms, particularly in distribution, this was not the case though there were still many, especially in South Wales, for whom it appeared to be so.

9.7 Those new industries of South Wales for which the South East was so important a market clearly stood to benefit from the improvement in communications. For those for whom the Midlands and more northerly regions were important, South Wales already had improved access, notably the M.5/M.50 Ross Spur, and the A.465 Heads of the Valleys route. The latter appeared to indicate little mileage advantage from the Bridge to firms in the uppermost section of the valleys and further west. In fact the switch of their traffic from the Gloucester route to the M.4/A.4 has been substantial while for coastal areas of South Wales the Bridge is used to reach the Midlands both along the A.38 and the A.46/A.433 route across the Cotswolds.

9.8 For those in the South West, the main improvements to the South East and the Midlands await the completion of the M.4 and M.5 motorways in 1972. The sections completed by 1970 were close to the river crossing; completion of the M.4 could have striking effects on movements from north and east of Bristol while the M.5 is the spine road so central to the transport strategy proposed for the region. In the short-run the motorways so far opened have given some relief around Bristol but have generated much new traffic while diverting South Wales traffic on to the A.4, thereby leading to serious congestion in North Wiltshire, one of the few disadvantages cited by respondents to our questions.

9.9 Inevitably, therefore, what follows is an interim assessment for several reasons. The first is the state of the motorway network of which the Bridge is a part. The critical adjacent gaps are now being closed and the original 1,000 miles target network is approaching completion. Already this is being superseded by the extensions such as the M.5 to Exeter by 1975 and the M.4/A.48(M) through South Wales. The second is that the rationalisation of the railway network is largely complete. The capacity of that network, especially in the study area, is being enhanced by important signalling and track improvement schemes affecting both the routes to London and the North East/South West spine route from York to Bristol and Cardiff. It is, therefore, a good moment at which to take the principal findings of this study, to set them against the hypotheses developed in Chapter 2 and then to speculate as to future outcomes.

9.10 Such speculation has, however, to be approached with caution for two important reasons. The first relates to the state of the economy in the period of study. The second concerns the assumptions that should be made as to future government policy on regional development and physical planning. Taking the state of the economy, the Bridge was opened within two months of the package of emergency measures of July 1966 and throughout the life of the facility to date national economic growth has been at a slower rate than previously. If a higher rate of growth in national income and output is resumed in the future, then the two regions are likely to share in this and the rate of growth of traffic, for example, might be higher. Certainly the benefits to be derived from the Bridge are underestimated for the period involved unless one assume that this country cannot do better before 2050. As for government policy on regional planning two assumptions can be made. One is that all government controls and inducements are removed and the second is what may follow if present policies remain unchanged.

9.11 The sequence followed is that of the chapters in which detailed findings have been set out, starting with traffic data, moving on to changes in industry and distribution and concluding with the wider effects on the two regions and the implications for the nation as a whole.

Traffic Changes

9.12 The speed, scale and nature of the traffic growth, when Bridge traffic is compared to that between the South Wales and the Bristol area before its opening, is very striking. It shows a massive movement with a fourfold increase in the first year alone. When allowance has been made for the novelty of the Bridge, as evidenced by facility created traffic, the really significant feature is the continual rate of growth in traffic and its relation-ship to that of other motorways and that of rural trunk roads. The slower adaptation of business to the new situation is evident from the later timing of the increase in heavy lorry traffic compared to private cars and light commercial vehicles. Compared to the motorways system, and subject to the limitations of the data on the latter, it appears that the full adjustment of traffic to and from South Wales may still be some way off. If the M.4 is comparable to the M.1 and M.6 then there is still some leeway to make up. Compared to rural trunk roads on the other hand, the growth especially of heavy vehicles is still sharply above the national average, though less so than in earlier years. The full adjustment may therefore follow only with the completion of the M.4 and allowing for "learning time" this could continue until 1974. However, the "learning time" is likely to be less in future now that firms have had their first real experience of what motorways can offer.

9.13 The sharp change in the first year included a substantial proportion of "facility created" traffic, mainly private cars but also coaches and motor cycles. The main element appears to have been "diverted" traffic. Now this can take several forms. One is traffic diverted from an alternative route of the same mode, in this case from the Gloucester route, the Beachley-Aust ferry and the Severn tunnel car train. If anything, this diversion has been even more pervasive than might have been expected as it extends to regions and destinations where there is no mileage saving though there may be some time and driving advantages. Diversions have meant sharply reduced traffic along the A.48 Chepstow-Gloucester route and increases along the A.4 through Wiltshire. As drivers have explored new opportunities the number of routes affected has increased. Welsh drivers have explored Cotswold roads to avoid congestion on the A.4 while Bristol drivers have used the Wye Valley route to Monmouth (A.466) as a speedier weekday route to the M.5 north of Tewkesbury. Some of these are temporary features pending motorway completions.

9.14 The second diversion is that between transport modes. At this stage one is only concerned with transfers to road transport and not within categories of road user. There has already been a diversion of goods traffic from rail to road which has ended an anomalous short-distance communication pattern by bringing cross-estuary traffic more in line with that over similar distances where no barrier exists. This switch is, however, in those freight traffics which the railways are not anxious to retain. Comparison of freight traffic changes shows that these are virtually as frequent on routes not affected by these motorway changes e.g. South West to South East as over the estuary. However, the railways retain a substantial volume of freight traffic both within and from South Wales, e.g. steel products.

9.15 The change in passenger traffic is even more striking. The loss of short-distance inter-city travel, particularly from North Bristol to South Wales stations, has been so severe as to be followed by the virtual elimination of local stopping services. An improved fast service inaugurated in May 1967, some six months after the opening of the Bridge, endured for three years before being cut back by almost 50% in May 1970. While the projected Stoke Gifford motorist station will permit some renewed rail travel to South Wales, the potential must be limited to city or town centre destinations in South Wales. The industrial surveys showed a marked switch and increase in business travel across the Severn. This was most marked over shorter distances. Traffic to and from London by fast inter-city services on standard schedules clearly gives a strong competitive advantage to the railways. Their future is to be judged by the experience of the London-Manchester-Liverpool electrification against the M.1/M.6 motorways.

9.16 As far as other media are concerned the diversions were of much smaller scale but were nevertheless important to those affected. The opportunity for pleasure travel by private car and coach, which was strongly in evidence as soon as the Bridge opened, dealt sharp blows to the seasonal pleasure steamer service. This was accentuated by the with-drawal of the traditional paddle steamers and led to the contraction of the tidal ferry services, the smaller fleet being used more further down the Channel. Subsequently there has been a feasibility study for a car ferry from Swansea to Ilfracombe. Coaster and barge traffic may have been affected.

9.17 The new traffic generated, apart from that which is facility created, can be reviewed in two stages. Private car traffic on Monday to Fridays shows a continued growth of business travel and the industry surveys revealed several sharp increases in the number of journeys made by staff. While private motoring is important at all times, its peak is at weekends and this offsets the weekday peak for commercial vehicles, especially heavy vehicles. The traffic generated includes some that results from diversions of yet another kind, switches in sources of products and services from other areas previously used to those involving a Bridge crossing. This applies to both private motorists who explore new excursions destinations and business firms that now draw more supplies from across the estuary at the expense of other sources.

9.18 The present Bridge was intended to be adequate for traffic growth to at least 1990. This will clearly depend on the response of both motorists and the Bridge management to such factors as peak period congestion, toll charges and traffic management. In Chapter 8 traffic has been assumed to grow to 17 million vahicles in the year 2000 and then to remain constant. Earlier estimates have put the capacity at 15 million but the critical factor is the nature of the peak demand. At present the traffic shows two distinct elements, the heavy commercial traffic having a weekday demand and the private motorist a weekend demand with the latter creating the greater peaks. For three reasons, assuming no changes in other factors, the pressure on the capacity of the Bridge may come earlier than 1990. The first is the low level of economic expansion that has been evident during most of the life of the Bridge so far. Any acceleration would lead to new pressures both from commercial users and from private motorists whose incomes have risen. The second is the likelihood of further spread of car ownership and greater use of cars by existing owners for leisure purposes.

The third is the possible development of the estuary to house part of the expected increase in the nation's population. This has led to the concurrent Severnside feasibility study with its task of establishing whether and how up to one million additional people could be accommodated in the study area after 1980. Depending on the siting of new development, the need for a second Bridge would be created independently of all other factors.

9.19 The sequence observed with the Severn Bridge — initial diversion and generation with a quick change by private motorists followed by a build up of heavier commercial traffic as the benefits are appreciated — can be expected to recur with each subsequent extension of the motorway network in the two regions. In particular the closing of the gaps in both M.4 and M.5 can be expected to trigger off new increases followed by those stimulated by the extension of the M.5 south-westwards. These are further explored in paragraphs 9.39–9.42 below. The latter will be more analogous to the effect of the north-west extensions of M.6 in so far as private motoring and tourist trade are concerned.

Manufacturing Industry

9.20 As expected there has been no significant relocation of manufacturing establishments in this period as a consequence of the Bridge. Capital investment committed to existing sites, problems of management and training and the prospects for expansion in the economy as a whole have combined to produce this result. This is not, however, to assert that there has been no change. On the contrary there have been at least five developments of interest.

9.21 The first is that both regions have become more attractive as sites for new development. In so far as labour supply is a critical factor, and taking governmental policies on the distribution of new industry into account, the gain in manufacturing is potentially greatest in South Wales for two reasons. One is the extent to which factories can now act as distribution points given access to the motorway system thereby obviating the establishment of separate depots across the estuary. The other is that managerial movement being greatly eased it becomes possible for firms in Bristol, North Wiltshire, etc., to consider establishments in South Wales as more easily integrated in their expansion plans. Given existing policies on industrial location, South Wales should now enjoy an even more attractive position as the development area closest to areas of new industrial overspill from the Midlands, London and the South of England. Even if these policies were to be relaxed then the presence of the Bridge would minimise any adverse consequences.

9.22 The second change has been one of production and of sources of new materials and components. While few firms have found entirely new sources, those firms that already drew some supplies from suppliers across the estuary have often increased their intakes from such sources at the expense of suppliers elsewhere. These intakes have been linked to better service and more competition leading in some cases to lower prices. Corroboration is seen in the increases in outputs to serve customers across the estuary and in the evidence offered as to services offered and obtained. Two trades where this has been particularly noticeable are food, drink and tobacco and building materials, the latter affecting the output of mining and quarrying and the trade in timber.

9.23 The element of service is not confined to deliveries. Increasing importance attaches to personal contacts of managers, sales and technical staffs of both suppliers and customers. The sharp increase in business travel is at least partly due to this element. This increased personal movement has brought about much more contact both within and between firms and has enabled more competition to emerge. The full implications of this change are difficult to assess. Firms have made comments such as "We now see trade representatives more often or even for the first time" and "We used to feel cut off; now we can shop around much more". As an important factor in business survival is learning about alternatives open to one, the importance of such a change could be considerable.

9.24 The fourth change is that of movements within companies between their establishments on both sides of the estuary. At first it was thought that the Severn had acted as a barrier so limiting the possibilities of such movements to a few firms. In fact slightly over 10% of firms responding to the first survey had establishments on both sides, Of those responding to the second survey,. 18% had establishments on both sides. The differences in the numbers surveyed and the response rates do not permit direct comparison. At the time of the first survey of such firms, 38% had movements between their establishments whereas of those in the second survey, 60% has some kind of movement between establishments. These movements were of many types ranging from components and semi-finished products to supplies originating elsewhere and managerial personnel. Where firms operated on both sides there were now many more internal linkages, partly directly connected with production, partly to do with their distributive functions, and partly arising from easier communications with a headquarters unit across the estuary. Overall, however, they represented only a slightly higher proportion of all firms in the two regions. This change has also been examined in the case of South Wales and the South East of England. Nearly half the firms in South Wales were subsidiaries of companies based in the South East. Among them there was a movement of goods to or from headquarters in less than a third of the cases, mainly for distribution to consumers from the present unit.

9.25 The fifth change has been in distribution. More manufacturing units were found to be engaged in distribution than there were firms solely concerned with it. The changes have been in areas served, in the channels and methods used and in the service offered, especially in frequency of delivery to cross-estuary customers. The result has been more competition and better services which has been generally welcomed. The precise changes are more fully discussed later.

9.26 The hypotheses set out in Chapter 2 have had some support. Thus the trades in which effects have been most noticeable are those meeting the criteria in paragraph 2.6, such as the food trades, perishable and other goods calling for speedy delivery and items where transport costs are of greater significance because of bulk and value, such as building materials. In nearly all cases the goods were already being produced for regional if not national consumption but the two markets are now treated as one. Consumers have more choice of alternative brands and so far there has been little evidence of take-overs to concentrate supply. The scale of takeovers has been almost exclusively at national level. Yet precisely because of this scale of reorganisation it is often difficult to ascribe specific changes in the areas studied to the Bridge as against any other factor.

9.27 The extent to which a single market now exists over a much wider area is linked to penetration by suppliers and this is still limited by local transport obstacles. The state of the internal road system in South Wales, especially west of Cardiff, does limit penetration from east of the Severn and thereby protects the position of firms located in the vicinity e.g. Cardiff. No data has been obtained from personal consumers but the evidence of business firms is clear. On both sides of the estuary there is evidence of better service, with in some cases lower prices and in others greater competition. The further hypotheses set out in paragraph 2.8 have been substantiated. Firms already trading across the estuary were able to use their knowledge to improve their penetration. The effect on other regions has been both a loss of supplies as firms switched to cross-estuary sources and new competition where areas could now be supplied from South Wales for the first time. The reorganisation of sales areas has been twofold, a grouping of the two regions in one for some purposes in some firms, and a redrawing of regional boundaries for further distribution in others.

9.28 As regards the location of industry, the hypotheses set out in paragraph 2.19 have been supported by the data obtained. There has been almost no relocation as such although there have been changes in production within establishments leading to a higher proportion of output being despatched to cross-estuary destinations. The attractiveness of South East Wales has been enhanced as factories can now act as distribution points avoiding the need for a depot east of the Severn. But the local road situation in South Wales is still cited as a difficulty by firms in central and western parts of the coalfield[2]. There is now some evidence that firms in the South West to whom closeness of managerial control over plants is important may now find South Wales a more acceptable area for expansion. Linkages both within and between firms have been strengthened as paragraph 9.24 above has shown but the overall position of the two regions relative to each other has not changed dramatically.

9.29 Without the industrial reconstruction of South Wales before 1966 much of what has occurred since then would have been impossible. But the reconstruction of South Wales is far from complete and for manufacturing industry, with or without present regional policies, South Wales now stands in a favourable position. For the South West its position is in no way weakened. On the contrary it is also enhanced as the distribution survey clearly indicates.

Distribution

9.30 Here a more rapid adjustment was anticipated and this has in fact occurred. The influence of the hierarchy of functions discussed in Chapter 2 emerges in Chapter 7 with the even stronger position of Bristol-South Gloucestershire as a centre for national and super-regional distribution. There has been widespread penetration of South Wales by firms from Bristol-Severnside and a more modest assault on the Bristol area by firms from Cardiff. Both sides consequently report increased competition and improved service both offered and received in particular trades. The main changes which are shown by distributors as such, and by manufacturers who distributed through their factories in the regions, are four in number.

9.31 The first has been a significant change in areas served as more firms now started trading across the Bridge. Among distributors trading across the Severn before the Bridge the most frequent change occurred in areas served and then in methods of distribution, notably frequency of delivery and of service offered. While these have been frequent among firms in both regions, the far larger number based in Bristol has meant that its influence has appeared to gain substantially. In this it has been assisted by three factors. To a considerable extent national distributors had already rationalised operations before the Bridge with the result that the only effects it could have would be improved delivery times at reduced cost where they supplied South Wales from the east bank or first entry into South Wales if they had hitherto left it out of their schemes. The fact that Bristol lay within that central zone of England bounded by London, Leeds, Liverpool and Bristol from which it was most economical to supply the bulk of consumers through a national network had led some firms to anticipate the Bridge in their planning. Lastly, there are few financial inducements or controls — other than local physical planning — to influence the choice of sites for depots.

9.32 These arguments are well illustrated by an analysis that has been made of 13 new firms that appeared after the opening of the Birdge. Altogether 13 firms were included in the second survey of distribution that were new to the survey area. There were more firms that had opened up for which data was not obtainable either because they were so new as not to be recorded or because they employed under 20 persons. Only one firm had located its depot in South Wales and this was intended to have a manufacturing operation later so that the special grants were an attraction. The other 12 were in the Bristol area. Questioned as to the importance of the Bridge to their decisions all but two served both sides of the Severn. Four would have opened a second depot in South Wales but for the Bridge, but three would not have considered the market there justified such a step. The Bridge was a significant but not the sole factor in their decisions. Access to a centre of business and to both M.4 and M.5 were among the reasons given.

9.33 The second change, as with manufacturers, was in sources of supplies. These were switched not only between suppliers in the two regions but also at the expense of other regions. The majority of the instances were in South Wales and given the greater emphasis on consumer industries in the South West this was to be expected. The improvement in service, notably through quicker and more frequent deliveries, but also with more frequent personnel contacts is reported from both regions. There have also been some clear indications that this new competition was viewed as a disadvantage by some firms in Cardiff. The only consumers whose views are known are manufacturers and other distributors but both communities have gained to some extent. The arguments already set out in respect of manufacturers apply here equally.

9.34 The volume of pre-Bridge movement by distributors belied the role of the Severn as a barrier and for them the benefit of the Bridge has come in reduced transport costs and ability to offer a better service and/or penetration even more deeply into the cross-estuary region. Yet the speed and scale of the increase in short-distance commercial traffic, particularly in light vans as well as heavier vehicles, is evidence of what a barrier the Severn remained for many firms and of the opportunities that were grasped from the first year of the Bridge onwards.

9.35 In terms of centres, Bristol and Cardiff dominate the scene with Gloucester, the former lowest crossing point, adversely affected by other factors such as oil pipelines as well as by the southerly migration of the ideal centre for super-regional distribution to the Yate-Patchway area.

9.36 The effect of these changes on employment has been studied within the limitations of the data available[3] Depot closures and associated changes have produced 206 redundancies, 40 in the South West and 166 in South Wales. These were confined to Bristol, Bath, Cardiff, Newport and Cwmbran. This is equivalent to 2% of those employed in the distributive trades in these areas. The main concentration has been in Cardiff. To these might be added a smaller change in establishments not surveyed or which are primarily manufacturing. At the same time, however, employment has increased in three localities, Avonmouth, Yate and Chepstow-Caldicot as follows:—

Avonmouth	1966—69	+	84 (12%)
Yate	1966—68	+	350 (432%)
Chepstow- Caldicot			
	1965—68	+	22 (28%)

9.37 These appear to confirm earlier conclusions as to the concentration of changes. However, in the case of Avonmouth and also to some extent of Yate, some of this is overspill from Central Bristol. The pressure to move from city centre sites partly with redevelopment has led to a number of movements to Avonmouth which remains within Bristol's city limits. From a planning standpoint, additional employment in distribution presents problems of land use. From data obtained in the distribution survey it is estimated that employment in a non-manufacturing activity on a trading estate requires 2,000 sq. ft. per person or 22 people per acre compared to 31 per acre in manufacturing as cited in the Severnside Study and 63 per acre on a Bristol trading estate as reported in a Bristol planning survey in 1962. Only highly capital intensive industries such as chemicals appear to offer a lower employment per acre than distribution. Building grants are only available in practice where employment in a warehouse or similar unit is to be offered to 50 or more persons. Given that the average size of such units is well below this figure little extra inducement can be given on the Welsh side even with the redefinition of the Development Area. Lastly the availability of suitable sites tends to favour new development close to the Bridge being to the east, notably at Avonmouth and Yate where the great majority of recent developments have been linked to warehousing.

9.38 The hypotheses as to areas which might benefit most in the short-run (paragraph 2.19(v) and (vi)), implying greater development east of the Bridge have been borne out and there has been clear evidence of new units being opened there. The further localised effects of highway improvements on precise local sites is supported by developments in the Bristol area and in South Gloucestershire. The fate of Gloucester is more complex as other factors such as oil pipelines have affected its role and that of its port.The question remains as to how far these changes can be projected forwards to take account of the completion of the

motorways that are so central to this study. Both surveys of industry and distribution attempted to get some indications of how firms expected the motorways to affect them. This data, not previously reported in this report, is set out in Tables 9.1 and 9.2 with further data in Appendices 49-52.

9.39 Any attempt to project these trends raises the question of expectations of motorway use. These were explored in both stages of the industry/distribution surveys. Table 9.1 shows the percentages of manufacturing firms expecting to use the four, as yet uncompleted, sections of motorways in 1966 and 1968. Table 9.2 shows the same information for distributors.

9.40 About three-quarters of firms in both regions expected to use the M.4 and M.5 in 1966 apart from South Wales firms that had a lower expectation of use of M.5. The change in 1968 was towards increased expectation of use of M.4 by firms in both regions but the increase in their expected use of M.5 was offset by similar proportions of firms reversing earlier expectations of its use.

TABLE 9.1   Manufacturers' Expectations of Use of M.4 and M.5, 1966 and 1968

Expectation	M.4		M.5	
	South Wales firms %	South West firms %	South Wales firms %	South West firms %
Use 1966 & 1968	67	69	33	63
Use 1966 Not 1968	6	7	19	13
No Use 1966 or 1968	14	8	32	10
No Use 1966 Use in 1968	14	16	17	14
No. of firms	162	219	62	219

TABLE 9.2   Distributors' Expectations of Use of M.4 and M.5, 1966 and 1968

Expectations	M.4		M.5	
	South Wales firms %	South West firms %	South Wales firms %	South West firms %
Use in 1966 & 1968	25	47	15	54
Use in 1966 not in 1968	6	7	6	4
No Use 1966 or 1968	47	22	70	18
No Use 1966, use 1968	23	24	9	24
No. of firms	53	117	53	117

9.41 While a much higher proportion of South West distributors in Table 9.2 expected to use the motorways in 1966 than was the use in South Wales, the proportion expecting to use the M.4 changed similarly in both regions. A higher proportion of South West firms expected to use the M.5 in 1968. These changes reflect the concentration of firms in distribution and the wider interests of those east of the Severn.

9.42 Firms were asked what particular benefits they expected to derive from specific motorways when completed, namely M.4 Bristol-London, M.4 west of Newport, M.5 Bristol-Gloucester and M.5 Bristol-Exeter. These have been analysed by region for both manufacturers and distributors and the data is set out in Appendices 49-52. The principal outcomes can be summarized as follows:—

(i)   Among manufacturers in South Wales the great majority — almost 85% — expect to use the M.4 east of Tormarton and over 75% a motorway west from Newport. The main benefit they expect is faster delivery of goods. Almost 50% expect to use the M.5 both north to Gloucester and south from Avonmouth.

(ii)   Among distributors in South Wales lower proportions expect to use three of the four motorways. The exception is that west of Newport a higher proportion expect to gain access to new markets than among manufacturers and 18% hope to rationalise distribution in South Wales with the motorway west of Newport.

(iii)   Turning to the South West, almost 90% of manufacturers expect to use the M.4 eastwards and 75% the M.5 northwards as compared to 68% using the M.4 in South Wales and 58% the M.5 to Exeter. Speedier delivery of goods is the principal benefit expected, followed by reduced transport costs.

(iv)   Among distributors in the South West the route of greatest interest is the M.5 northwards (84%) followed by the M.4 eastwards (78%), the M.5 southwards (73%) and last the M.4 in South Wales (59%). Reduced transport costs are expected and over 10% expect further rationalisation of distribution and/or access to new markets.

9.43 The first survey of industry and distribution covered the whole of the South West Economic Planning Region. At that time (1967), firms in West Somerset, Dorset, Devon and Cornwall were asked what use they expected to make of motorways when completed. Among manufacturers the highest proportion (57%) expected to use the M.5 and virtually equal proportions the M.4 eastwards and the Severn Bridge — 45% and 44% respectively. This was far greater than the use expected by distributors, 23% of whom expected to use the M.4 and M.5 and 25% the Bridge. Bearing in mind the timing of this part of the survey, even higher proportions can be expected to use both motorways if only because of experience of existing motorways in the intervening years.

Changes in Demand for Transport

9.44 As expected there have been large diversions of demand from one form of transport to another as well as from route to another; but it is clear that there has been a substantial new demand for road travel and transport — the various forms of traffic generation. Taking the hypotheses advanced in paragraph 2.25, all five have been present though some of the changes may have been due to factors other than the Bridge. Thus the first expectation, a limited switch of freight traffic from rail to road, has occurred. But how much of this is attributable to the Bridge, how much to changes in the use of railways by consignors that is evident on routes other than those affected by highway improvements, and how much to the policy of the railway management in hiving off less attractive traffic? In so far as an anomalous situation existed while there was no road bridge, then this has ended and movements at least between South Wales and the South West are now in line with those over similar distances elsewhere.

9.45 The switch in short to medium-distance passenger movements has been severe and has been accompanied by a sharp increase in demand for travel both on business and for private purposes by car. The new demand for passenger movement is almost exclusively for car travel. While there was a temporary element of facility created traffic in the first 15 months, much of the increase has been permanent. The fact that the Forth Bridge had been opened at virtually the same period of a year enabled a very accurate prediction to be made of the period of increased "novelty" travel in the autumn of 1966 and of its recurrence in the spring of 1967.

9.46 The effect on types of commercial road use has also been as expected. There has been some switch from hauliers to own vehicle operation and further relaxation of licensing may increase this. However, any fear that the combination of such switches and the reduced mileages required using the Bridge would lead to surplus capacity appearing the haulage industry has not been well founded. On the contrary, the increased demands of industry coupled with a limited switch over longer distances from both rail and own vehicles to hauliers has at least absorbed any temporary "surplus" capacity in road haulage. The results of the special study of hauliers show that they were able to achieve operating economies and there is a suggestion that the larger operators were the more successful in seeking new business.

9.47 The road passenger transport industry was affected in similar ways. An initial switch from other destinations together with largely excursion and charter traffic generated by the novelty of the Bridge produced a temporary increase in business in 1966—67 after which movements tended to be in line with national trends for this type of traffic with an enduring switch of business from other destinations to those reached by the Bridge, notably for journeys originating in South Wales. One sufferer from this is the seasonal pleasure steamer traffic in the upper Bristol Channel.

Highway Improvements and Physical Planning Questions

9.48 As indicated in Chapter 2, it proved impracticable to undertake any investigation of changes in land values consequent upon the Bridge, while there is fragmentary evidence of changes in isolated instances in locations such as Thornbury and Chepstow these do not offer a basis for significant comment. The wider issues of the extent to which developments have been able to take their "natural" course and the extent to which physical planning has prevented this can be commented upon.

9.49 The economic pressures set up by the new transport facilities provide an additional impetus to future development and this in turn poses questions of land use planning. The various controls and inducements have their greatest impact on new industrial establishments. Evidence from this and other studies proceeding concurrently supports the view that South Wales, in particular the Newport-Cwmbran-Pontypool area, is favoured by these factors when taken in conjunction with improved access given the M.4. During the period of the study the Development Area was extended to cover all of Monmouthshire except the Chepstow and Monmouth districts; Special Development Area status was granted to areas close to Newport and, following the Hunt report, the position of Cardiff and Newport was changed to that of an "intermediate area" so that they ceased to be at so much disadvantage compared to their neighbouring areas in terms of inducements.

9.50 For new distribution establishments — as indicated in paragraph 9.37 above — their average size has meant that they could not qualify for grants. This, coupled with the strong attractions of the area east of the Severn as a centre for distribution, has been one factor in the rapid expansion of such activities at places like Yate. It is, however, difficult to isolate either the Bridge or the highway improvements as the main factor when redevelopment and local planning pressures point to such a move. In Bristol the move to Avonmouth was already afoot with such other influences at work as the decline of the City Docks and the possible development of Portbury — itself at the first intersection of the M.5 after the Avon crossing which will be open in 1974. The argument as to these influences in Cardiff is even more complex. The pressure to move out is certainly present. Cardiff is concerned with its further development as a capital city; there has been the attraction of industry to the nearby Development Area now alleviated somewhat by the inclusion of Cardiff in the South East Wales Intermediate Area; but most notable of all is the fact that the redevelopment has been quite independent of any projected motorway extension through the area. There has, therefore, been a coincisence of pressures which have tended to favour development at locations close to the motorway system in the Bristol-Yate area but the same cannot be said of Cardiff.

Leisure Activities

9.51 The growth of car ownership and the new opportunities open to the private motorist, as outlined in Chapter 2, have important consequences for both regions. Three aspects of this call for comment — tourism, shopping and the role of "environment" factors in the attractiveness and, therefore, the economic chances of a region, a point first made in the Toothill report to the Scottish Council for Development and Industry.

9.52 One feature of tourism is the role of sightseeing as a leisure activity. The private motorist is interested in new destinations for day and half-day trips. The two regions have long offered different types of leisure opportunities. South Wales offers the mountains and valleys of Breconshire and with them access to much of Central and West Wales, as well as the border area of the Wye Valley and the Forest of Dean which have been prime targets for excursionists from the east bank. Conversely, the West Country offers the Cotswolds, the coastal and inland attractions of Somerset and Wiltshire. Already both regions received many visitors from the Midlands and further motorway improvements can be expected to augment this traffic especially east of the Severn. This poses two questions. First what is the capacity of existing facilities and areas such as the Brecon Beacons National Park? How should its administrators react?

9.53 When interviewed at an early stage in the study, they were uncertain as to whether to promote the National Park through publicity in the South West or to protect it from too ready an access. Restrictions of the type already introduced in the Lake District and the Peak District are examples of what may become necessary in the Brecon Beacons and on Dartmoor when the M.5 is completed. Such problems are already experienced at peak weekends in such popular destinations as Bristol Zoo and Longleat. The attendances at stately homes, the development of several such estates as recreational centres close to the M.4 and the interest in places such as the Wildlife Park and the Wildfowl Trust at Slimbridge exphasise the growing demand for outdoor facilities.

9.54 The seaside resorts may be faced with growing competition but they remain major destinations. One factor in attracting such visitors is their ability to cater for large numbers and the evidence in this study is that those to the east of the Severn were better placed to do so. Even so they may expect a further wave of business when the M.5 and M.4 are completed. While some of this will be traffic diverted from other destinations much of it will be newly generated traffic.

9.55 The range of opportunities is not confined to the country nor to outdoor summer activities. Bristol has acted as a focal point for indoor entertainment with its theatres, entertainment centres and other facilities. It is sightseeing and entertainment that has brought the spin-off of shopping expenditure to Bristol, itself one of the principal destinations throughout the period since the Bridge opened.

9.56 While to the general public in Cardiff or Bristol the sound of accents from "across the water" in shopping centres is thought to be evidence of an invasion of buyers, the evidence of sales confounds this view. The net effect on most stores and shops has been slight and largely swamped by general movements in sales independent of the new customers. Nevertheless, in resorts and leisure destinations the effect has been more obvious. The overall result in their case could be summed up as a bringing forward of growth that they might otherwise have expected and in some cases bringing much nearer the point of saturation at peak periods.

9.57 Improved access to leisure activities and new opportunities to reach areas of greater amenity can be important factors in attracting new firms and their managers to an area. In so far as the mining valleys of South Wales may have an image — whatever its justification — of not being in the top rank for amenity, the improved access to other parts of the country may help to tip the balance in some cases.

9.58 People have been voting with their feet in these two regions for close on half a century. The emigration from South Wales and the imigration into the South West are of long standing. The Bridge may help to arrest this process so far as South Wales is concerned. One of its subsidiary benefits has been to make easier and possibly more frequent the returns of "exiles" to visit families at weekends and holiday periods. But ultimately the outcome depends on where job opportunities arise and these depend on the decisions of government and more particularly of business.

9.59 Future development of the Severnside area is linked to its possible use for large scale projects after 1980 as covered in the Severnside Study. If present national policies on regional development and the distribution of industry continue unchanged, then some restraint on new industrial expansion may be expected there unless there is a major employment problem such as a further contraction of the aircraft industry. If, for whatever reason, the present national controls and pressures were to be eased then the pressures on local physical planning controls could be severe as the Severnside belt from Yate and Bristol to Newport and Cardiff remains an attractive site for new industry and services. The reactions of planners and administrators are one factor; the other is the likely reaction of business men.

Organisation Studies

9.60 At several points in this report attention has been given to the differing ways and speeds with which firms react to an external change. Here was a predictable event with uncertain consequences. Some firms chose to ignore it. There was the managing director who replied to a request for his views with the words "bridges have been built in the past without statistics and studies; long may it be so! This bridge cannot possible have any effect upon us". This attitude is more prosaically put in the expectations of firms as to their likely use of the Bridge and the motorways already analysed earlier in this chapter. There were many who thought the estuary was an obstacle because they had never attempted to trade with the area across the Severn. But there were many more who had already done so despite the obstacle and who were among the first to grasp the new opportunities presented with the Bridge.

9.61 The particular hypotheses advanced in paragraph 2.44 have been found to hold good with one exception. Those that reacted soonest were drivers, both motorists and commercial drivers. Often the latter were using the Bridge when their managers still thought they were going via Gloucester. The distributors reacted more quickly but, as the traffic data analysed in Chapter 3 shows, a very material reason for delayed reaction was the fact that the Newport by-pass was not opened until

the spring of 1967. Once there was experience of the use of motorways their possibilities were more fully realised and future completions will not have so slow a reaction.

9.62 The one exception concerns amalgamations. The period of this study has been one of intense take-over activity nationally and this is seen in the proportions of firms surveyed that were involved in concluded take-overs 16% of manufacturers and 15% of distributors. It is argued in Chapter 7 that there is little evidence of takeovers to consolidate the particular market amalgamation produced by the Bridge. If anything this change had already been anticipated. Internal changes within firms have occurred as expected and these have been linked to a review of marketing areas in some cases. But given the proportions involved in take-overs alone, quite apart from other reorganisations due to policy changes independent of the Bridge, it is impossible to assess the full impact of the Bridge in this context.

Benefits Conferred

9.63 Chapter 8 sets out the problems encountered in any attempt to estimate the benefits conferred. Whereas the cost of the Bridge is relatively easy to determine, the benefits are much more difficult to quantify for two reasons. The first is obtaining data of any kind; the second is putting a value on a particular benefit. How does one measure the gains to different classes of road user of time saved when travelling on business, let alone how does one value time saved on a pleasure trip? The exclusion of many benefits through lack of sufficiently reliable data and the arbitrary valuations tend to underestimate the benefits throughout. To this reservation three others must be added. The first concerns the estimates of traffic growth. Both estimates used in Chapter 8 assume that traffic growth rises with car ownership. This increase, arising from the spread of car ownership to lower income groups, and the growth of "two-car" households, is unlikely to produce a higher mileage for car than existing vehicles. However, as leisure increases and leisure spending becomes more important it is possible that expenditure on leisure may rise leading to more journeys than have been allowed for. The second is the link between the state of the economy and the growth of heavy vehicle traffic. The period since the Bridge was opened has been one of very slight growth. Faster economic growth would mean more traffic and the rise in real incomes would reinforce the effect on car usage. The third is the full effect of the completion of the M.4 to London and the M.5 to Brimingham. Such allowances as have been made in Chapter 8 even at the higher estimate have the same characteristics as the rest of the data discussed here.

9.64 On the most severe set of assumptions, namely a 10% discount rate, which is Treasury's current Test Discount Rate, the slower rate of traffic growth implied by a decline to the long-term growth rate by 1975 and the lower level of light vehicle running costs, the estimate of net benefit stands at £99.8 million — virtually £100 million. This is after allowing for the cost of the Bridge plus its maintenance through to 2050. Still retaining a 10% discount rate but taking the less severe assumptions as to traffic growth and running costs, the benefit shoots up to £123.9 million. At a discount rate of 8%, a level adopted by the Treasury as a guide-line in the years when the Bridge was being built, the lowest benefit on the basis used before stands at £132.2 million while the upper forecast now reaches £162.6 million. Finally at a discount rate of 5%, the lower forecast is £224.5 million and the upper stands at £273 million. On a project costing £21.5 million when discounted at 10%, £20.6 million at 8% and £19.7 million at 5% this is clearly a massive benefit to the nation.

9.65 But these calculations assume no further traffic growth beyond 2000. Whether the Bridge will then be able to withstand unaided the pressure of traffic has already been questioned. As soon as any of the short-term constraints are removed, such as a faster economic growth rate of the extensions of M.4 being completed, this investment stands out as an even greater bargain for the nation.

9.66 But this is only a beginning. The slow rate of national economic growth during the survey period has accentuated the inter-regional adjustments and minimised the potential benefit given more rapid economic growth. When that expansion occurs the position of both regions is enhanced, whatever the national policy on distribution of industry. Given policies of the type operative in the 1960s, the attractive position of South Wales is substantial and the benefits may be felt more deeply in that region than if a less tough approach was adopted. Even if the policy were relaxed, however, South Wales is now in a far better position in relation to the Midlands and the South East than almost any other present development area. The attractive power of the South West is also enhanced, especially in distribution and services, and the improved communications ensure that it will be well placed to withstand any adverse change in those of its present activities that are vulnerable. This could be important for a region in which aircraft and tobacco are important sources of industrial employment. On the other hand, a greater diversity with less dependence on such large lumps of sensitive industry would be the basis for a much healthier regional economy.

9.67 A relaxation of present controls would favour the South West and that part of South Wales nearest to the crossing. The extent to which the two communities might react to such a change is more dangerous to predict. It is clear that firms on both sides have often reacted strongly to the new situation and neither side has a monopoly of either initiative or protectionist complacency. Yet this could be a decisive factor. The new competition which both have experienced has been more keenly felt in the Welsh capital. All that this study can show is the creation of new opportunities and the record of their first three years of operation. It is, therefore, dangerous to argue which community has gained relatively more. The nation and the two regions are the richer for the opening of the Bridge.

Wider Implications

9.68 The terms of reference of this study included a mention of the possible relevance of the conclusions to future investment in communications elsewhere. The only guides that were available to this study were the traffic growth patterns of the Tay Tamar and Forth Road Bridges. The pattern in the early months of the Bridge's existence closely resembled those on the Forth Bridge but the scale of the change and the volume of traffic have been so much greater that the financial position of the two projects has been very different. The Forth Bridge already has higher and differential charges for crossings.

9.69 Allowing for specific features of particular projects in terms of the areas linked, the lessons of the Severn Bridge are that change may be much greater than previously estimated, that traffic growth and adaption by users may be spread over several years, and that these will occur most quickly among private motorists, less quickly among commercial users and least quickly with major adaptations by firms in manufacturing industry. The areas affected are not confined to those immediately connected and the full exploitation of the new facility will be influenced by such factors as previous knowledge of the areas across the estuary or other obstacle that is removed. Above all the potential pay-off from this type of investment is very great even on the very conservative tests applied in this study.

REFERENCES

1. The first agreed charge ever negotiated, which anticipated the Road and Rail Traffic Act 1933, was Messrs, Robinson, and Great Western Railway 1931. Cited by G. Walker 'Road and Rail' (Allen and Unwin, 1942, p.77 ff.)

2. Dissertation (unpublished) by T. Farmer on New Industrial Employment in Three Selected Areas within the South Wales Coalfield. Bath University School of Management, 1971.

3. These are considerable for three reasons: the first is the extent to which manufacturing establishments also act as distribution centres; the second is the large switch in the classification of firms from distribution to manufacturing following S.E.T. which was introduced in the survey period; and the third is the lack of data on sales staff and administrative workers.

Methodology

Traffic Surveys

1.   Basically the same team of trained interviewers was used at all the traffic interview surveys. While the number of interviews per hour varied a little over the day it normally dropped below 50 only before 7 a.m. and after 9 p.m., when the volume of traffic was very low, so that a total of nearly 900 vehicles was the usual outcome for a day, though on 31st March 1969 (east-bound) a total of 1020 was achieved.

2.   As noted in Chapter 1, an hourly count of both light and heavy vehicles was kept so that the fraction of

both total light and heavy vehicles interviewed each hour was known and the reciprocal of these factors was applied to the characteristics of the interviewed vehicles to give a separate picture of all light and heavy vehicles. Refusals, at under 1%, were neglected. The following table sets out the hourly pattern of interviews in relation to total traffic for two randomly chosen survey days. They are for the first day of interviews in March 1967 (Monday, eastbound) and one of the pre-Easter days in 1969 (Friday, westbound) —

| Hour Beginning | March 1967 | | | | March 1969 | | | |
| | Light Vehicles | | Heavy Vehicles | | Light Vehicles | | Heavy Vehicles | |
	Interviewed	Total	Interviewed	Total	Interviewed	Total	Interviewed	Total
6 a.m.	24	61	12	50	18	57	31	101
7 a.m.	32	159	15	82	26	203	30	167
8 a.m.	47	268	20	119	33	325	22	205
9 a.m.	38	247	27	100	38	320	16	213
10 a.m.	46	266	12	83	28	283	27	169
11 a.m.	55	248	9	120	28	329	28	162
12 noon	46	255	11	104	35	235	11	135
1 p.m.	48	204	16	98	31	275	11	151
2 p.m.	42	260	10	90	45	406	9	137
3 p.m.	35	268	13	95	53	535	8	145
4 p.m.	42	290	5	95	41	589	7	117
5 p.m.	48	380	9	79	50	630	18	113
6 p.m.	56	280	5	64	60	630	8	96
7 p.m.	44	158	7	42	57	557	5	64
8 p.m.	44	91	6	28	59	350	8	44
9 p.m.	13	45	5	15	41	256	7	34
Total	660	3,480	182	1,264	643	5,980	246	2,053

3.   At the summer weekend surveys when, as noted in Chapter 1, traffic densities were too high to permit a lane at the toll area being reserved for interviews, reply-paid post-card questionnaires were distributed to every fifth light vehicle crossing.[1] The cards were numbered so that the proportion returned that were distributed at any hour was known and this combined with the hourly count of traffic (which provided some separate check

that every fifth light vehicle was receiving a card) enabled hourly sampling factors to be calculated and the characteristics of the returned cards to be grossed appropriately to give a picture of the whole population. The details of this operation for one day's distribution in each direction (Saturday 12th August, 1967 eastbound and Sunday 20th August, 1967 westbound) were as follows —

Hour Beginning	Saturday 12th August 1967 Eastbound			Sunday 20th August 1967 Westbound		
	Total Vehicles	Post-Cards Distributed	Post-Cards Returned	Total Vehicles	Post-Cards Distributed	Post-Cards Returned
6 a.m.	280	55	13	30	6	4
7 a.m.	513	100	25	85	25	8
8 a.m.	807	160	57	130	26	21
9 a.m.	851	162	52	460	92	47
10 a.m.	1,149	229	83	880	176	46
11 a.m.	1,206	239	77	966	191	73
12 noon	1,078	215	77	835	165	47
1 p.m.	966	187	68	669	133	39
2 p.m.	881	174	69	1,190	237	78
3 p.m.	984	183	65	1,239	246	95
4 p.m.	858	171	67	1,240	245	76
5 p.m.	695	137	54	1,155	230	64
6 p.m.	705	140	49	1,195	238	72
7 p.m.	650	127	45	1,240	247	91
8 p.m.	555	111	45	965	193	70
9 p.m.	270	54	14	605	121	47
Total	12,448	2,444	860	12,984	2,581	878

Returned as percentage of distributed: Saturday 35.2, Sunday 34.0. (The table excludes unusable returned cards, of which there were 38 on the Saturday and 28 on the Sunday).

4.   The percentages of post-cards returned and the percentages returned and analysed for the August weekends in 1967 and 1968 are given below. The proportion of returned cards with incomplete information that were not analysed was small, less than 5%. The low percentage of returned cards analysed for eastbound traffic in 1968 was the result of having to enforce an earlier cut-off date for returns to meet a computer deadline.

	Saturday		Sunday	
	% Returned	% Returned and Analysed	% Returned	% Returned and Analysed
1967 Westbound	39.9	38.8	34.9	34.1
Eastbound	36.7	35.3	37.1	35.5
1968 Westbound	40.2	37.9	40.4	38.8
Eastbound	41.1	31.9	40.3	31.2

Household Interviews

5.   A sample of households was interviewed in Bristol, Newport, Ebbw Vale, Chepstow and Thornbury. Chepstow and Thornbury Urban Districts were selected as the nearest urban areas of reasonable size to the west and east of the Bridge. Newport and Bristol were chosen as the two largest centres nearest to the Bridge on each bank of the Severn: although differing greatly in size and consequently in variety of facilities offered, residents in both centres have easy access to at least a fairly high level of shopping, entertainment and similar services.

Cardiff was an obvious alternative on the west bank of the Severn, but if chosen there would have remained a size discrepancy compared with Bristol; the arguments of proximity and the practical one of availability of interviewers resulted in the choice of Newport. Ebbw Vale, with no similar sampled equivalent on the east side of the Bridge was included as representing small industrial valley towns with moderate levels of central area services and of very different accessibility to the Bridge than Chepstow or Thornbury.

H

6. The samples were selected in late 1966 before the results of the 1966 Sample Census were available so that selection was on the basis of the 1961 Census populations. In order to include in the sample a high probability of a reasonable number of Bridge users it was decided to take a 10% sample of households.

7. In all towns the sampling frame was a numbered list of all residential addresses in the appropriate area. A set of random numbers of the required size was then applied to this frame to choose the sample. In Chepstow and Thornbury all addresses in the area constituted the frame. In Bristol, Newport and Ebbw Vale a 10% sample of all households would have given an absolute number of households too large, given the limitations imposed by cost and time, so that these towns were first stratified by wards.

8. In Ebbw Vale the wards were divided into low and high rateable value classes and one ward selected at random from each class. This resulted in one ward at the extreme north of the town and one to the south. In Newport the wards were stratified by rateable value and by location, east and west of the River Usk, with a high and low rateable value ward then being chosen at random from each side of the river.

9. As the average size of wards in Bristol was over 4,000, twice the size of Newport, resources would have permitted at most a 10% sample of two wards, which might have been very poorly representative of the whole city. Thus, in Bristol a 5% sample of four wards was taken. The wards were stratified by rateable value and position and one ward of high and one of low rateable value was chosen at random from the Severn side of Bristol with a similar choice of two wards from the other (south and east) side of the city.

10. To obtain some information about the influence of time on the extent of use of the Bridge, interviews in Newport were conducted in two stages. In the autumn of 1967, 15 to 18 months after the Bridge opened, interviews were conducted in one high and one low rateable value ward to the west of the River Usk and, a year later, in a similar pair of wards to the east of the river. Interviews in Ebbw Vale and Bristol were carried out 15 to 18 months after the Bridge opened and those in Chepstow and Thornbury in the spring of 1968, 18 to 20 months after the opening.

11. The number of households in the sample for each of the five towns was as follows —

Area	Number of Selected Households	Total Households	Sample As % of Total
Bristol	1,069	139,747	.8
Thornbury	119	1,064	11.18
Newport (Stage 1)	490	32,866	1.5
Newport (Stage 2)	450		1.3
Ebbw Vale	204	8,778	2.3
Chepstow	193	1,730	11.16

12. No substitution of addresses was allowed, and where two or more households were found at one address interviewers were instructed to interview all households and then omit the next 1, 2 or 3 addresses on their list. A household was defined as a group of people who all live at the same address and who are catered for (having at least one meal a day) by the same person: this, of course, is the usual definition used by the Government Social Survey.

13. After the selection of the households in the samples and prior to interviewing, an introductory letter was sent to each selected household explaining the purpose of the survey, asking for co-operation and indicating that an interviewer would be calling during the next few days. Trained and experienced interviewers were available for all the interviews in Newport, Ebbw Vale, Chepstow and Thornbury and for about half the interviews in Bristol. The remainder of the Bristol interviews were in the hands of second-year university students who were able to take part thanks to the co-operation of Bristol University. These students were all studying survey methods and while they thus knew something of the problems involved, they were inexperienced and their youthful appearance may sometimes have had disadvantages. There was supervision of at least two

interviews in most cases.

14. The response rates in Newport were 96% for the first stage and 93% for the second; in Ebbw Vale it was 95%, in Chepstow 91%, in Thornbury 89% and in Bristol 91%.

15. The reason for the lower response rates in Chepstow, Thornbury and the second stage in Newport was the number of non-contacts as a result of a time limit necessitated by the need to have the data available for computer processing. This limited the repetition of calls on selected households. These non-contacts were later investigated and found not to differ from the contacted households in personal characteristics and use of the Bridge.

16. The lower response rate in Bristol may be accounted for by two factors. First, the general lowering of response in non-Welsh areas, confirmed by the experience of interviewers who worked in both areas reporting that the response in Bristol was 'less enthusiastic' and that there was a tendency to 'doorstep' interviews. This was reflected in their higher individual refusal rates — a difference of 1% for Bristol compared with Wales. The second and more important reason for the lower response rate in Bristol was the use of students as interviewers for about half of the Bristol interviews. The refusal and non-

contact rate for student interviewers was considerably higher than that of the experienced personnel. This was probably due to lack of confidence to carry on after a 'semi' refusal. Despite their knowledge the students lacked confidence when confronted with indifference and even mild hostility, and they retreated where the trained interviewers would have persisted. Also the students were not helped by their youthful appearance which tends to 'put off' some people.

17.   From a statistical view it is better that the reason for the lower response rate was interviewer effect than because of something in the respondents themselves. This latter reason would indicate that the refusers were different from the rest, and this difference might be connected with travel habits and thus the interviewed part of the sample not including these 'different ones' would be biased.

18.   Refusal and non-contact households did not differ in type of house occupied, age group, area or social class from the rest of the sample. However, from the recorded verbatim refusals it is possible that a high proportion of the refusers were non-users of the Bridge as this was sometimes given as the reason for refusing. The response rate in Bristol (91%), while lower than in the Welsh areas, is still satisfactorily high.

Manufacturing and Distribution Surveys

19.   The data for the manufacturing and distribution surveys was collected by postal questionnaires and interviews from firms in South Wales and the South West region. All mining, manufacturing industries and the distributive trades were surveyed. The geographical locations, populations and response rates of firms investigated varied in each stage; details are given in Appendix 1A. A pilot survey of the pre-Bridge situation was carried out in 1965 and was reported on in a separate but unpublished paper. The main purpose of the questionnaire was to discover the type of data that firms could readily supply. The results of the survey enabled a set of hypotheses to be formulated which were the foundations of the subsequent surveys.

20.   The main surveys were carried out in two stages. The first stage (1966–67) examined the pre-Bridge situation and had these objectives —
(i)   To provide general background information about the structure of industry, particularly for the distributive trades and base data on inter-regional flows of commodities prior to the opening of the Bridge. This was important as experience showed that "historical" data is very difficult to obtain after a change has taken place since replies tend to be influenced by later events.
(ii)   To measure the immediate impact of the Severn Bridge on industrial and commercial activity in South Wales and the South West region and to check that the factors being studied were the most significant ones, and also whether the information collected would be adequate to test the hypotheses.

21.   The second stage (1968–69) had the major objective of identifying and quantifying the changes that had taken place because of the Severn Bridge during the first two years after the Bridge opened. Unlike the first stage, information on changes for other reasons were not requested although other causes of change were of far greater significance for the vast majority of firms than the opening of the Bridge.

22.   Lists of employers were provided by the Department of Employment and Productivity. Before the Bridge opened, because registration was not obligatory before S.E.T. started in 1966, these lists were only approximately 90% complete and many small firms were omitted. The surveys do not cover all firms as the lists excluded firms with fewer than 20 employers. Because of the small numbers of firms in each geographical area and industrial groups (details of these groupings are shown on Map C and in Appendix 1B), total populations of firms were studied except in the second stage when a 25% sample of manufacturers with 20 to 99 employees was surveyed.

23.   Although most of the data was obtained by post a large number of interviews was carried out which yielded valuable case study material. They were also useful in cases where the firm's activities did not fit the standardised questionnaire forms. For the first stage separate questionnaires were used for manufacturers and distributors but for the second an identical questionnaire was used for both surveys. The numbers of interviews conducted were —
Stage I   manufacturing 40 (7%),
Stage I   distribution 41 (13%),
Stage II   manufacturing 226 (30%),
Stage II   distribution 157 (45%).

24.   Planning the first stage commenced in July 1966. Constructing, testing and printing the questionnaire took two months and it was not until two days before the Bridge opened that the questionnaires were posted. The initial response was so encouraging that, with the agreement of the sponsors, the area covered by the survey was twice extended until eventually the whole of the South West region and South East Wales was covered. Hence the data collection proceeded in three overlapping stages from September 1966 to July 1967. Although most of the questionnaires were returned after the Bridge opened, respondents were asked to provide data on the pre-Bridge situation. In the early stages the road haulage, construction and retail distribution industries were covered. Early replies showed that the questionnaire was not suitable for these sectors of the economy and data collection was suspended. Swansea University took over and expanded the road haulage survey. Because it is composed of small units mostly with fewer than 20 employees the D.E.P. lists were not appropriate. The retail distribution survey was subsequently investigated by interviews and the construction industry survey left in abeyance. This was because of lack of resources, not because the Severn Bridge had had no effect on firms' activities. In fact the reverse was the case but its effects were different from those on manufacturing.

25.   The second stage occupied two years. Questionnaires were first posted in November 1968 and data

collection proceeded until August 1969. Because of a lower initial response rate a high proportion of replies were obtained by interview. Computer programming and data analysis was undertaken between September 1969 and September 1970. The areas surveyed in both the manufacturing and distribution surveys were identical.

26.   There were, however, differences between the two stages. In the first stage the whole of the South West Economic Planning Region and South East Wales, i.e. Newport, Cardiff, Bridgend, the Lower and Upper Valleys of Monmouthshire and Glamorgan and non-industrial Monmouth — see Map C at the end of this report — were covered. In the second stage three sub-regions of the South West Region, North Gloucestershire, Bristol—Severnside (Areas 16—18 on Map C) and North Wiltshire which comprise the South West Northern sub-division, plus the Wellington—Westbury sub-region were covered. South East Wales was covered and, for the first time, Industrial West Wales was included i.e. Swansea—Port Talbot, the Neath and Swansea Valleys and Industrial Carmarthen. In the analysis of vehicle movements data on the Forest of Dean, that area of the South West region on the west bank of the Severn, has been segregated. Comparisons between the first and second stages refer only to those areas common to both stages of the survey unless otherwise stated.

27.   There were considerable changes in the population of firms surveyed in the two stages. Most of these were due to changes in classification with the introduction of the Selective Employment Tax. This resulted in an increase in the registration of firms with the D.E.P. and, in some cases, re-classification of industries and trades. In the area common to both stages of the surveys there were in the first stage, 776 manufacturers with over 100 employees and 454 distributors. Of these original populations by the time the second stage started 188 (15%) of manufacturers and 114 (25%) of distributors had closed, contracted to less than 100 employees in the case of manufacturers or to less than 20 if distributors, or changed their main activity from either manufacturing or distribution. Of those surveyed in 1968—69, 105 (13%) of the manufacturers and 219 (38%) of distributors were new starts in the area, newly registered with the D.E.P., re-classified by the D.E.P. or had grown in employment from below the minimum in that period. The population common to the two surveys was 73% of the manufacturers and 63% of the distributors. Of all firms replying to the second stage of the surveys (including West Wales not surveyed in the first stage) 399 (69%) of manufacturers and 181 (51%) of distributors completed a questionnaire in the first stage.

28.   The response rates to the different stages of the surveys are given in Appendix 1A. In each survey the response rates were, in most categories, satisfactory. There was the usual tendency for more large firms to reply than small ones. Between 65% and 76% of large manufacturers replied to all stages, whereas the sample of small manufacturers yielded response rates ranging from 40% to 58%. Distributors, which are predominately small firms, had response rates ranging from 43% to 69%. Distance from the Bridge affected the response.

The response rates from South West Wales and South West South were lower than the two areas adjacent to the Bridge. Apart from the two factors of geographical location and size of firm, a more detailed examination of non-respondents and response rates did not show any clear bias. A comparison in the first stage of expected usage of the Bridge and the response rate in each area showed no direct correlation. The degree of local owner-ship of firms also did not seem to be a significant factor. Analysis by industries showed that the lowest response rates were from the quarrying (Stage I, 51%) and vehicle manufacturing (Stage I, 57%) firms. The latter industry is a special case since the finished products either do not travel by road (aircraft, ships and railway rolling stock) or are self-propelled and the questionnaire is not appropriate. In the case of the quarrying industry this is partly because of the small size of the units (all firms with 20+ employees were included) and partly because of the structure of the industry in the Severnside area which makes distribution a highly localised activity usually less than 20 miles for aggregates. The nationalised coal, gas and electricity generation industries were surveyed only in the second stage.

Coach Traffic

29.   Three surveys were undertaken. The first in June 1967 which was repeated in November and December 1967. A smaller follow-up survey was conducted in April 1970. The data was obtained by interviews with the larger "territorial" companies and postal question-naires of the small firms. In the first stage covering the seven months period after the Bridge opened question-naires were sent to all operators appearing on lists supplied by the Traffic Commissioners for the Western and South Wales Areas. The Traffic Commissioners' areas follow county boundaries. The South West Area includes Gloucester, Somerset, Wiltshire, Dorset, Devon and Cornwall and the South Wales area, Monmouth, Glamorgan, Brecon, Carmarthenshire, Pembroke, Cardigan and Radnor. The survey was repeated to cover the summer period March 1st to 30th September, 1967. The sample frame was different and up-to-date lists of operators were obtained. Those firms that had stated in the first stage that they would never use the Bridge because they ran only school or municipal services were deleted and questionnaires sent to 50% of the remainder except that all territorial operators were contacted separately.

30.   The response rate to the first survey was 36% and to the second survey stage 39%. The higher response rate to Stage II was partly because of simplification of the questionnaire and partly because November was a less busy period than June for operators to spare time to complete the questionnaires.

31.   The third stage of the survey was carried out in April 1970.[1] This was on a much smaller scale than the first two. The previous surveys had indicated that 70% of the passengers were carried by the 20 major operators and these together with the 15 next largest operators were approached. The response rate was 43%.

Retail Shopping

32. The questionnaire used for the first stage of the distributive trades survey in 1966 was also sent to all retail establishments with more than 50 employees in the first part of that survey. Most replies came from stores and shops located in the major urban areas of Cardiff, Newport, Bristol and Bath with a few replies from smaller centres such as Weston-super-Mare. Because the questionnaire was not wholly appropriate for retailers most of the data was obtained by interview and the survey was not extended to other centres such as Gloucester or Taunton when the main survey was extended in March 1967.

33. In April 1969 the survey was repeated[2] focussing on departmental stores in the four main urban centres close to the Bridge. Data was obtained by interviews with managers of seven departmental stores located in Bristol and Bath and three in Cardiff. Several of these had more than one establishment but no store in Newport participated in the survey.

REFERENCES

1.   Mr J Hood, Survey of Coach Traffic using the Severn Bridge, Bath University DIA project Report 1970.
2.   Mr T Horrobin: The Effects of the Severn Bridge on the Retail Trade in the South West England and South Wales, Bath University DIA project Report 1969.

GEOGRAPHICAL LOCATION, POPULATIONS & RESPONSE RATES TO MANUFACTURING & DISTRIBUTION SURVEYS

Geographical location		Stage 1		Response Rate☆		Stage 2		Response Rate	
		No. of Firms	No. of Questionnaires completed	No.	%	No. of Firms	No. of Questionnaires completed	No.	%
South West North*	Man. 100+φ	368	231	263	72	467	295	343	73
Gloucestershire, North Somerset	Man. 20–99θ	N.S.	N.S.	N.S.	N.S.	224	112	123	55
North Wiltshire	Dis. 20+	255	130	143	56	398	238	275	69
South West South	Man. 100+	303	142	202	67	N.S.	N.S.	N.S.	N.S.
South Somerset, South Wilts,	Man. 20+99	N.S.	N.S.	N.S.	N.S.	N.S.	N.S.	N.S.	N.S.
Dorset (excl. Poole), Devon & Cornwall	Dis. 20+	269	91	127	47	N.S.	N.S.	N.S.	N.S.
South East Wales	Man. 100+	331	191	219	66	317	216	241	76
Monmouthshire, East Glamorgan,	Man. 20–99	N.S.	N.S.	N.S.	N.S.	96	48	56	58
Cardiff and South (industrial) Breconshire	Dis. 20+	154	69	78	51	183	99	115	63
South West Wales	Man. 100+	N.S.	N.S.	N.S.	N.S.	121	65	78	65
West Glamorgan (Swansea) and	Man. 20–99	N.S.	N.S.	N.S.	N.S.	38	14	15	40
East (industrial) Carmarthen	Dis. 20+	N.S.	N.S.	N.S.	N.S.	44	15	19	43
TOTALS	Man. 100+	1002	564	684	68	905	576	662	73
	Man. 20–99	N.S.	N.S.	N.S.	N.S.	358	174	194	54
	DIS. 20+	678	290	348	51	625	352	409	65

Notes: * In Stage II South West North included Wellington—Westbury, whereas in Stage I Wellington—Westbury was part of South West South.
φ Man. 100+ in all areas includes quarrying firms with 20+ employees. ☆No. of replies includes multiple responses.
θ Man. 20—99 in all areas includes quarrying firms with 20+ employees.
25% sample of firms, numbers not aggregated.
N.S. — Not surveyed.

Industries Included in the Manufacturing and Distribution Surveys and Categories Used in the Analysis

The classification of industries used in this survey was based upon the Standard Industrial Classification, 1958 with certain amendments as listed below.

MANUFACTURING SURVEY

S.I.C. Order

Order II Mining and quarrying Coal mining was excluded from the survey in the first stage.

Order III Food, drink and tobacco The whole order was included.

Order IV Chemicals and Allied Industries The whole order was included.

Order V Metal Manufacture The whole order was included.

Order VI Engineering and Electrical Goods The whole order was included.

Orders VII and VIII Shipbuilding and Marine Engineering and Vehicles The shipbuilding and ship preparing industries are very little represented in the area of study, and Orders VII and VIII were combined. The resulting group of industrues included shipbuilding, motor vehicle and motor cycle manufacture, aircraft manufacture and repair, locomotive and railway rolling-stock manufacture and prams and other hand-drawn vehicles.

Order IX Metal Goods not Elsewhere Specified This group of industries includes all hand tools and nuts and bolts, wire, cans and boxes etc. It also included jewellery and the refining of precious metals (including the minting of money).

Orders X and XI Textiles and leather, leather goods and Fur This group is a rather mixed group of industries, including processes from the basic manufacture of man-made fibres to the manufacture of finished products, such as carpets, lace, hosiery and other knitted goods. There were very few firms in the leather goods industry and this order was included.

Order XII Clothing and Footwear The whole order was included.

Order XIII "Building Materials" i.e. Bricks, Pottery, Glass, Cement, etc. As well as the industries mentioned in the title, this group included the manufacture of abrasives and other building materials, such as plasterboard.

Order XIV Timber, Furniture, etc. The whole order was included.

Order XV Paper, Printing and Publishing The whole order was included except newspaper publishing in the South West South subdivision studied in the first stage.

Order XVI Other Manufacturing Industries This miscellaneous group included rubber manufacture, linoleum, brushes and brooms, toys, games and sports equipment, miscellaneous stationers goods and plastics moulding and fabricating.

DISTRIBUTION SURVEY

Order IXX MLH 704 Miscellaneous Transport Services of goods by road haulage firms warehousing and distribution.

Order XX MLH 810 Wholesale Distribution grocery provisions and other food; tobacco; clothing footwear and textiles; paper, stationery and books; petroleum products; other non-food goods and general wholesale merchants.

Order XX MLH 831 Dealing in Coal, Builders' Materials, Grain and Agricultural supplies (wholesale or Retail) Coal merchants; builders' merchants; corn, seed and agricultural merchants; Dealing in horses and livestock.

Order XX MLH 832 "Industrial Suppliers" i.e. Dealing in other industrial materials and machinery Ores and metals; timber; hides, skin and leather; textiles materials and yarn; industrial machinery; scrap and waste materials; other industrial materials.

A Note on the Reliability of Returned Post-Card Samples

1.   On Monday 20th March 1967 a sample of eastbound and on Tuesday 21st March a random sample of westbound light vehicles was interviewed from 6 a.m. to 10 p.m. At the same time vehicles not selected for interview were given a reply-paid post-card questionnaire. All light vehicles should thus have been interviewed or have received a questionnaire; refusals were very few.

2.   Because of the shortage of space at the toll collection booths reinforced by shortage of staff due to the demands of the interviewing, the distribution of cards had to be left to the toll collectors, who generously took on this extra burden. However, in periods of pressure cards were not distributed to all cars not interviewed. Also cars sometimes strayed unwanted into the lane being interviewed causing congestion which could only be dispersed without causing inconvenience to travellers by letting a few cars through the interview lane uninterviewed. Since cards were not being distributed in that lane, they also received no card. The occupancy of the interviewed vehicles was recorded, but this information was not available for the vehicles receiving cards. In all, of 7416 light vehicles, 1379 were interviewed and 5460 cards distributed leaving some 557 vehicles which escaped both nets.

3.   The object of the post-card enquiry was to find out something of the reliability of this method, compared with the random sample interview method, as a basis for finding out the characteristics of traffic crossing the Bridge. Of the 5460 cards distributed, 2112 (38.7%) were returned, of which 48 were not completed or spoiled, leaving 2064 (37.8%) available for analysis.

4.   The hourly pattern in each direction of cards distributed and returned was known, and in the analysis the cards returned were multiplied by an appropriate factor, so that they represented the total cards distributed in that hour. The hourly percentage of cards returned varied from 0% 6 a.m. westbound when none of the 7 cards distributed was returned to 69% eastbound 1 p.m. when 96 cards distributed produced 66 returned. The following table gives the distribution of these hourly percentages of useable cards returned. On the first day, eastbound, 39.25% of cards were returned and on the second day, westbound, 36.52%.

Percentage of Cards Returned

	0–10%	–20%	–30%	–40%	–50%	–60%	–70%
No. of Hours with given percentage	1	1	3	17	7	2	1

5.   The questions asked at the interview and on the card were directed at finding the purpose of the trip the traveller was making and the origin and destination of that trip. With regard to origins and destinations the cards, completed at the travellers' leisure, tended to give more precise locations than the interview. Except in the case of Bristol this did not create any great difficulty. However, with Bristol there was a problem. Given the pressure of time and the overriding need to cause as little inconvenience to travellers as possible, an interviewer may reasonably accept Bristol as a reply to the origin or destination question. Had the same traveller returned a post-card, it would be clear that the location lay on the fringe of Bristol, designated the Rest of Bristol Conurbation in our classification. Thus the post-card sample will contain many fewer responses than the interview sample for Bristol, and vice-versa for the Rest of the Bristol Conurbation. This was met by combining Bristol, Avonmouth and the Rest of Bristol Conurbation as a single location.

6.   With regard to journey purpose the need for speed at interviews, to avoid inconvenience, and the need for brevity with return post-cards, to obtain as large a response as possible, creates difficulties in the very clear and specific delineation of categories. For instance, the distinction between a journey on firm's business (in the firm's time, paid by the firm) and a journey to work (in the respondent's own time, unpaid) is not always clear. Again, a visit to friends or relations leads into a holiday spent with them or a holiday during which a visit may be made to relations or friends. Circumstances make it impossible for these sort of journeys to be precisely typed as visiting friends and relations on the one hand or holidaying on the other. Similarly problems can arise, though perhaps less often, with sightseeing and paid entertainment. These problems were needlessly increased on this occasion by an unfortunate error. Holidays were omitted from the purposes specified on the return post-card. Thus travellers who, if interviewed, would have given holidays as the purpose of the journey, if given a card might feel that a return was not called for, since their clear purpose was not specifically mentioned. If the post-card was returned, then no purpose might be stated or, as in the holiday example above, visiting friends and relations could be given as the purpose, although the visit was for a period of days and seen as a holiday. A blank space was left for other purposes than those specifically mentioned. Few people completed this, but of those who did so, holidays was the largest group. Among the interview sample, holidays was given as the main purpose of 8% of journeys. It seems that in the card sample a substantial number of those going on

holiday returned their purpose as visiting friends and relations. Since the survey was made at the beginning of the week before Easter — away from the main holiday period — and during the school holidays, a good deal of such holiday visiting is a reasonable possibility.

7.   In considering the reliability of the post-card sample, two hypotheses (A and B) were tested. First (A); assuming that the interview sample gives an accurate description of the characteristics of the population of light vehicles crossing the Bridge, that the card sample is in fact a random sample from this population. Second (B); since the interviews were only of a sample of the population, and the resulting description of population characteristics is subject to sampling error, that the card and interview samples are both random samples of a population whose characteristics are those given by pooling the card and interview samples. The first hypothesis could be regarded as too rigorous a test since it ignores the fact of sampling fluctuations in the interview sample. The second test could be regarded as too lax since it ignores the reasonable judgment that, because the interview sample was randomly selected and the card sample self-selected, the interview sample is a better guide to population characteristics than the card sample.

8.   The following table gives the results of testing hypothesis A (that the card sample is a random sample of 2064 from the population of 7416 vehicles, whose characteristics are as found in the interview sample) and hypothesis B (that the interview and card samples are both random samples of a population whose characteristics are given by the pooled results of the two samples) for the pattern of journey purposes.

tenability of the hypothesis. As this figure rises the hypothesis becomes less and less tenable. Values as high as 1 are very probable, that is, will occur as a result of sampling fluctuations about two out of every three times such samples are taken; values of 2 are fairly unlikely, occurring only about once in twenty times. Values above 2.5 are so unlikely as to make the hypothesis untenable.

10.   Clearly neither hypothesis is consistent with the data, there is clear evidence of bias in the information and given the method of selection of the two samples, it is the card sample that is biased.

11.   Travel on firm's business is the largest single purpose and also subject to the greatest error. The number of cards returned by business travellers was in much greater proportion than their numbers, perhaps because business travellers are more conscious of transport improvement and are more familiar with questionnaires. There may possibly have been a slightly different line drawn between firm's business (over represented) and work (under represented) in the card sample compared with the interviews.

12.   The picture of shopping and recreational travel is at least a little more reliable than those purposes connected with work. This is some comfort in that we have had to rely on cards, only for estimating the characteristics of weekend travel, when there are few journeys for 'work' purposes. For recreational travel the greatest defect is the under-representation of sightseeing and entertainment.

Purpose of Vehicle Journeys

| Purpose | PI | PC | A Hypothesis B | |
			PI−PC SA	PI−PC SB
Firm's Business	.3603	.4670	− 12.9	− 7.3
Collection & Delivery	.0569	.0264	+ 7.1	+ 5.3
Service & Maintenance	.1538	.0303	− 6.5	− 3.2
Work	.1567	.1017	+ 8.1	+ 5.6
Shopping	.0221	.0217	+ 0.1	+ 0.1
Sightseeing & Entertainment	.1408	.1076	+ 6.8	+ 3.4
Visiting	.1407	.2012	− 9.9	− 5.5
Holidays & Visiting	.2207	.2066	+ 1.9	+ 1.2
Others & Multiple	.0146	.0301	− 7.1	− 3.3

9.   PI is probability that any vehicles will have the stated purposes as found from the interview sample, PC similarly for the card sample and PO for the two samples combined. SA is the standard deviation of the distribution of values of PC for samples of 2064 from a population of 7416. SB is the standard deviation of differences between PI and PC for samples of 1379 and 2064 respectively, drawn from a population where PO gives the probability of any vehicle having the stated characteristic. The size of $\frac{PI-PC}{SA}$ and $\frac{PI-PC}{SB}$ is a measure of the

13. It is of some importance to know whether the purpose biases are greater for travellers in one direction, say westbound, than the other. Testing the stronger of the two hypotheses (that the card sample of travellers for a particular purpose are a random sample as far as direction is concerned of the population travelling for that purpose) the data was found to be quite consistent with that hypothesis for all purposes except service and maintenance. Given that the vast majority of travellers are making a round trip,

---

Direction of Travel, Westbound

	PI (Westbound)	PC	Hypothesis A PI—PC / SA
Firm's Business	0.5556	0.5571	− 0.1
Goods Coll. & Del.	0.5450	0.5103	+ 0.1
Service & Maintenance	0.5439	0.4731	− 2.3
Work	0.3761	0.3712	+ 0.2
Shopping	0.5366	0.5630	− 0.4
Sightseeing & Ent.	0.5915	0.5621	+ 1.0
Visiting	0.5211	0.5287	− 0.5

---

crossing the Bridge on both the outward and return journey, travellers for each purpose were just as likely to return a card if they received it when travelling eastward on Monday (when cards were distributed to eastbound travellers) as when travelling westward on the Tuesday. The low figure for work is the result of eastbound travellers being questioned on Monday when the flow was augmented by those returning from weekend visits to friends and relations, thus the eastbound Monday figure was higher than that for Tuesday westbound.

14. The following tables consider the efficiency of the card sample as a description of the origin and destination of the light vehicles using the Bridge, as measured by the tenability of the two hypotheses. The probabilities here are that any vehicle chosen at random will have a given origin or destination.

15. The fit between the card and interview samples is far from perfect, but that they are both random samples of the same population is at least a tenable hypothesis. The fit for origins is a little better than that for destinations. A minus means the card sample is overstating the importance of an area as origin (or destination) and a plus implies underestimation. Looking at the pattern of differences (PI—PC) areas in Wales tend to be minus, with the very large exception of the Rest of Monmouthshire. Near areas to the east of the Bridge tend to be plus and more distant areas minus. The figures for London and Outer London are consistent with the suggestion that to some degree, the imprecision of response at the interview discussed above with reference to Bristol leads to some overestimation of the importance of London compared with Outer London on the interview sample.

16. The next question is whether the differences between the estimates based on the interviews and those on returned cards of origins and destinations is merely the consequence of the different purpose pattern of trips between different areas. Since we know that, for instance, business purposes are overestimated in the card sample, that sample will overestimate the importance of areas where business travel is important. To consider this question the probability that a particular traveller has a given purpose can be taken as that established at the interview, but the probability that the traveller for that purpose has, say, Cardiff as his origin (or destination) can be taken as that established by the returned cards. The result is a table of origins and destination corrected for the deficiencies in the card sample as regards purpose of travel. The following table gives the results of comparing this corrected distribution with the interview sample for the stronger hypothesis, i.e. that this corrected distribution is a random sample of a population with origin and destination characteristics as indicated by the interview sample.

Origins

	PI	PC	PI—PC / SA	PI—PC / SB
Newport	.0616	.0663	− 1.0	− 0.6
Cardiff	.1187	.1214	− 0.4	− 0.3
Rest of Mon.	.1268	.0951	+ 5.1	+ 3.4
Rest of Glam.	.6473	.0621	− 3.7	− 2.1
Swansea	.0251	.0255	− 0.1	− 0.1
West Wales	.0097	.0140	− 2.4	− 1.3
West Glos.	.0280	.0308	− 0.9	− 0.5
East Glos.	.0144	.0110	+ 1.5	+ 1.0
Bristol Con.	.2758	.2651	+ 1.3	+ 0.9
Somerset	.0941	.0916	+ 0.5	+ 0.3
Wiltshire	.0158	.0275	− 5.1	− 2.7
Devon & Cornwall	.0305	.0297	+ 0.2	+ 0.2
London	.0260	.0224	+ 1.2	+ 0.8
Outer London	.0271	.0277	− 0.2	− 0.1
S.E. Coast	.0140	.0151	− 0.5	− 0.3
Central Southern England	.0357	.0457	− 2.9	− 1.7
Rest	.0492	.0501	− 0.2	− 0.1

Destinations

	PI	PC	PI—PC / SA	PI—PC / SB
Newport	.0573	.0714	− 3.3	− 1.9
Cardiff	.1299	.1388	− 1.4	− 0.8
Rest of Mon.	.1349	.1033	+ 4.9	+ 3.2
Rest of Glam.	.0717	.0576	+ 2.9	+ 1.9
Swansea	.0357	.0376	− 0.5	− 0.3
West Wales	.0199	.0246	− 1.8	− 1.0
West Glos.	.0213	.0266	− 2.0	− 1.1
East Glos.	.0102	.0185	− 4.4	− 2.2
Bristol Con.	.2671	.2651	+ 0.2	+ 0.1
Somerset	.0684	.0673	+ 0.2	+ 0.1
Wiltshire	.0197	.0192	+ 0.2	+ 0.1
Devon & Cornwall	.0361	.0257	+ 3.0	+ 2.0
London	.0311	.0193	+ 3.7	+ 2.5
Outer London	.0070	.0275	− 12.8	− 4.9
S.E. Coast	.0057	.0110	− 3.8	− 1.8
Central Southern England	.0321	.0400	− 2.4	− 1.4
Rest	.0520	.0457	+ 1.5	+ 1.0

Corrected Distribution of Origin and Destination

Hypothesis A   PI−PC (corrected)
             SA

	Origin	Destination
Newport	− 1.0	− 2.7
Cardiff	+ 0.3	+ 0.8
Rest of Mon.	+ 3.2	+ 3.4
Rest of Glam.	− 4.6	+ 3.1
Swansea	− 0.8	0.0
West Wales	− 2.3	− 2.6
West Glos.	− 0.5	− 2.0
East Glos.	+ 1.5	− 4.1
Bristol Con.	+ 1.3	− 0.7
Somerset	+ 1.1	− 0.7
Wiltshire	− 4.0	− 0.7
Devon & Cornwall	+ 0.4	+ 3.2
London	+ 1.6	+ 4.2
Outer London	+ 0.9	− 13.9
S.E. Coast	− 0.7	− 3.4
Central Southern England	− 1.8	− 1.2
Rest	− 0.5	+ 1.9

17. Comparing this table with the previous origin and destination tables for the same hypothesis, it is clear that the correction for purpose does little to improve the fit although in the case of some of the larger deviations there is a sharp improvement. It seems clear that the under representation of the Rest of Monmouth both as origin and destination is partly the result of the under representation of sightseeing as a purpose in the card sample because this is an important purpose in the Rest of Monmouth.

18. There is the further possibility that the omission of holidays as a specified purpose on the cards has upset the results. This is not a strong possibility since only 8% of the total traffic interviewed specified this purpose. The following table gives for the interview sample the percentage of all holiday traffic with a given origin and the percentage of total traffic with that origin, and similarly for destinations.

Holiday Traffic

	Origin		Destination	
	% of Holiday	% of All	% of Holiday	% of All
Newport	1.7	6.2	3.4	5.7
Cardiff	3.5	11.9	9.6	13.0
Rest of Mon.	8.0	12.7	8.3	13.5
Rest of Glam.	4.2	4.7	10.1	7.2
Swansea	5.7	2.5	11.3	3.6
West Wales	1.3	1.0	6.2	2.0
West Glos.	1.2	2.8	2.5	2.1
East Glos.	0.0	1.4	0.0	1.0
Bristol Con.	12.1	27.6	6.9	26.7
Somerset	9.6	9.4	4.4	6.8
Wiltshire	1.0	1.6	2.2	2.0
Devon & Cornwall	10.6	3.0	14.0	3.6
London	12.4	2.6	3.0	3.1
Outer London	4.2	2.7	1.3	0.7
S.E. Coast	6.0	1.4	1.5	0.6
Central Southern England	7.2	3.6	2.7	3.2
Rest	11.2	4.9	12.5	5.2

19. The assumption is that if an area has a higher percentage of holiday traffic than total traffic the return card sample will under represent that area. This table of holiday traffic does little to explain the differences between interviews and cards, though it probably has something to offer at a few points. It helps to explain the under representation of Devon and Cornwall both as origin and (especially) destination and surprising perhaps, the Bristol conurbation. The concentration of holiday traffic on the major urban centres adds strength to the earlier suggestion that in late March much of this traffic bordered on visiting friends and relations.

20. The investigation during the two weekends in August showed that holidays, visiting, sightseeing and paid entertainment were the predominant purposes. To find where travellers accomplish any purpose, say sightseeing, the number of vehicles making return journeys from sightseeing with a given point as origin are combined with those on outward journeys for the same purpose with the given area as destination. The two tables which follow make a comparison between the interview and card samples as indicators of 'place of accomplishment'. Again the strong (A) and weak (B) hypotheses are tested.

Place of Accomplishment, Sightseeing

	PI	PC	A Hypothesis B	
			PI−PC SA	PI−PC SB
Newport & Cardiff	.1103	.0597	+ 2.4	+ 1.9
Rest of Mon. & W. Glos.	.3733	.3086	+ 2.0	+ 1.4
Rest of South Wales	.0318	.0617	− 2.5	− 1.5
Bristol Con.	.2577	.2756	− 0.6	− 0.4
Somerset & East Glos.	.0874	.1173	− 1.1	− 0.7
Devon & Cornwall, Wiltshire & Central Southern England	.0584	.0700	− 0.7	− 0.5
Rest	.0468	.0864	− 2.8	− 1.7

21. As with the other comparisons hypothesis A does not fare too well being untenable in about a third of all cases, and this includes some areas with substantial traffic. Differences as large as those observed are compatible with hypothesis B; the largest difference could arise about once in one hundred samples due to sampling fluctuations above. The card questionnaire did not include holidays as a separate purpose, and while, as noted above, this does not account for the differences between the samples in patterns of origins and destinations for traffic as a whole, it will be a more substantial force where only holiday and visiting traffic is considered. Where an area has a larger share of holiday than of total traffic then as suggested above, this will tend to make PI larger than PC and vice versa. A number of the larger differences in the first of these two tables fit this pattern. Newport and Cardiff with lowish holiday traffic give card probabilities for holidays and visiting much higher than the interview probabilities. In the opposite direction are Devon and Cornwall, Swansea and the South East Coast.

22. While the first of the tables suggests a reasonable fit between the two samples (PI—PC/SB less than 1 in half the cases), it must be remembered that when dealing with a particular purpose the sample size is small, in this case 396 vehicles going to or from visiting and holidays. With samples of this size even if the sample is randomly chosen, the resulting estimates have the possibility of a high margin of error. Thus, to take an example, in the case of Devon and Cornwall which according to the interview sample was the place of accomplishment for 8.5% of visiting and holiday traffic, samples of 396 will give a figure as low as 5.1% about once in twenty times.

23. With sightseeing and paid entertainment the card sample drops to 184 vehicles. The place of accomplishment for sightseeing is considered in the second table which follows. Sightseeing tends to be short-distance traffic and to give reasonable frequencies in areas away from the Bridge, the data has been grouped.

Place of Accomplishment — Visiting and Holidays

| | PI | PC | A Hypothesis B | |
			$\dfrac{PI-PC}{SA}$	$\dfrac{PI-PC}{SB}$
Newport	.0390	.0823	− 5.1	− 2.6
Cardiff	.0890	.1483	− 4.7	− 2.7
Rest of Mon.	.1164	.1110	+ 0.4	+ 0.2
Rest of Glam.	.0645	.1110	− 4.3	− 2.4
Swansea	.0603	.0421	+ 1.7	+ 1.4
West Wales	.0505	.0555	− 2.0	− 0.3
West Glos.	.0268	.0306	− 0.5	− 0.3
East Glos.	.0073	.0029	+ 1.2	+ 0.9
Bristol Con.	.1359	.1321	+ 0.3	+ 0.2
Somerset	.0731	.0488	+ 2.1	+ 1.5
Wiltshire	.0201	.0133	+ 1.1	+ 0.8
Devon & Cornwall	.0853	.0392	+ 3.8	+ 2.8
London	.0256	.0133	+ 1.8	+ 1.4
Outer London	.0244	.0277	− 0.5	− 0.3
S.E. Coast	.0317	.0133	+ 2.4	+ 1.9
Central Southern England	.0615	.0364	+ 2.4	+ 1.8
Rest	.0884	.0919	− 0.3	− 0.2

London and areas beyond have practically no observations. The pattern is much the same as before with it being very unlikely that hypothesis A is true, but hypothesis B being consistent with the data, though there are some substantial differences between the two samples.

24. The data was similarly tested for other purposes and for the pattern of destinations from those origins that generated substantial traffic. The pattern is very much the same, differences between the results of the two samples are always substantial for at least a few of the cells. The differences do not exhibit an explicable firm pattern. One is left with the conclusion that a card sample provides a picture of the characteristics of the population that has the same broad outlines as presented by the interview sample. However, the data is not to be trusted in great detail and for particular purposes data regarding particular origins or destinations are subject, as is shown above, to substantial ranges of error.

REFERENCES

1. See Appendix 1C: A Note on the reliability of returned post-card samples.

APPENDIX 2

TOTAL VEHICLES, MONTHLY BY CLASS CROSSING THE BRIDGE, 1966-1970

Thousands and Percentages

	Motor Cycles		Cars and Vans		Lorries		Buses		Total
	No.	%	No.	%	No.	%	No.	%	No.
1966									
Sept.									468.3
Oct.									484.5
Nov.	1.1	.4	237.0	78.9	58.5	19.5	3.9	1.3	300.5
Dec.	1.1	.4	236.8	79.5	56.9	19.1	3.2	1.1	298.0
Total									1,551.3
1967									
Jan.	1.1	.4	223.4	77.2	61.9	21.4	3.1	1.0	289.5
Feb.	1.4	.5	242.8	78.9	60.6	19.7	2.8	.9	307.6
Mar.	2.9	.6	394.6	82.5	76.5	16.0	4.4	.9	478.4
Apr.	2.7	.6	355.6	82.0	71.9	16.6	3.4	.8	433.6
May	2.9	.5	441.4	81.4	88.7	16.4	9.5	1.8	542.5
June	3.4	.6	425.9	79.6	86.7	16.2	18.9	3.5	534.9
July	5.4	.8	570.8	83.8	87.5	12.8	17.7	2.6	681.4
Aug.	5.6	.7	677.9	87.1	82.2	10.6	12.6	1.6	778.3
Sept.	2.3	.4	454.1	80.8	98.1	17.4	7.6	1.4	562.1
Oct.	1.8	.4	372.5	78.6	95.3	20.1	4.2	.9	473.8
Nov.	1.2	.3	279.0	72.5	100.9	26.2	3.6	.9	384.7
Dec.	1.1	.3	263.9	74.6	86.5	24.4	2.5	.7	354.0
Total	31.8	.5	4,701.9	81.0	996.8	17.1	90.3	1.6	5,820.8
1968									
Jan.	1.0	.3	255.0	71.2	98.7	27.6	3.3	.9	358.0
Feb.	1.0	.3	279.7	73.6	96.1	25.3	3.1	.8	379.9
Mar.	1.8	.4	360.3	76.1	108.3	22.9	3.2	.7	473.6
Apr.	2.7	.5	468.9	81.4	99.1	17.2	5.1	.9	575.8
May	2.1	.4	389.3	76.2	112.3	22.0	7.3	1.4	511.0
June	3.7	.6	536.3	82.6	95.5	14.7	13.9	2.1	649.4
July	3.9	.6	561.2	81.3	111.7	16.2	13.3	1.9	690.1
Aug.	3.7	.5	687.4	85.3	103.0	12.8	11.5	1.4	805.6
Sept.	2.8	.4	518.2	82.1	100.1	15.9	10.0	1.6	631.1
Oct.	1.5	.3	398.6	76.8	114.4	22.0	4.7	.9	519.2
Nov.	1.1	.3	331.0	75.1	105.0	23.8	3.5	.8	440.6
Dec.	.9	.2	314.0	75.0	101.2	24.2	2.6	.6	418.7
Total	26.2	.4	5.099.9	79.0	1,245.4	19.3	81.5	1.3	6,453.0

See continuation sheet

	Motor Cycles		Cars and Vans		Lorries		Buses		Total
	No.	%	No.	%	No.	%	No.	%	No.
1969									
Jan.	1.0	.2	293.1	70.6	118.9	28.6	2.6	.6	415.6
Feb.	.7	.2	252.3	71.0	99.7	28.1	2.5	.7	355.2
Mar.	1.2	.3	355.5	75.2	112.6	23.8	3.3	.7	472.6
Apr.	2.3	.4	488.3	80.7	109.1	18.1	4.7	.8	604.4
May	2.3	.4	492.8	79.7	117.2	18.9	6.5	1.0	618.8
June	2.9	.5	493.3	78.9	118.3	18.9	10.4	1.7	624.9
July	3.5	.4	603.9	82.6	113.9	15.6	10.6	1.4	731.9
Aug.	4.2	.5	716.8	84.6	113.9	13.6	11.1	1.3	846.0
Sept.	2.4	.4	522.3	80.1	119.0	18.3	7.5	1.2	651.2
Oct.	2.2	.4	445.7	77.1	125.7	21.8	4.3	.7	577.9
Nov.	0.9	.2	347.7	73.3	122.6	25.8	3.5	.7	474.7
Dec.	0.8	.2	325.3	73.5	113.6	25.7	3.0	.6	442.7
Total	24.4	.4	5,337.0	78.2	1,384.5	20.4	70.0	1.0	6,815.9
1970									
Jan.	0.8	0.2	305.9	71.5	118.1	27.6	2.9	0.7	427.7
Feb.	0.7	.2	313.9	73.2	111.4	25.9	3.0	.7	429.0
Mar.	1.7	.3	458.8	78.6	119.0	20.4	4.4	.7	583.9
Apr.	1.3	.2	411.8	74.3	137.5	24.8	4.1	.7	554.7
May	2.9	.4	548.8	80.1	125.6	18.4	7.8	1.1	685.1
June	2.4	.4	506.2	77.6	133.7	20.5	10.2	1.5	625.5
July	2.9	.4	637.3	80.7	138.7	17.6	10.3	1.3	789.2
Aug.	3.8	.4	760.6	85.3	116.8	13.1	10.9	1.2	892.1
Sept.	2.4	.4	530.3	78.7	134.7	20.0	6.3	0.9	673.7
Oct.	1.6	.3	461.4	75.9	140.1	23.1	4.4	0.7	607.5
Nov.	1.0	.2	379.6	73.0	136.3	26.2	3.2	0.6	520.1
Dec.	0.9	.2	347.8	70.8	139.3	28.4	2.9	0.6	490.9
Total	22.4	.3	5,662.4	77.5	1,551.2	21.2	70.4	1.0	7,306.4

APPENDIX 3

DIVERTED, GENERATED AND FACILITY CREATED TRAFFIC BY AREAS: AUGUST 1967

No. of vehicles per week

		Bristol	East Glos.	Somerset	Wilts.	Devon & Cornwall	Central Southern England	London & Outer London	South East Coast	Rest Great Britain	Total
Newport	Diverted	2,135	147	1,604	537	820	377	1,108	169	67	6,964
	Generated	3,960	44	1,778	1,087	98	230	414	15	—	7,626
	Facility created	202	13	595	179	—	13	273	—	—	1,275
Rest Mon.	Diverted	3,246	127	1,896	916	543	997	1,710	210	54	9,699
	Generated	8,521	95	2,448	391	293	218	180	108	172	12,426
	Facility created	3,051	325	1,332	179	408	191	146	32	32	5,664
West Glos.	Diverted	1,838	206	939	99	242	55	324	170	80	3,953
	Generated	2,060	101	1,113	255	56	—	122	11	—	3,718
	Facility created	513	212	515	157	15	13	246	—	32	1,811
Cardiff	Diverted	6,500	608	2,877	996	1,706	1,207	3,407	609	215	18,125
	Generated	4,893	260	2,736	606	156	134	344	28	—	9,157
	Facility created	963	31	681	127	—	219	46	—	29	2,087

See continuation sheet

APPENDIX 3 (Continued)

No. of vehicles per week

		Bristol	East Glos.	Somerset	Wilts.	Devon & Cornwall	Central Southern England	London & Outer London	South East Coast	Rest Great Britain	Total
Rest Glam.	Diverted	2,867	535	1,295	595	583	582	2,603	347	31	9,438
	Generated	2,708	77	1,042	455	86	55	224	38	40	4,725
	Facility created	361	23	206	13	—	—	14	—	29	646
Hereford & Brecon	Diverted	2,322	74	876	206	320	54	171	17	13	4,053
	Generated	1,141	27	136	45	171	—	70	—	—	1,590
	Facility created	485	—	62	—	—	—	17	—	—	564
Swansea	Diverted	1,205	65	738	337	140	162	1,621	252	28	4,608
	Generated	1,594	—	116	134	14	14	122	16	12	2,022
	Facility created	121	—	123	—	—	—	27	—	17	288
West Wales	Diverted	1,286	54	782	262	545	518	2,161	520	295	6,423
	Generated	537	28	144	30	176	13	193	—	300	1,421
	Facility created	220	—	209	11	—	153	82	—	14	689
Rest Great Britain	Diverted	1,705	13	1,739	200	2,035	201	608	183	—	6,684
	Generated	120	—	688	15	69	—	11	15	15	933
	Facility created	818	330	497	—	228	43	149	—	—	2,065
Total	Diverted	23,164	1,829	12,746	4,148	6,934	4,153	13,713	2,477	783	69,947
	Generated	25,534	632	10,201	3,018	1,119	664	1,680	231	539	43,618
	Facility created	6,734	934	4,220	666	651	623	1,000	—	261	15,089

HOME ORIGINS AND PLACES OF ACCOMPLISHMENT OF WEEKDAY TRAFFIC, 1968

Purpose — Firm's Business

Thousands

*	Newport	Rest Mon.	West Glos.	Cardiff	Rest Glam.	Hereford & Brecon	Swansea	West Wales	Rest Great Britain	Total
Bristol	55 67	35 69	17 32	113 155	27 64	5 26	21 36	3 8	13 1	289 458
East Glos.	6 4	— 7	— —	6 22	— —	1 1	2 —	2 —	— —	16 34
Wiltshire	5 6	2 2	1 —	9 13	8 7	— 3	1 6	6 7	— 4	32 39
Somerset	8 25	7 6	4 —	4 45	4 14	1 12	— 6	— —	16 4	44 119
Devon and Cornwall	3 1	2 —	5 2	3 5	3 1	— 1	3 3	4 4	2 3	20 19
Central Southern England	4 5	3 —	3 3	21 —	4 9	— 1	— 4	4 —	— —	35 26
London and Outer London	6 13	4 11	— 3	26 47	3 12	1 6	1 4	5 5	— —	41 101
South East Coast	1 5	2 1	— —	3 6	— 7	— —	— 2	2 —	2 4	8 25
Rest Great Britain	8 2	— 1	— —	1 10	3 1	— 1	— 2	— —	— 1	12 18
Total	96 128	55 97	30 40	186 303	52 115	7 51	28 62	13 28	30 15	497 839

* The figures to the left of each column relate to eastbound traffic and those to the right to westbound

APPENDIX 5

HOME ORIGINS AND PLACES OF ACCOMPLISHMENT OF WEEKDAY TRAFFIC, 1968

Purpose — Work

Thousands

*	Newport		Rest Mon.		West Glos.		Cardiff		Rest Glam.		Hereford & Brecon		Swansea		West Wales		Rest Great Britain		Total	
Bristol	36	35	66	42	10	13	18	45	4	11	—	2	—	6	—	1	—	—	134	155
East Glos.	—	1	—	2	—	2	3	2	—	2	—	—	—	—	—	—	—	—	3	9
Somerset	3	2	7	5	—	1	3	—	—	—	—	3	—	1	—	—	—	—	13	13
Wiltshire	1	2	—	—	—	—	—	1	—	1	—	—	—	—	—	—	—	—	1	4
Devon and Cornwall	—	—	—	—	—	—	—	1	—	—	—	—	—	—	—	—	—	—	—	1
Central Southern England	—	3	2	—	—	—	—	—	—	—	—	—	—	—	—	—	—	—	2	3
London and Outer London	—	—	1	—	—	—	—	1	—	1	—	—	—	—	—	—	—	—	1	2
South East Coast	—	—	—	—	—	—	—	—	—	—	—	—	—	—	—	—	—	—	—	0
Rest Great Britain	1	—	—	—	—	—	—	—	—	—	—	—	—	—	—	—	—	—	1	0
Total	41	43	76	49	10	16	24	50	4	16	—	5	—	7	—	1	—	0	155	187

* The figures to the left of each column relate to eastbound traffic and those to the right to westbound

HOME ORIGINS AND PLACES OF ACCOMPLISHMENT OF WEEKDAY TRAFFIC, 1968

Purpose — Shopping

Thousands

*	Newport		Rest Mon.		West Glos.		Cardiff		Rest Glam.		Hereford & Brecon		Swansea		West Wales		Rest Great Britain		Total	
Bristol	19	5	26	3	12	12	23	6	9	–	4	1	1	–	–	–	–	–	94	27
East Glos.	–	–	1	–	–	–	2	2	1	–	–	–	–	–	–	–	–	–	4	2
Somerset	1	–	1	–	–	–	2	2	–	–	–	–	–	–	–	–	–	–	4	2
Wiltshire	1	–	–	–	–	–	–	–	–	–	1	–	–	–	–	–	–	–	2	–
Devon and Cornwall	–	–	–	–	–	–	–	–	–	–	–	–	–	–	–	–	–	–	–	–
Central Southern England	–	–	–	–	–	–	–	–	1	–	–	–	–	–	–	–	–	–	1	–
London and Outer London	–	–	–	–	–	–	–	–	–	–	–	–	1	1	1	1	–	–	2	2
South East Coast	–	–	–	–	–	–	–	–	–	–	–	–	–	–	–	–	–	–	–	–
Rest Great Britain	–	–	–	–	–	–	–	–	–	–	–	–	–	–	–	–	–	–	–	–
Total	21	5	28	3	12	12	27	10	10	–	6	1	2	1	1	1	–	–	107	33

* The figures to the left of each column relate to eastbound traffic and those to the right to westbound

125

APPENDIX 7

HOME ORIGINS AND PLACES OF ACCOMPLISHMENT OF WEEKDAY TRAFFIC, 1968

Purpose — Holidays

Thousands

*	Newport		Rest Mon.		West Glos.		Cardiff		Rest Glam.		Hereford & Brecon		Swansea		West Wales		Rest Great Britain		Total	
Bristol	2	–	11	4	2	–	11	–	–	6	2	–	5	–	–	6	5	14	38	30
East Glos.	1	–	–	2	–	–	–	1	–	1	–	1	–	1	–	1	–	2	1	8
Somerset	6	4	8	7	5	–	–	8	–	5	–	5	2	3	2	6	13	3	36	41
Wiltshire	–	1	3	–	–	1	–	3	–	1	–	1	–	1	–	2	3	–	6	10
Devon and Cornwall	–	5	5	4	–	3	5	5	9	–	4	4	9	–	–	3	22	2	54	26
Central Southern England	–	3	5	5	–	–	–	5	–	5	1	3	–	–	–	10	6	1	12	32
London and Outer London	–	4	4	5	–	1	–	8	–	17	2	1	–	6	–	6	2	3	8	51
South East Coast	–	3	–	–	1	1	–	1	2	4	–	–	–	5	–	3	–	–	3	17
Rest Great Britain	–	1	–	1	–	–	–	3	–	–	–	–	–	1	–	2	–	–	–	8
Total	9	21	36	28	8	6	16	34	11	38	9	15	16	17	2	39	51	25	158	223

* The figures to the left of each column relate to eastbound traffic and those to the right to westbound

HOME ORIGINS AND PLACES OF ACCOMPLISHMENT OF WEEKDAY TRAFFIC, 1968

Purpose — Visiting

Thousands

*	Newport		Rest Mon.		West Glos.		Cardiff		Rest Glam.		Hereford & Brecon		Swansea		West Wales		Rest Great Britain		Total	
Bristol	19	6	12	11	2	5	9	28	6	4	2	5	5	9	4	3	4	3	63	74
East Glos.	—	3	—	1	—	4	—	2	—	1	1	1	1	—	1	—	1	—	4	12
Somerset	2	5	15	2	—	1	19	9	9	2	—	1	1	4	1	—	—	13	47	32
Wiltshire	—	3	2	2	—	1	2	4	2	8	—	2	—	8	3	—	—	—	23	28
Devon and Cornwall	—	1	7	—	—	2	5	—	5	5	—	7	2	2	1	—	9	—	18	—
Central Southern England	—	5	5	1	—	1	9	6	12	5	3	—	—	8	7	—	—	1	29	33
London and Outer London	10	2	6	4	—	1	17	14	4	6	—	—	4	—	1	—	—	—	41	28
South East Coast	—	4	3	—	—	—	—	7	2	2	—	—	—	2	—	—	—	—	5	15
Rest Great Britain	—	—	—	—	—	—	—	1	1	1	—	—	—	1	—	—	—	—	1	2
Total	31	29	50	21	2	14	61	66	36	33	6	16	13	34	9	12	14	17	222	242

* The figures to the left of each column relate to eastbound traffic and those to the right to westbound

APPENDIX 9

HOME ORIGINS AND PLACES OF ACCOMPLISHMENT OF WEEKDAY TRAFFIC, 1968

Purpose — Sightseeing

Thousands

*	Newport		Rest Mon.		West Glos.		Cardiff		Rest Glam.		Hereford & Brecon		Swansea		West Wales		Rest Great Britain		Total	
Bristol	6	4	2	48	–	8	18	1	–	5	–	10	4	6	2	–	–	3	32	85
East Glos.	1	–	3	3	–	–	–	5	–	–	–	5	–	–	–	–	–	–	4	13
Somerset	–	7	–	21	3	2	8	–	5	–	–	5	–	4	–	–	2	–	18	39
Wiltshire	3	–	–	2	–	–	3	–	2	–	–	–	–	–	–	–	–	–	8	2
Devon and Cornwall	–	–	–	–	–	–	–	–	–	1	–	–	–	1	–	1	–	–	–	3
Central Southern England	1	–	–	4	–	–	–	2	–	–	–	–	–	–	–	–	–	–	1	7
London and Outer London	–	–	–	1	–	–	–	2	–	3	–	–	–	–	–	–	–	–	–	6
South East Coast	–	1	–	–	–	–	–	1	–	–	–	–	–	–	–	1	–	–	–	3
Rest Great Britain	–	–	–	1	–	–	–	2	–	1	–	–	–	–	–	–	–	–	–	4
Total	11	13	5	80	3	10	29	13	7	10	–	20	4	11	2	2	2	3	63	162

* The figures to the left of each column relate to eastbound traffic and those to the right to westbound

HOME ORIGINS AND PLACES OF ACCOMPLISHMENT OF WEEKDAY TRAFFIC, 1968

Purpose — Paid Entertainment

Thousands

*	Newport	Rest Mon.	West Glos.	Cardiff	Rest Glam.	Hereford & Brecon	Swansea	West Wales	Rest Great Britain	Total
Bristol	8 4	15 6	— —	27 —	5 —	2 —	1 —	— —	1 —	59 10
East Glos.	— —	— —	— —	— —	— —	— —	— —	— —	— —	— —
Somerset	— —	— 2	— —	— —	— —	— —	— —	— —	— —	— 2
Wiltshire	— —	— 1	— —	— —	— 1	— —	— —	— —	— —	— 2
Devon and Cornwall	— —	— —	— —	— —	— —	— —	— —	— —	— —	— —
Central Southern England	— —	— —	— —	— —	— —	— —	— —	— —	— —	— —
London and Outer London	— —	— —	— —	— —	— —	— —	— —	— —	— —	— —
South East Coast	— —	— —	— —	— —	— —	— —	— —	— —	— —	— —
Rest Great Britain	— —	— —	— —	— —	— 1	— —	— —	— —	— —	— 1
Total	8 4	15 9	— —	27 —	5 2	2 —	1 —	— —	1 —	59 15

* The figures to the left of each column relate to eastbound traffic and those to the right to westbound

APPENDIX 11A

EXPENDITURE ON TRIPS TO OR FROM HOLIDAYS: SATURDAY AND SUNDAY, AUGUST 1968

Expenditure per head		Main meals & snacks	Ice-Cream & sweets	Drinks	Entrance Fees	Amuse-ments	Parking Fees	Souvenirs	Other	Groceries & other food	Clothes	Furn-iture	Domestic App. veh & access	Other Purchases	Total
Nil	Cars	49	63	86	126	126	116	110	112	87	127	129	128	124	1,383
	People	176	213	308	455	452	418	394	397	316	457	466	461	453	4,966
1d-1/3d	Cars	3	48	24	1	3	13	6	11	6	—	—	1	1	117
	People	13	196	94	3	13	51	24	46	26	—	—	4	3	473
1/4d-2/3d	Cars	18	16	11	2	—	—	5	5	12	1	—	—	2	72
	People	66	51	45	7	—	—	22	19	44	4	—	—	6	264
2/4d-5/-	Cars	21	3	6	1	—	1	4	—	6	—	—	1	3	46
	People	77	10	14	5	—	1	15	—	24	—	—	5	8	159
5/1d-10/-	Cars	21	—	2	—	1	—	3	1	8	1	—	—	—	37
	People	75	—	8	—	5	—	11	4	29	5	—	—	—	140
10/--£1	Cars	13	—	1	—	—	—	1	—	9	1	1	—	—	26
	People	48	—	1	—	—	—	3	—	28	4	4	—	—	88
Over £1	Cars	5	—	—	—	—	—	1	1	2	—	—	—	—	9
	People	12	—	—	—	—	—	1	4	3	—	—	—	—	20
Total	Cars	130	130	130	130	130	130	130	130	130	130	130	130	130	1,690
	People	470	470	470	470	470	470	470	470	470	470	470	470	470	6,110
Total Expend.	(shgs)	2,080	333	308	35	51	55	278	234	925	106	60	22	43	4,528
Expend. per car	All trips	16.0	2.6	2.4	0.3	0.4	0.4	2.1	1.8	7.1	0.8	0.5	0.2	0.3	34.8
Expend. per head		4.4	0.7	0.7	0.1	0.1	0.1	0.6	0.4	2.0	0.2	0.1	—	0.1	9.6
Expend. per Car	Trips on which item was purchased	25.7	5.0	7.0	8.8	12.8	3.9	13.9	13.0	21.5	35.3	60.0	10.8	7.2	
Expend. per head		7.1	1.3	1.9	2.3	2.8	1.1	3.7	3.2	6.0	8.2	15.0	2.4	2.5	

EXPENDITURE ON VISITING TRIPS: SATURDAY AND SUNDAY, AUGUST 1968

Expenditure per head		Main meals & snacks	Ice-Cream & sweets	Drinks	Entrance Fees	Amuse-ments	Parking Fees	Souvenirs	Other	Groceries & other food	Clothes	Furniture	Domestic App. veh & access	Other Purchases	Total
Nil	Cars	56	46	56	80	83	72	79	79	79	85	87	86	77	964
	People	155	110	153	218	218	203	213	215	212	228	235	234	205	2,599
1d-1/3d	Cars	2	22	7	1	1	10	4	1	1	1	—	—	2	52
	People	8	72	26	3	4	25	12	4	4	3	—	—	7	168
1/4d-2/3d	Cars	3	11	11	3	3	3	—	4	3	—	—	—	1	43
	People	9	36	32	7	13	5	—	7	8	1	—	—	2	119
2/4d-5/-	Cars	9	6	9	1	—	2	1	1	1	1	—	1	1	34
	People	25	14	15	2	—	2	4	4	4	4	—	1	4	83
5/1d-10/-	Cars	8	2	1	2	—	—	2	1	3	—	—	—	4	21
	People	20	3	3	5	—	—	5	4	7	—	—	—	10	49
10/- -£1	Cars	5	—	1	—	—	—	—	1	—	—	—	—	1	9
	People	13	—	1	—	—	—	1	1	—	—	—	—	4	23
Over £1	Cars	4	—	2	—	—	—	1	—	—	—	—	—	1	8
	People	5	—	5	—	—	—	1	1	—	—	—	—	3	14
Total	Cars	87	87	87	87	87	87	87	87	87	87	87	87	87	1,131
	People	235	235	235	235	235	235	235	235	235	235	235	235	235	3,055
Total Expend.	(shgs)	608.5	215.5	330.0	61.5	30.0	42.0	131.0	53.5	86.5	17.0	—	3.5	250.0	1,829
Expend. per Car	All trips	7.0	2.5	3.8	0.7	0.3	0.5	1.5	0.6	1.0	0.2	—	—	2.9	21.0
Expend. per head		2.6	0.9	1.4	0.3	0.1	0.2	0.6	0.2	0.4	0.1	—	—	1.1	7.8
Expend. per Car	Trips on which item was purchased	19.6	5.3	10.6	8.9	7.5	2.8	16.4	6.8	10.9	8.5	—	3.5	25.0	21.0
Expend. per head		7.6	1.7	4.0	3.6	1.8	1.3	6.0	2.7	3.8	2.4	—	3.5	8.3	

APPENDIX 11C

EXPENDITURE ON SIGHTSEEING TRIPS: SATURDAY AND SUNDAY, AUGUST 1968

Expenditure per head		Main meals & snacks	Ice-Cream & sweets	Drinks	Entrance Fees	Amuse-ments	Parking Fees	Souvenirs	Other	Groceries & other food	Clothes	Furniture	Domestic App. veh & access	Other Purchases	Total
Nil	Cars	29	28	34	43	57	43	45	56	56	62	66	64	58	637
	People	1U2	68	119	141	192	140	144	189	194	214	225	220	197	2,145
1d-1/3d	Cars	1	29	16	4	2	19	10	6	3	1	—	—	2	93
	People	4	118	60	20	8	75	46	25	13	3	—	—	7	379
1/4d-2/3d	Cars	3	11	7	9	2	3	3	1	2	—	—	—	—	41
	People	11	35	22	27	6	7	11	5	7	—	—	—	—	131
2/4d-5/-	Cars	10	2	7	7	3	—	3	1	1	—	—	1	1	36
	People	42	4	18	29	11	—	8	4	1	—	—	1	6	124
5/1d-10/-	Cars	8	—	1	2	1	—	3	—	2	2	—	1	2	22
	People	32	—	3	5	5	—	12	—	7	7	—	4	7	82
10/--£1	Cars	11	—	—	—	—	—	—	1	—	—	—	—	3	15
	People	25	—	—	—	—	—	—	1	—	—	—	—	8	34
Over £1	Cars	4	—	—	—	—	—	2	1	2	1	—	—	—	10
	People	9	—	—	—	—	—	4	1	3	1	—	—	—	18
Total	Cars	66	66	65	65	65	65	66	66	66	66	66	66	66	854
	People	225	225	222	222	222	222	225	225	225	225	225	225	225	2,913
Total Expend.	(Shgs)	1,058	202	190	213	96	89	306	94	173	86	—	34	201	2,740
Expend per Car		16.0	3.1	2.9	3.3	1.5	1.4	4.6	1.4	2.6	1.3	—	0.5	3.0	41.5
Expend per Head	All trips	4.7	0.9	0.9	1.0	0.4	0.4	1.4	0.4	0.8	0.4	—	0.2	0.9	12.2
Expend. per Car	Trips on which item was purchased	28.6	5.3	6.1	9.7	12.0	4.0	14.6	9.4	17.3	2.2	—	17.0	25.0	
Expend per Car		8.6	1.3	1.8	2.6	3.2	1.1	3.8	2.6	5.6	7.8	—	6.8	7.2	

AVERAGE HOUSEHOLD EXPENDITURE PER HEAD ON LAST TRIP & TRIP PURPOSE

Last Journey Purpose	Area	Amount Spent						Number of Households
		Nil	Up to 5/-	Up to 10/-	Up to 20/-	Up to 100/-	100/- Plus	
		Percentages						
Sightseeing	Bristol	27	26	23	16	7	1	491
	Thornbury	27	35	18	16	4	—	55
	Newport	21	24	24	24	6	1	241
	Chepstow	17	35	24	17	4	3	78
Visiting	Bristol	45	29	10	9	6	1	131
	Thornbury	48	28	5	14	5	—	21
	Newport	66	14	10	10	—	—	71
	Chepstow	44	37	4	15	—	—	77
Shopping	Bristol	48	23	16	7	2	4	14
	Thornbury	—	—	33	33	34	—	3
	Newport	10	7	20	34	17	12	41
	Chepstow	2	17	15	32	13	21	47
All Purposes	Bristol	31	26	20	14	7	2	693
	Thornbury	32	31	14	18	5	—	84
	Newport	31	21	19	21	6	2	378
	Chepstow	19	29	17	21	6	8	156

TYPE OF EXPENDITURE AND AVERAGE HOUSEHOLD EXPENDITURE PER HEAD

Type	Area	Amount Spent						Number of Households
		Nil	Up to 5/-	Up to 10/-	Up to 20/-	Up to 100/-	100/- plus	
		Percentages						
Meals and Snacks	Bristol	34	29	19	13	4	1	693
	Thornbury	36	41	11	10	2	—	84
	Newport	34	37	15	13	1	—	378
	Chepstow	26	54	13	6	1	—	156
Purchases	Bristol	90	6	1	1	1	1	693
	Thornbury	82	9	8	—	1	—	84
	Newport	87	5	4	2	2	—	378
	Chepstow	67	7	10	6	6	4	156
Entrance Fees	Bristol	91	6	2	1	—	—	693
	Thornbury	89	9	2	—	—	—	84
	Newport	64	18	11	7	—	—	378
	Chepstow	60	30	7	3	—	—	156

GROWTH OF TRAFFIC BY PURPOSE, WEEKDAYS

Each column represents one day's traffic

Purpose	March 1967 No.	%	Aug. 1967 No.	%	April 1968 No.	%	Aug. 1968 No.	%	Nov.1968 No.	%	March 1969 No.	%
Firm's Business	2,671	36.0	3,674	23.1	4,884	48.3	3,609	23.4	3,494	35.4	3,976	37.6
Goods Collection & Delivery	424	5.7	304	1.9	425	4.2	191	1.2	256	2.6	167	1.6
Service & Maintenance	114	1.5	—	0.0	162	1.6	140	0.9	112	1.1	75	0.7
Work — Daily commuters	{1,162	15.7	{530	3.3	862	8.5	{751	4.9	826	8.4	891	8.4
— Others					172	1.7			616	6.2	609	5.8
Shopping	164	2.2	368	2.3	203	2.0	270	1.8	418	4.2	185	1.7
Holidays	592	8.0	3,878	24.4	881	8.7	5,617	36.4	90	0.9	1,029	9.7
Visiting	1,044	14.1	1,808	11.4	1,349	13.3	1,498	9.7	3,558	36.0	2,321	21.9
Sightseeing	{1,136	15.3	3,750	23.6	760	7.5	2,469	16.0	138	1.4	419	4.0
Paid Entertainment			1,342	8.4	200	2.0	517	3.3	160	1.6	235	2.2
Other & Multiple	106	1.4	230	1.4	217	2.1	353	2.3	216	2.2	674	6.4
Total	7,413		15,884		10,115		15,415		9,884		10,581	

APPENDIX 15

GROWTH OF TRAFFIC BY PURPOSE, WEEKENDS

Each column represents one day's traffic

Purpose	August 1967				August 1968				November 1968		May 1969	
	Saturday		Sunday		Saturday		Sunday		Saturday		Saturday	
	No.	%	No.	%	No.	%	No.	%	No.	%	No.	%
Firm's Business	567	2.3	356	1.4	440	1.6	430	1.6	800	9.8	1,055	9.1
Goods Collection & Delivery	73	0.3	41	0.2	130	0.5	40	0.2	144	1.7	} 417	3.6
Service and Maintenance	35	0.1	15	0.1	85	0.3	0	0	24	0.3		
Work	93	0.4	132	0.5	485	1.8	315	1.2	600	7.4	220	1.9
Shopping	725	2.9	123	0.5	725	2.7	65	0.2	1,283	15.8	789	6.8
Holidays	14,164	56.6	6,517	24.8	17,065	57.0	7,330	27.6	86	1.1	2,379	20.5
Visiting	4,961	19.9	9,033	34.4	5,065	19.0	9,965	37.6	3,162	6.6	3,539	30.5
Sightseeing	2,740	10.9	7,964	30.3	2,640	10.0	6,525	24.6	532	11.0	1,311	11.3
Paid Entertainment	696	2.8	1,058	4.0	730	2.6	655	2.4	896	38.8	1,044	9.0
Other and Multiple	980	3.9	1,001	3.8	1,265	4.4	1,190	4.5	614	7.6	847	7.3
Total	25,034		26,240		28,630		26,515		8,144		11,601	

PRE-EASTER WEEKDAY TRAFFIC BETWEEN AREAS 1967-69, LIGHT VEHICLES

(Each row represents traffic for one day)

		Newport	Rest Mon.	West Glos.	Car-diff	Rest Glam.	Here-ford & Brecon	Swan-sea	West Wales	Rest G.B.	Total
Bristol	1967	569	1,180	270	948	438	94	183	98	251	4,031
	1968	827	1,226	377	1,389	462	231	403	114	220	5,249
	1969	790	1,229	340	1,622	528	286	233	26	307	5,361
E. Glos.	1967	6	31	29	43	19	11	15	6	16	176
	1968	45	66	13	156	18	70	58	18	20	464
	1969	32	82	33	146	115	9	18	177	—	612
Somerset	1967	116	376	36	296	137	75	54	28	188	1,306
	1968	230	240	48	347	188	113	78	28	140	1,412
	1969	41	109	34	119	45	60	36	20	41	505
Wilts.	1967	26	65	17	84	23	—	30	—	12	257
	1968	89	90	18	197	79	10	49	13	7	552
	1969	88	72	5	95	114	48	76	20	16	534
Devon Cornwall	1967	43	121	—	94	80	22	18	21	95	494
	1968	22	32	30	75	48	44	68	41	89	449
	1969	64	75	22	144	91	34	9	28	159	626
Central Southern England	1967	21	53	9	130	35	6	38	17	45	354
	1968	34	76	15	92	90	30	24	21	30	412
	1969	122	182	41	358	179	29	100	108	81	1,200
London	1967	69	168	—	205	104	—	83	39	44	712
	1968	140	101	22	367	169	21	58	61	11	950
	1969	47	150	40	445	296	—	188	62	—	1,228
South East Coast	1967	13	34	—	17	40	—	19	11	64	198
	1968	51	36	19	71	37	19	52	12	27	324
	1969	20	39	20	53	39	20	23	45	10	269
Rest G.B.	1967	19	18	—	29	7	—	12	—	4	89
	1968	37	14	7	72	45	10	14	11	—	210
	1969	61	12	—	65	38	—	12	—	7	195
Total	1967	882	2,046	361	1,846	883	208	452	220	719	7,617
	1968	1,475	1,881	549	2,766	1,136	548	804	319	544	10,022
	1969	1,265	1,950	535	3,047	1,445	486	695	486	621	10,530

TRAFFIC BETWEEN AREAS: AUGUST 1967 AND AUGUST 1968, WEEKENDS

		Bristol	East Glos.	Somerset	Wilts	Devon & Cornwall	Central Southern England	London	Outer London	South East Coast	Rest Great Britain	Total
Newport	Aug. 1967	1,482	154	977	373	248	250	111	504	184	67	4,350
	Aug. 1968	1,710	170	1,000	505	470	605	135	280	135	35	5,045
Rest Mon.	Aug. 1967	5,623	377	2,938	946	594	436	172	854	238	109	12,287
	Aug. 1968	4,890	615	2,315	1,120	770	1,230	175	445	330	165	12,055
West Glos.	Aug. 1967	1,891	169	637	247	313	68	—	140	11	—	3,476
	Aug. 1968	1,025	240	445	150	310	225	—	15	30	60	2,500
Cardiff	Aug. 1967	3,703	429	1,801	1,041	732	525	402	1,429	295	186	10,543
	Aug. 1968	2,420	500	1,615	975	880	1,225	400	995	595	225	9,830
Rest Glam.	Aug. 1967	2,426	265	1,193	803	509	347	239	1,192	275	60	7,309
	Aug. 1968	1,930	395	1,270	580	750	1,305	415	1,085	495	165	8,390
Hereford & Brecon	Aug. 1967	1,101	101	744	237	221	54	49	169	17	13	2,706
	Aug. 1968	1,455	140	680	305	520	265	40	110	40	15	3,570
Swansea	Aug. 1967	827	65	457	191	110	66	153	447	158	57	2,531
	Aug. 1968	665	130	515	340	310	565	290	445	225	55	3,540
West Wales	Aug. 1967	1,003	82	485	163	261	144	202	724	90	39	3,193
	Aug. 1968	1,190	75	615	405	240	600	280	775	250	40	4,470
Rest Great Britain	Aug. 1967	983	13	1,514	55	1,232	94	37	207	13	15	4,163
	Aug. 1968	1,100	80	1,670	235	1,835	275	45	80	—	—	5,320
Total	Aug. 1967	19,039	1,655	10,746	4,056	4,220	1,984	1,365	5,666	1,281	546	50,558
	Aug. 1968	16,385	2,345	10,125	4,615	6,085	6,295	1,780	4,230	2,100	760	54,720

AUGUST 1967-68/NOVEMBER 1968 WEEKDAY TRAFFIC BETWEEN AREAS, LIGHT VEHICLES

(Each row represents traffic for one day)

		New-port	Rest Mon.	West Glos.	Car-diff	Rest Glam.	Here-ford & Brecon	Swan-sea	West Wales	Rest G.B.	Total
Bristol	Aug'67	972	1,830	484	1,784	718	570	466	177	332	7,333
	Aug'68	863	1,393	307	1,659	457	246	304	190	331	5,750
	Nov'68	1,012	1,162	290	1,562	510	176	314	62	88	5,176
E. Glos.	Aug'67	10	34	72	96	74	—	—	—	66	352
	Aug'68	69	121	75	215	18	40	22	12	24	596
	Nov'68	84	48	26	142	—	—	—	—	—	300
Somerset	Aug'67	578	544	386	926	268	66	104	130	284	3,286
	Aug'68	431	655	137	630	276	148	196	174	252	2,899
	Nov'68	150	246	32	302	88	46	38	32	256	1,190
Wilts.	Aug'67	268	172	52	156	52	28	58	28	32	846
	Aug'68	70	118	19	187	96	40	43	36	23	632
	Nov'68	52	—	—	30	180	42	122	76	34	536
Devon & Cornwall	Aug'67	114	128	—	126	32	56	8	92	220	776
	Aug'68	70	193	51	206	188	102	221	105	389	1,525
	Nov'68	32	72	42	86	44	80	22	—	96	474
Central Southern England	Aug'67	130	194	30	304	78	—	34	154	108	1,032
	Aug'68	145	229	8	208	127	59	145	199	101	1,221
	Nov'68	84	54	26	240	192	22	108	92	—	818
London	Aug'67	238	182	180	388	298	8	234	304	95	1,927
	Aug'68	96	176	31	391	245	15	238	263	80	1,535
	Nov'68	166	174	—	508	100	28	16	34	—	1,026
South East Coast	Aug'67	—	54	34	50	11	—	22	86	64	321
	Aug'68	84	17	11	45	95	23	69	63	27	434
	Nov'68	46	30	—	108	68	—	13	—	26	291
Rest G.B.	Aug'67	—	22	44	8	—	—	—	54	—	128
	Aug'68	52	25	2	149	58	9	39	12	19	365
	Nov'68	26	—	—	—	—	—	—	—	—	26
Total	Aug'67	2,310	3,160	1,282	3,838	1,531	728	926	1,025	1,201	16,001
	Aug'68	1,880	2,927	641	3,690	1,560	682	1,277	1,054	1,246	14,957
	Nov'68	1,652	1,786	416	2,978	1,182	394	633	296	500	9,837

The August 1967 and November 1968 figures are based on a survey in one direction for one day doubled to represent the two way flow. August 1968 is based on a survey for one day in each direction.

AUGUST WEEKDAY TRAFFIC 1966 AND 1967 CROSSING SCREENLINE, LIGHT VEHICLES

Origin / Dest.		New-port	Rest Mon.	West Glos.	Car-diff	Rest Glam.	Here-ford & Brecon	Swan-sea	West Wales	Rest G.B.	Total
Bristol	1966	165	221	267	329	141	344	133	146	35	1,781
	a 1967	946	1,200	575	1,455	469	318	469	339	305	6,076
	b 1967	5	14	109	11	—	77	2	3	23	244
E. Glos.	1966	310	675	6,770	567	92	1,319	122	177	27	10,059
	a 1967	63	131	107	108	99	56	39	19	24	646
	b 1967	177	586	7,353	256	108	1,628	134	157	89	10,488
Somerset	1966	68	77	67	132	40	123	65	102	50	724
	a 1967	327	404	398	500	152	123	169	139	261	2,473
	b 1967	2	21	24	13	—	26	6	9	8	109
Wilts.	1966	41	77	43	49	21	160	18	55	54	518
	a 1967	144	165	110	176	99	71	49	44	69	927
	b 1967	3	12	53	—	6	47	3	11	23	158
Devon & Cornwall	1966	40	56	12	110	54	91	40	37	90	530
	a 1967	98	156	26	214	154	114	9	214	385	1,370
	b 1967	—	1	12	11	—	32	2	3	23	84
Central Southern England	1966	149	304	81	320	108	323	159	254	82	1,780
	a 1967	140	216	166	334	179	91	139	139	65	1,469
	b 1967	31	90	175	137	79	263	97	112	76	1,060
London	1966	249	328	141	514	297	286	364	469	39	2,687
	a 1967	173	130	87	241	108	24	185	181	14	1,143
	b 1967	75	149	129	188	135	178	177	352	60	1,443
South East Coast	1966	66	108	29	136	79	152	88	171	13	842
	a 1967	54	57	15	107	91	31	73	77	13	518
	b 1967	7	43	45	35	18	94	29	60	18	349
Rest G.B.	1966	333	536	309	845	350	738	317	197	4	3,629
	a 1967	5	2	40	37	24	10	14	13	14	159
	b 1967	342	547	243	794	392	632	271	228	21	3,470
Total	1966	1,421	2,382	7,719	3,002	1,182	3,536	1,306	1,608	394	22,550
	a 1967	1,950	2,461	1,524	3,172	1,375	838	1,146	1,165	1,150	14,781
	b 1967	642	1,463	8,143	1,445	738	2,977	721	935	341	17,405

a Crossing the screenline at the Bridge
b Crossing the screenline at other points

AVERAGE NUMBER OF OCCUPANTS FOR EACH PURPOSE, ALL SURVEYS

Purpose	Weekdays							Weekends				
	Mar '67 Mon & Tues.	Aug '67 Tues.	Ap. '68 Mon & Tues.	Aug '68 Mon & Tues.	Nov '68 Fri.	Mar '69 Fri.	Mar '69 Mon.	Aug '67 Sat.	Aug '67 Sun.	Aug '68 Sat.	Aug '68 Sun.	Nov '68 Sat.
Firm's Business	1.4	1.5	1.4	1.4	1.8	1.3	1.3	2.0	2.2	1.6	2.1	1.7
Collection & Delivery	1.3	1.9	1.3	1.9	1.2	1.0	1.3	1.9	4.1	1.8	2.3	2.0
Service & Maintenance	1.2	–	1.3	1.5	1.0	1.3	1.6	1.8	–	1.5	–	2.1
Work	1.6	1.8	1.7	1.6	1.7	1.7	1.6	1.5	1.4	1.6	1.6	1.5
Shopping	2.6	2.9	2.1	3.1	2.6	2.3	2.0	3.0	2.2	3.2	2.7	3.0
Holidays	2.2	2.7	2.4	2.8	2.3	2.3	2.5	3.3	3.1	3.3	3.0	2.5
Visiting	2.2	2.7	2.2	2.6	2.1	2.3	2.2	2.8	2.8	2.7	2.7	2.6
Sightseeing	2.6	3.2	3.6	3.4	1.6	2.7	2.3	3.4	3.4	3.2	3.3	2.5
Paid Entertainment		3.3	2.5	3.6	2.3	2.6	2.0	3.3	3.7	3.1	3.6	2.7
Other & Multiple	1.9	1.9	2.2	2.1	1.6	1.8	1.8	2.4	2.8	2.8	2.7	2.6
Overall Average	1.8	2.5	1.8	2.5	1.9	1.9	1.7	3.1	3.1	3.0	2.9	2.5

APPENDIX 21

AGE AND SEX GROUPS OF SAMPLE POPULATIONS

Area	Children under 15 years (1)	(2)	Females 15–24 (1)	(2)	25–39 (1)	(2)	40–65 (1)	(2)	65 plus (1)	(2)	Males 15–24 (1)	(2)	25–39 (1)	(2)	40–65 (1)	(2)	65 plus (1)	(2)	Total Number of People In Households (1)	(2)
Bristol	24	29	5	5	10	12	17	13	6	7	4	4	12	12	17	13	5	5	2,045	793
Thornbury	26	22	4	5	12	12	16	15	5	8	6	4	12	12	15	15	4	7	252	60
Newport Stage 1	24	21	4	—	11	9	16	13	7	17	4	3	10	10	17	15	5	12	972	210
Newport Stage 2	17	12	4	3	12	11	18	18	8	22	3	—	14	10	17	15	7	9	983	103
Ebbw Vale	21	24	7	5	6	7	15	10	9	15	6	9	9	8	16	9	11	12	424	162
Chepstow	21	17	6	—	10	—	17	22	8	17	5	11	10	—	16	27	7	5	468	51

Percentages

(1) Users
(2) Non-Users

SOCIO-ECONOMIC GROUP OF HEAD OF HOUSEHOLD USERS & NON-USERS

Percentages

Socio-Economic Group	Bristol		Thornbury		Newport Stage 1		Newport Stage 2		Ebbw Vale		Chepstow	
	(1)	(2)	(1)	(2)	(1)	(2)	(1)	(2)	(1)	(2)	(1)	(2)
(1) Employers & Managers of over 25 Employees	5	—	1	—	5	1	4	—	—	—	1	—
(2) Professional Workers	7	5	20	—	15	2	7	2	4	2	5	—
(3) Intermediate Non-Manual & Employers & Managers of less than 25 Employees	24	10	23	—	26	9	28	17	9	6	15	28
(4) Junior Non-Manual	5	2	5	—	6	2	4	12	6	—	5	—
(5) Foremen & Skilled Manual	27	24	21	—	16	22	22	11	19	17	30	29
(6) Semi-Skilled Manual	17	25	13	45	17	20	21	13	42	46	25	—
(7) Unskilled Manual	5	16	5	—	4	19	5	10	11	16	7	29
(8) Personal Service & Agricultural Workers, Widows etc	10	18	12	55	11	25	9	35	9	13	12	14
	100	100	100	100	100	100	100	100	100	100	100	100

| Total Number of Households | 693 | 280 | 84 | 21 | 371 | 98 | 378 | 40 | 135 | 59 | 156 | 18 |

(1) Users
(2) Non-Users

APPENDIX 23

HOUSE AND CAR OWNERSHIP OF HOUSEHOLDS

	Bristol		Thornbury		Newport Stage 1		Newport Stage 2		Ebbw Vale		Chepstow	
	(1)	(2)	(1)	(2)	(1)	(2)	(1)	(2)	(1)	(2)	(1)	(2)
Owner Occupied	61%	39%	56%	22%	89%	77%	76%	57%	59%	53%	42%	15%
Local Authority Rented	34%	57%	44%	77%	2%	3%	20%	38%	29%	42%	50%	77%
Private Rented	5%	4%	—	1%	9%	20%	4%	5%	12%	5%	8%	8%
Total Number of Households	693	280	84	21	371	98	378	40	135	59	156	18
Car Owner	70%	41%	78%	22%	63%	28%	66%	25%	50%	24%	58%	29%
Non-Car Owner	30%	59%	22%	78%	37%	72%	34%	75%	50%	76%	42%	71%
Total Number of Households	693	280	84	21	371	98	378	40	135	59	156	18

(1) Users

(2) Non-Users

GEOGRAPHICAL AREA AND AVERAGE TRIPS FOR HOUSEHOLD BY PURPOSE

Area	Total Households in Sample	User Households as Percentage of Total			Average Trips Per Household					
					User Households			All Households		
		Sightseeing and Paid Ent.	Visiting	Shopping	Sightseeing and Paid Ent.	Visiting	Shopping	Sightseeing and Paid Ent.	Visiting	Shopping
Bristol	973	57	17	6	3.6	7.2	2.4	2.0	1.2	0.2
Thornbury	103	68	68	11	4.2	7.6	4.5	2.9	5.2	0.5
Newport Stage 1	468	56	26	21	4.0	6.9	3.5	2.3	1.8	0.7
Newport Stage 2	418	77	29	24	7.4	9.3	5.2	5.7	2.7	1.3
Ebbw Vale	194	56	18	26	2.5	3.2	3.0	1.4	0.6	0.6
Chepstow	174	80	37	72	7.9	8.5	8.7	6.4	3.2	6.2

SOCIO-ECONOMIC GROUP AND AVERAGE TRIPS PER HOUSEHOLD BY PURPOSE

Socio-Economic Group	Total Households in Group	User Households as Percentage of Total			Average Trips Per Household					
					User Households			All Households		
		Sightseeing and Paid Ent.	Visiting	Shopping	Sightseeing and Paid Ent.	Visiting	Shopping	Sightseeing and Paid Ent.	Visiting	Shopping
(1) Employers & Managers of over 25 Employees	72	79	42	21	6.9	4.9	4.5	5.5	2.0	0.9
(2) Professional Workers	179	67	39	28	5.8	8.5	5.2	3.9	3.3	1.5
(3) Intermediate Non-Manual Workers & Employers & Managers of less than 25 Employees	475	71	31	20	5.7	8.2	5.2	4.0	2.5	1.0
(4) Junior Non Manual	105	65	32	16	4.7	8.2	4.0	3.0	2.7	0.6
(5) Foremen & Skilled Manual	527	65	22	21	4.9	7.9	5.7	3.2	1.7	1.2
(6) Semi-Skilled Manual	498	63	15	16	4.9	7.3	5.2	3.1	1.1	0.9
(7) Unskilled Manual	181	45	10	11	2.9	6.6	5.1	1.3	0.7	0.6
(8) Personal Service & Agricultural Workers, Widows	295	54	30	12	3.1	6.2	3.4	1.5	1.9	0.4

PRE AND POST-BRIDGE METHOD OF TRAVEL BY AREA AND PURPOSE

A. Post-Bridge Method of Travel

Sightseeing and Entertainment

Area	No. of User households	Method of Travel %		
		Car	Special Bus	Scheduled Bus
Bristol	551	76	16	5
Thornbury	70	89	9	3
Newport (1 & 2)	587	78	16	6
Ebbw Vale	109	35	64	1
Chepstow	140	61	18	21

Visiting

Area	No. of User households	Method of Travel %		
		Car	Special Bus	Scheduled Bus
Bristol	165	86	3	11
Thornbury	32	97	3	—
Newport (1 & 2)	216	89	2	9
Ebbw Vale	35	74	3	23
Chepstow	65	71	3	25

Shopping

Area	No. of User households	Method of Travel %		
		Car	Special Bus	Scheduled Bus
Newport (1 & 2)	198	82	3	15
Ebbw Vale	50	58	40	2
Chepstow	125	47	4	49

B. Pre-Bridge Method of Travel of Post-Bridge Users

Sightseeing and Entertainment

Area	No. of User households	Method of Travel %		
		None	Rail	Car
Bristol	551	84	2	14
Thornbury	70	84	3	13
Newport (1 & 2)	587	71	4	25
Ebbw Vale	109	94	2	4
Chepstow	140	68	11	21

Visiting

Area	No. of User households	Method of Travel %		
		None	Rail	Car
Bristol	165	16	35	49
Thornbury	32	28	13	59
Newport (1 & 2)	216	23	19	58
Ebbw Vale	35	11	40	49
Chepstow	65	22	22	57

Shopping

Area	No. of User households	Method of Travel %		
		None	Rail	Car
Newport (1 & 2)	198	84	5	11
Ebbw Vale	50	96	2	2
Chepstow	125	76	14	10

APPENDIX 27   NET MOVEMENTS OF BUS AND COACH PASSENGERS BY SUB-AREA

Area	1966-67		1968		1969	
	Gain	Loss	Gain	Loss	Gain	Loss
North Gloucestershire						
Bristol	49,246	8,710	5,619	947	1,101	1,010
North Wiltshire	229		1,900		1,859	
Bath	11,178		2,970		3,953	
Weston, Cheddar, Wells	41,896			2,544	3,941	
Central Somerset	8,998		2,971		4,102	
Dorset	7,789		5,869		6,074	
Torbay – Exeter	87		4,569		8,140	
Bodmin – Exmoor	10,197		5,105		4,419	
Plymouth	270		1,102		1,102	
West Cornwall		117	3,334		2,918	
South East (incl. London)			17,676		21,278	
	129,890	8,827	51,115	3,491	58,887	1,010
Forest of Dean, Wye Valley						
Newport	21,619	25,211	24,263	6,807	20,536	6,165
Cardiff		76,167		22,025		23,346
North Monmouthshire		900	226		295	
Central & Eastern Valleys		127,408		33,455		33,906
Barry		3,000		4,740		7,229
Bridgend, Porthcawl		229		1,337		1,370
Swansea, Port Talbot		66,472		32,723		29,611
Brecon	81		200		108	
Carmaerthen, Pembroke		5,791				
Cardigan, Radnor		98	4,550	4,330	4,223	4,230
	21,700	305,276	29,239	105,417	25,162	105,857

ESTIMATED COMMODITIES CROSSING 1968

	Commodity	No. of vehicles	% Empty	Average carrying cap. of vehicles Tons
1.	Food, Drink, Tabacco	205,400	36	10.2
2.	Metal Manufacturers	157,900	28	8.8
3.	Steel	137,700	31	14.6
4.	Other	82,600	39	9.0
5.	Building Materials	82,200	35	12.6
6.	Coal	78,900	40	14.2
7.	Agricultural Requisites	78,200	38	11.3
8.	Chemicals	67,200	41	11.9
9.	Non Metal Manufacturers	64,400	16	7.2
10.	Petrol	60,100	38	15.2
11.	Paper	55,400	33	10.4
12.	Furniture (incl. Removals)	46,000	28	5.4
13.	Wood	44,500	20	11.1
14.	Road Making Materials	33,500	39	12.1
15.	Multiple - Not Known	24,500	45	9.6
16.	Other Raw Materials	14,600	36	13.5
17.	Livestock	10,700	30	9.3
	Total	1,244,000	34	10.9

AUGUST WEEKDAY 1966 AND 1967 TRAFFIC CROSSING SCREENLINE, HEAVY VEHICLES

Origin	Dest.	New-port	Rest Mon.	West Glos.	Car-diff	Rest Glam.	Here-ford & Brecon	Swan-sea	West Wales	Rest G.B.	Total
Bristol	1966	123	99	76	176	30	225	75	104	2	910
	a 1967	397	190	156	388	124	61	128	62	37	1,543
	b 1967	—	2	47	1	—	120	—	—	20	190
E. Glos.	1966	148	268	1,235	165	75	427	77	37	3	2,465
	a 1967	18	22	7	44	12	—	14	9	—	126
	b 1967	65	168	1,044	88	98	356	34	48	28	1,929
Somerset	1966	14	20	16	60	13	54	12	10	2	201
	a 1967	133	37	8	20	27	11	12	21	14	283
	b 1967	—	6	14	—	1	9	—	2	8	40
Wilt-shire	1966	18	3	32	37	10	39	33	5	3	180
	a 1967	50	—	16	85	37	7	28	11	—	234
	b 1967	—	2	40	7	—	23	—	2	1	75
Devon & Cornwall	1966	37	8	10	16	8	11	17	—	9	116
	a 1967	18	20	12	23	—	14	—	9	2	98
	b 1967	—	1	4	2	—	5	—	—	7	19
Central Southern England	1966	82	85	74	125	91	55	42	13	12	579
	a 1967	55	14	3	62	71	1	9	—	4	219
	b 1967	31	45	33	49	30	38	29	32	—	287
London	1966	150	169	83	200	81	84	112	42	15	936
	a 1967	120	15	—	110	85	7	28	34	—	399
	b 1967	65	144	95	60	71	111	56	42	2	646
South East Coast	1966	29	27	26	46	19	31	4	33	—	215
	a 1967	15	4	—	46	13	—	—	13	—	91
	b 1967	20	12	16	7	2	16	6	10	—	89
Rest G.B.	1966	467	338	270	561	234	153	197	54	4	2,078
	a 1967	16	5	—	63	—	—	4	—	—	88
	b 1967	569	316	212	491	274	185	145	14	14	2,220
Total	1966	1068	1,017	1,822	1386	361	1079	569	296	50	7,650
	a 1967	822	307	202	841	369	101	223	159	57	3,081
	b 1967	750	696	1,505	705	476	863	270	150	80	5,495

a Crossing the screenline at the Bridge.
b Crossing the screenline at other points.

See continuation sheet

PRE-EASTER WEEKDAY TRAFFIC BETWEEN AREAS 1967-68, HEAVY VEHICLES

(Each row represents traffic for one day)

		New-port	Rest Mon.	West Glos.	Car-diff	Rest Glam.	*Here-ford & Brecon	Swan-sea	West Wales	Rest G.B.	Total
Bristol	1967	273	153	33	267	91	—	139	57	113	1126
	1968	273	250	73	489	170	97	168	147	25	1692
E. Glos.	1967	67	31	0	32	25	—	8	7	9	179
	1968	79	11	7	93	65	0	27	7	0	289
Somerset	1967	110	54	27	40	32	—	26	20	22	331
	1968	39	40	22	74	31	11	4	20	5	246
Wilts	1967	28	13	6	36	33	—	24	26	4	170
	1968	69	37	15	100	44	3	84	8	0	360
Devon Cornwall	1967	28	26	26	2	34	—	34	0	21	171
	1968	42	2	13	27	19	0	10	0	3	116
Central Southern England	1967	27	41	0	48	36	—	11	5	0	168
	1968	109	43	25	137	114	11	77	6	4	526
London	1967	92	20	0	77	45	—	42	20	0	296
	1968	194	42	14	144	85	15	89	7	0	590
South East Coast	1967	38	18	0	29	22	—	5	5	0	117
	1968	53	3	0	25	10	0	3	0	0	94
Rest G.B.	1967	21	6	0	11	9	—	5	0	7	59
	1968	26	7	0	52	10	0	3	0	0	98
Total	1967	684	362	92	542	327	—	294	140	176	2617
	1968	884	435	169	1141	548	137	465	195	37	4011

(*Hereford and Brecon included with Rest in 1967)

151

TRANSPORT METHODS USED TO CARRY GOODS TO EACH DESTINATION
(Manufacturers Employing 100+, First and Second Surveys)

Destination	Survey	Firms Located in South East Wales								Firms Located in South West North							
		Own Vehicles		Road Hauliers		British Rail		Other Methods		Own Vehicles		Road Hauliers		British Rail		Other Methods	
		No.	%	No.	%	No.	%	No.	%	No.	%	No.	%	No.	%	No.	%
South Wales	1st survey Pre-Bridge	123	65	83	44	55	29	13	7	107	47	101	45	74	33	14	6
	2nd survey 1968-69	129	60	118	55	49	23	16	7	147	60	123	50	52	21	21	9
South West	1st survey Pre-Bridge	80	43	89	47	61	32	16	9	160	71	123	54	74	33	22	10
	2nd survey 1968-69	101	47	119	55	52	24	16	7	191	78	145	59	58	24	20	8
Other	1st survey Pre-Bridge	115	61	123	65	100	53	22	12	134	59	146	65	108	48	30	13
London and South East	2nd survey 1968-69	104	48	127	59	70	32	16	7	152	62	160	65	74	30	21	9
Rest of England and Wales	2nd survey 1968-69	97	45	137	63	76	35	17	8	136	55	161	66	78	32	21	9

ORIGINS AND DESTINATIONS OF COMMODITIES – FOOD, DRINK AND TOBACCO

Number of loaded vehicles, 1968.

		Newport	Rest Mon.	West Glos.	Cardiff	Rest Glam.	Hereford & Brecon	Swansea	West Wales	Rest G.B.	Total
Bristol	e'bnd	3,057	1,960	569	5,702	2,951	548	978	—	144	15,910
	w'bnd	6,873	7,444	1,228	16,918	3,791	2,553	6,593	480	144	45,423
East Glos.	e'bnd	394	—	—	1,568	—	—	—	—	—	1,962
	w'bnd	1,277	—	290	3,167	—	—	2,054	277	—	6,890
Somerset	e'bnd	701	175	428	685	492	—	432	—	—	2,914
	w'bnd	336	—	—	2,002	394	—	1,812	384	—	4,948
Wilts	e'bnd	525	288	—	995	958	144	724	292	—	3,924
	w'bnd	1,056	511	—	4,746	234	—	3,931	192	—	10,670
Devon & Cornwall	e'bnd	213	788	—	788	—	—	—	292	—	2,471
	w'bnd	876	—	—	1,326	868	—	—	—	—	3,070
Central Southern England	e'bnd	691	—	175	851	—	—	—	1,168	—	2,885
	w'bnd	1,094	—	—	3,492	234	—	1,082	—	388	6,138
London	e'bnd	1,015	332	—	415	2,087	388	—	1,167	499	5,090
	w'bnd	3,131	432	611	6,294	2,602	—	826	—	—	12,784
South East Coast	e'bnd	528	117	—	—	—	—	144	527	—	1,924
	w'bnd	—	—	—	462	336	—	—	—	—	798
Rest G.B.	e'bnd	476	—	—	—	—	—	394	—	—	870
	w'bnd	726	—	—	1,246	—	—	—	—	—	1,972
Total	e'bnd	7,602	3,661	1,173	9,955	7,762	1,080	2,673	1,343	1,031	37,001
	w'bnd	15,098	8,357	2,116	39,698	8,459	2,553	15,645	1,333	144	93,800

APPENDIX 32

ORIGINS AND DESTINATIONS OF COMMODITIES – METAL MANUFACTURE

Number of loaded vehicles, 1968.

		Newport	Rest Mon.	West Glos.	Cardiff	Rest Glam.	Hereford & Brecon	Swansea	West Wales	Rest G.B.	Total
Bristol	e'bnd	401	3,007	475	5,140	4,833	325	2,062	–	676	16,921
	w'bnd	8,645	2,705	954	7,930	3,341	271	3,075	2,688	–	29,610
East Glos.	e'bnd	1,885	–	–	2,149	–	–	–	–	–	4,035
	w'bnd	596	–	138	–	822	–	276	379	–	2,214
Somerset	e'bnd	929	–	–	688	163	–	1,024	–	–	2,804
	w'bnd	1,136	–	–	1,507	–	–	735	–	431	3,808
Wilts	e'bnd	–	431	–	1,306	–	–	276	230	–	2,243
	w'bnd	2,082	–	–	1,773	677	276	1,718	–	–	6,525
Devon & Cornwall	e'bnd	230	–	–	108	–	–	–	–	–	338
	w'bnd	764	138	–	688	309	–	597	–	–	2,470
Central Southern England	e'bnd	476	751	–	334	163	–	–	944	230	2,898
	w'bnd	2,200	542	–	4,138	1,068	–	643	276	–	8,868
London	e'bnd	1,583	815	–	2,294	2,093	–	421	–	–	5,782
	w'bnd	3,924	1,576	414	5,747	1,102	276	4,214	431	–	17,967
South East Coast	e'bnd	661	414	–	1,055	276	–	–	–	–	2,404
	w'bnd	–	–	–	785	–	–	–	–	–	785
Rest G.B.	e'bnd	–	–	–	459	–	–	–	–	–	459
	w'bnd	345	–	263	792	–	–	–	551	–	1,964
Total	e'bnd	6,164	5,418	475	13,698	7,527	325	3,371	1,174	906	40,606
	w'bnd	19,691	4,961	1,781	23,334	7,322	822	11,268	4,326	430	73,928

ORIGINS AND DESTINATIONS OF COMMODITIES — STEEL

Number of loaded vehicles, 1968.

		Newport	Rest Mon.	West Glos.	Cardiff	Rest Glam.	Hereford & Brecon	Swansea	West Wales	Rest G.B.	Total
Bristol	e'bnd	3,515	912	156	3,680	1,959	156	2,276	218	602	13,476
	w'bnd	2,356	546	1,063	2,637	421	—	2,200	372	104	9,702
East Glos	e'bnd	3,945	956	—	370	602	—	—	—	—	5,959
	w'bnd	946	—	—	1,725	—	—	164	—	—	2,836
Somerset	e'bnd	1,453	764	783	736	104	—	562	—	109	4,511
	w'bnd	—	361	—	1,470	—	—	218	—	—	2,050
Wilts	e'bnd	3,617	241	—	405	1,080	—	261	—	—	5,604
	w'bnd	2,769	—	—	261	—	—	1,782	—	—	4,812
Devon & Cornwall	e'bnd	578	—	—	491	—	—	327	—	—	1,396
	w'bnd	—	261	—	783	209	—	261	—	—	1,513
Central Southern England	e'bnd	2,818	301	—	903	3,620	—	1,338	—	—	8,817
	w'bnd	3,317	—	436	1,076	1,058	—	538	—	—	5,989
London	e'bnd	8,520	104	—	3,127	740	—	2,776	—	—	15,239
	w'bnd	156	—	—	1,092	1,443	—	709	261	—	3,880
South East Coast	e'bnd	365	—	—	956	—	—	—	—	—	1,321
	w'bnd	—	156	—	—	—	—	—	—	—	156
Rest G.B.	e'bnd	5,598	104	—	—	—	—	722	—	—	6,425
	w'bnd	1,295	363	—	—	—	—	261	—	—	1,919
Total	e'bnd	30,492	3,382	1,376	10,669	7,476	156	8,263	218	711	62,745
	w'bnd	10,840	1,686	1,063	8,927	3,131	—	6,133	633	104	32,855

L

ORIGINS AND DESTINATIONS OF COMMODITIES – BUILDING MATERIALS

Number of loaded vehicles, 1968.

		Newport	Rest Mon.	West Glos.	Cardiff	Rest Glam.	Hereford & Brecon	Swansea	West Wales	Rest G.B.	Total
Bristol	e'bnd	1,708	681	291	1,340	1,187	834	221	–	–	5,810
	w'bnd	2,778	1,562	821	744	1,420	313	251	–	233	8,122
East Glos.	e'bnd	901	233	–	–	–	–	231	–	–	1,365
	w'bnd	–	416	–	–	175	–	–	462	–	1,063
Somerset	e'bnd	324	811	–	879	139	–	–	–	–	2,639
	w'bnd	736	648	–	694	–	369	–	291	–	2,737
Wilts.	e'bnd	786	–	466	291	–	–	–	–	–	1,543
	w'bnd	590	1,262	233	648	–	–	–	–	–	2,732
Devon & Cornwall	e'bnd	1,403	1,568	369	–	–	–	–	–	–	3,339
	w'bnd	324	–	–	231	–	855	811	–	–	2,221
Central Southern England	e'bnd	347	546	–	503	–	–	–	–	–	1,396
	w'bnd	2,075	394	–	2,397	1,970	277	116	–	–	7,227
London	e'bnd	1,246	–	–	766	1,475	–	–	–	–	3,486
	w'bnd	768	302	–	590	1,881	139	721	1,114	–	5,340
South East Coast	e'bnd	815	151	–	–	–	–	–	–	–	966
	w'bnd	959	175	–	590	–	–	–	694	–	2,098
Rest G.B.	e'bnd	93	6	–	–	–	–	–	–	–	93
	w'bnd	302	–	–	–	–	–	–	–	–	302
Total	e'bnd	8,109	3,990	1,126	3,779	2,800	834	452	–	–	21,090
	w'bnd	8,212	4,759	1,054	5,894	5,442	1,953	1,900	2,562	233	32,036

ORIGINS AND DESTINATIONS OF COMMODITIES — COAL

Number of loaded vehicles, 1968.

		Newport	Rest Mon.	West Glos.	Cardiff	Rest Glam.	Hereford & Brecon	Swansea	West Wales	Rest G.B.	Total
Bristol	e'bnd w'bnd	2,669	612	—	3,500	2,842	164	249	—	—	10,037
East Glos.	e'bnd w'bnd	—	750	—	461	1,938	—	374	748	—	4,122
Somerset	e'bnd w'bnd	701	1,635	—	494	2,315	—	556	414	—	6,116
Wilts.	e'bnd w'bnd	450	219	164	225	2,257	—	522	557	375	4,772
Devon & Cornwall	e'bnd w'bnd	1,152	—	—	219	910	—	225	—	—	2,503
Central Southern England	e'bnd w'bnd	658	—	—	2,147	2,486	—	688	476	444	6,902
London	e'bnd w'bnd	906	749	—	351	742	—	707	—	—	4,114
South East Coast	e'bnd w'bnd	—	—	262	311	289	—	—	—	—	863
Rest G.B.	e'bnd w'bnd	225	—	—	488	384	—	—	595	—	1,692
Total	e'bnd w'bnd	7,442	4,186	427	8,125	14,602	164	3,322	2,704	819	41,271

ORIGINS AND DESTINATIONS OF COMMODITIES – AGRICULTURAL REQUISITES

Number of loaded vehicles, 1968.

		Newport	Rest Mon.	West Glos.	Cardiff	Rest Glam.	Hereford & Bracon	Swansea	West Wales	Rest G.B.	Total
Bristol	e'bnd	138	1,675	528	1,016	–	893	639	397	–	5,286
	w'bnd	1,030	10,002	1,145	1,737	3,322	4,823	1,592	6,793	449	30,893
East Glos.	e'bnd	–	–	–	–	–	–	–	–	–	–
	w'bnd	–	265	–	323	506	–	–	–	–	1,093
Somerset	e'bnd	–	–	–	–	276	–	159	–	317	752
	w'bnd	528	–	–	838	–	1,166	–	–	–	2,534
Wilts.	e'bnd	–	–	–	317	634	–	–	–	–	951
	w'bnd	–	397	–	317	397	–	138	265	–	1,514
Devon & Cornwall	e'bnd	–	317	–	–	–	–	184	–	–	501
	w'bnd	–	–	–	159	–	–	–	–	–	159
Central Southern England	e'bnd	–	–	–	–	–	–	–	–	–	–
	w'bnd	370	460	–	–	–	–	–	138	–	968
London	e'bnd	414	–	–	–	–	–	–	–	–	414
	w'bnd	1,091	–	–	–	441	230	–	177	–	2,112
South East Coast	e'bnd	–	–	–	–	–	–	–	–	–	–
	w'bnd	221	–	–	–	–	–	–	–	–	221
Rest G.B.	e'bnd	–	–	–	–	–	–	–	–	–	–
	w'bnd	265	–	221	317	88	–	–	–	–	891
Total	e'bnd	551	1,992	528	1,333	910	893	982	397	317	7,904
	w'bnd	3,678	9,818	1,366	3,690	4,755	6,219	1,730	7,372	449	40,385

ORIGINS AND DESTINATIONS OF COMMODITIES — CHEMICALS

Number of loaded vehicles, 1968.

		Newport	Rest Mon.	West Glos.	Cardiff	Rest Glam.	Hereford & Brecon	Swansea	West Wales	Rest G.B.	Total
Bristol	e'bnd	827	834	—	2,343	1,161	—	536	—	431	5,252
	w'bnd	1,920	1,492	1,095	2,959	590	391	—	491	313	9,251
East Glos.	e'bnd	—	—	—	1,229	—	—	1,083	—	—	2,312
	w'bnd	—	—	590	—	548	—	—	—	—	1,137
Somerset	e'bnd	—	—	431	262	431	—	1,027	—	216	2,367
	w'bnd	590	—	—	1,570	1,081	—	—	—	—	3,241
Wilts.	e'bnd	556	156	—	365	287	327	328	—	—	2,020
	w'bnd	1,081	491	—	590	—	—	—	—	—	2,162
Devon & Cornwall	e'bnd	—	—	—	—	—	—	—	—	—	—
	w'bnd	—	—	—	—	—	—	491	—	—	491
Central Southern England	e'bnd	412	—	—	131	574	—	359	—	—	1,477
	w'bnd	804	—	—	—	1,587	—	—	—	—	2,391
London	e'bnd	1,416	393	—	1,027	131	—	353	—	—	3,321
	w'bnd	1,685	—	—	491	704	—	786	—	—	2,962
South East Coast	e'bnd	—	—	—	—	—	—	—	—	—	—
	w'bnd	—	—	—	—	—	—	—	—	—	—
Rest G.B.	e'bnd	—	—	—	—	—	—	—	—	—	469
	w'bnd	—	—	—	—	—	—	—	—	—	—
Total	e'bnd	3,259	1,384	431	5,257	2,586	327	3,686	—	647	17,679
	w'bnd	5,959	1,983	1,685	5,610	4,509	391	1,277	491	313	22,220

ORIGINS AND DESTINATIONS OF COMMODITIES – NON-METAL MANUFACTURE

Number of loaded vehicles, 1968.

		Newport	Rest Mon.	West Glos.	Cardiff	Rest Glam.	Hereford & Brecon	Swansea	West Wales	Rest G.B.	Total
Bristol	e'bnd	2,203	1,808	569	3,818	1,050	1,279	1,767	987	1,687	14,763
	w'bnd	2,921	2,264	341	2,628	2,544	–	1,371	1,782	–	13,852
East Glos.	e'bnd	–	–	–	328	–	–	–	–	–	328
	w'bnd	459	–	–	–	256	–	262	–	–	977
Somerset	e'bnd	230	–	–	–	307	–	262	–	–	799
	w'bnd	–	1,025	–	407	–	–	230	–	–	1,662
Wilts.	e'bnd	407	–	–	602	262	–	262	–	–	1,533
	w'bnd	604	882	–	197	1,411	–	342	–	–	3,443
Devon & Cornwall	e'bnd	–	747	339	262	–	–	–	–	–	1,348
	w'bnd	–	–	–	–	339	–	–	–	–	339
Central Southern England	e'bnd	131	–	–	768	459	–	–	383	–	1,742
	w'bnd	460	262	–	407	–	–	–	341	–	1,471
London	e'bnd	512	569	154	339	1,109	–	1,877	–	–	4,560
	w'bnd	407	–	–	3,058	–	–	998	–	–	4,464
South East Coast	e'bnd	285	–	–	407	998	–	–	–	–	1,690
	w'bnd	–	512	–	–	–	–	–	–	–	512
Rest G.B.	e'bnd	–	–	–	683	–	–	–	–	–	683
	w'bnd	–	–	–	–	341	–	–	–	–	341
Total	e'bnd	3,769	2,717	1,062	6,801	4,186	1,279	4,168	1,370	1,687	27,040
	w'bnd	4,859	4,946	341	6,698	5,082	–	3,203	2,140	–	27,260

APPENDIX 39

ORIGINS AND DESTINATIONS OF COMMODITIES — PAPER

Number of loaded vehicles, 1968.

		Newport	Rest Mon.	West Glos.	Cardiff	Rest Glam.	Hereford & Brecon	Swansea	West Wales	Rest G.B.	Total
Bristol	e'bnd	1,534	1,005	—	3,108	918	—	—	408	—	6,974
	w'bnd	1,814	1,239	1,321	4,456	1,592	255	1,210	—	274	12,162
East Glos.	e'bnd	—	336	—	—	173	—	—	—	—	539
	w'bnd	713	—	—	—	—	—	—	—	—	713
Somerset	e'bnd	115	361	594	255	—	—	—	—	—	1,325
	w'bnd	—	357	548	2,553	646	—	—	921	—	5,025
Wilts.	e'bnd	—	—	—	—	—	—	—	—	—	—
	w'bnd	—	—	—	153	—	—	—	—	—	153
Devon & Cornwall	e'bnd	—	—	1,160	—	—	—	—	—	—	1,160
	w'bnd	—	—	—	—	—	—	—	—	—	—
Central Southern England	e'bnd	102	274	—	—	—	—	—	—	—	376
	w'bnd	—	1,371	—	848	1,019	—	—	—	—	3,239
London	e'bnd	—	713	—	115	1,036	—	—	—	—	1,864
	w'bnd	289	—	—	1,810	390	—	—	—	—	2,489
South East Coast	e'bnd	204	—	—	—	—	—	548	—	—	752
	w'bnd	—	—	—	255	—	—	—	—	—	255
Rest G.B.	e'bnd	—	—	—	—	—	274	—	—	—	274
	w'bnd	—	—	—	—	—	—	—	—	—	—
Total	e'bnd	2,229	2,720	1,754	3,478	2,126	274	548	408	—	13,264
	w'bnd	2,816	2,967	1,869	9,982	3,647	255	1,210	921	274	24,036

CHANGES IN DISTRIBUTIVE SYSTEMS IN SEVERNSIDE AREA
EXPECTED IN 1966

	Types of Change	South Wales		South West		All Companies	
		No.	%	No.	%	No.	%
Gloucester Cheltenham Companies	No changes expected in distributive system	–	–	12	10	12	7
	Distribution area to be extended southwards to South West or South Wales	–	–	9	7	9	5
Companies supplying only one side pre-Bridge	Distribution area not expected to be extended across estuary	23	41	24	20	47	26
	Distribution area expected to be extended from existing location	8	14	5	4	13	7
	Depot expected to be opened on other side of estuary	3	5	2	2	5	3
Companies supplying both sides from one point pre-Bridge	No changes expected in distributive system	4	7	18	15	22	12
	Distribution area on other side expected to be extended or depot opened	9	16	25	21	34	19
Companies supplying both sides from two or more points pre-Bridge	No changes expected in distributive system	7	13	17	14	24	13
	Depot expected to take over part of distribution area of depot on other side of estuary	1	1	9	7	10	6
	Depot on other side expected to be closed and area taken over	–	–	1	1	1	1
	Depot expected to be relocated to serve both sides of estuary	1	1	–	–	1	1
Total All Companies		56	100	122	100	178	100

CHANGES IN DISTRIBUTIVE SYSTEMS IN SEVERNSIDE AREA, 1966-68

Type of Change		South Wales		South West		All Companies	
		No.	%	No.	%	No.	%
Gloucester-Cheltenham Companies	No changes made in distributive system	–	–	20	10	20	7
	Distribution area extended southwards in South West or South Wales	–	–	8	4	8	3
Companies supplying only one side pre-Bridge	Distribution area not extended across estuary	25	32	36	18	61	22
	Distribution area not extended but company expects to do so by 1970	3	4	7	3	10	3
	Distribution area extended from existing location	10	13	10	5	20	7
	Depot opened on other side of estuary	1	1	1	1	2	1
Companies supplying both sides from one point pre-Bridge	No changes made in distributive system	10	13	30	15	40	14
	Distribution area on other side extended or depot opened	3	4	24	12	27	10
Companies supplying both sides from two or more points pre-Bridge	No changes made in Distributive system	21	27	34	17	55	19
	Depot has taken over part of distribution area of depot on other side of estuary	2	3	14	7	16	6
	Depot on other side has been closed and area taken over	3	4	12	6	15	5
	Depot has been relocated to serve both sides of estuary including cases where a depot has been opended and the use of contractors' depots ceased	1	1	8	4	9	3
Total All Companies		79	100	204	100	283	100

COMBINED STARTS AND INTENSIFICATIONS OF DELIVERY
SERVICES REPORTED BY DISTRIBUTORS IN SOUTH WALES
ANALYSED BY TRADE.

Percentages

Distribution Zones †	Contract Distrib- utors	Whole- salers	Coal, Builders & Agricultural Suppliers	Industrial Suppliers	All Firms
North Gloucester	11	10	—	6	8
Greater Bristol	11	15	13	24	16
Bath	11	8	13	12	10
Weston-super-Mare & Mendips	11	10	—	12	9
North Wiltshire	11	4	7	12	6
Wellington-Westbury	11	7	—	6	6
South Somerset, South Wiltshire and Dorset	11	3	7	6	4
Exmoor, Devon & Cornwall	11	3	—	12	4
Hampshire	—	—	—	6	1
Berkshire & Oxfordshire	—	—	7	—	1
London (G.L.C.)	11	—	7	—	2
Rest of South East England	11	—	—	—	1

† See Map C.

COMBINED STARTS AND INTENSIFICATIONS OF
DELIVERY SERVICES REPORTED BY DISTRIBUTORS
IN THE SOUTH WEST ANALYSED
BY TRADE.

Percentages

Distribution Zones†	Contract Distrib- utors	Wholesalers	Coal, Builders & Agricultural Suppliers	Industrial Suppliers	All Firms
Forest of Dean	27	13	10	23	15
Herefordshire	27	9	4	15	10
Newport and South East Monmouthshire	47	24	18	31	26
Cardiff	40	21	16	31	23
Lower and Upper Valleys & North Monmouthshire	40	12	14	21	15
Bridgend and Porthcawl	27	11	10	23	14
Swansea and Port Talbot	40	13	12	26	16
Neath and Swansea Valleys	27	9	8	15	12
Brecon and Radnorshire	20	5	6	13	8
East Carmarthen	27	6	8	10	8
West Carmarthen, Pembroke & Cardigan	33	6	10	10	9
Rest of Wales	7	4	6	8	6

† See Map C.

FATSTOCK MARKETS — ANIMALS FROM WEST OF THE SEVERN CERTIFIED AT WINFORD AND CHIPPENHAM

Period	Winford			Chippenham		
	Cattle	Sheep	Pigs	Cattle	Sheep	Pigs
1 (April 1967)	–	–	–	–	–	–
2 (July 1967)	–	–	–	–	–	–
3 (Oct. 1967)	–	–	–	24	20	–
4 (Jan. 1968)	9	180	–	49	79	–
5 (April 1968)	–	–	–	–	53	3
6 (July 1968)	–	–	–	–	–	–
7 (Oct. 1968)	–	39	–	16	262	–
8 (Jan. 1969)	–	–	–	–	–	–
Percentage of all animals certified at market, periods 3–8	0.8	6.2	–	3.6	14.0	0.3

FATSTOCK MARKETS – ANIMALS FROM WEST OF THE SEVERN CERTIFIED AT THORNBURY AND THEIR RELATIVE IMPORTANCE

Period	No. of Animals from west of the Severn			Total certified at Thornbury in period and percentage from west of the Severn					
	Cattle	Sheep	Pigs	Cattle	%	Sheep	%	Pigs	%
1 (April 1967)	15	2	–	143	10	113	2	568	–
2 (July 1967)	–	–	–	137	–	521	–	338	–
3 (Oct. 1967)	40	280	–	167	24	779	36	606	–
4 (Jan. 1968)	147	487	16	334	42	809	60	453	3
5 (April 1968)	72	69	22	208	35	185	37	686	3
6 (July 1968)	37	250	51	141	26	702	40	362	14
7 (Oct. 1968)	129	1,162	17	246	52	1,235	94	641	3
8 (Jan. 1969)	254	632	99	408	62	723	87	837	12

APPENDIX 46

FATSTOCK MARKETS – AREA OF ORIGIN OF ANIMALS FROM WEST OF THE SEVERN CERTIFIED AT THORNBURY

Area of Origin	Totals for the eight periods analysed		
	Cattle	Sheep	Pigs
Chepstow	227	1,364	64
Newport	144	622	27
Usk	57	349	26
Lydney	173	160	45
Monmouth	60	143	3
Abergavenny	12	130	40
Others	6	112	–

APPENDIX 47

TONNAGE PASSING THROUGH THE BRISTOL CHANNEL PORTS IN 1965 & 1968

Thousand tons

Commodity	Bristol 1965	Bristol 1968	Sharpness/* Gloucester 1965	Sharpness/* Gloucester 1968	Newport 1965	Newport 1968	Cardiff 1965	Cardiff 1968	Barry 1965	Barry 1968	Swansea 1965	Swansea 1968	G.B. Total 1965	G.B. Total 1968
Foodstuffs														
Meat Products	24	28	—	—	—	—	3	3	—	—	—	—	1,528	1,544
Dairy & Eggs	40	38	—	—	4	36	24	16	—	—	—	—	903	942
Fruit & Veg.	137	92	—	—	5	25	42	63	133	141	2	3	3,513	3,956
Sugar & Molasses	137	139	—	—	—	—	—	—	—	—	—	—	2,643	2,496
Cereals	950	834	65	79	—	—	64	72	89	69	1	—	7,980	7,561
Agric. Supplies														
Animal Feedstuffs	475	525	—	—	—	—	—	—	—	—	—	—	1,815	1,581
Oil Seeds & Nuts	47	48	—	—	—	—	—	—	—	—	—	—	878	713
Chemical Fertilizers	142	151	—	—	—	—	—	—	—	—	—	—	Not available	
Wood & Timber	217	133	62	49	91	143	106	85	58	33	45	16	6,698	6,287
Petroleum Products	3,282	3,072	556	332	259	295	650	849	475	336	627	683	Not available	
All goods	7,069	6,906	788	595	3,059	3,915	2,016	2,226	1,007	497	1,112	1,040	201,183	228,725

* from British Transport Docks Board's Annual Reports

— nil or under 1,000 tons.

Source: Digest of Port Statistics

CHANGES IN QUANTITIES IMPORTED THROUGH
VARIOUS BRISTOL CHANNEL PORTS 1965-68

(Percentage increase or decrease in trade)

Commodity	Bristol	Sharpness/* Gloucester	Newport	Cardiff	Barry	Swansea	National Average
Foodstuffs							
Meat Products	+ 17	—	—	no change	—	—	+ 1.0
Dairy & Eggs	− 5	—	+ 900	− 33	—	—	+ 4
Fruit & Veg	−33	—	+ 500	+ 50	+ 6	+ 50	+ 13
Sugar & Molasses	+ 1.5	—	—	—	—	—	−6
Cereals	−14	+ 22	—	+ 13	−23	—	−5
Agric. Supplies							
Animal Feed— stuffs	+ 11	—	—	—	—	—	−13
Oil Seeds & Nuts	−17	—	—	—	—	—	−19
Chemical Fertilizers	+ 6	—	—	—	—	—	Not avai-lable
Wood & Timber	−39	−21	+ 57	−20	−43	−64	−6
Petroleum Products	− 6	−40	+ 14	+ 31	−29	+ 9	+ 25 (est.)
All goods	− 2	−24	+ 28	+ 91	−20	− 6	+ 12

*From Bristish Transport Docks Board's
Annual Reports

Source: Digest of Port
Statistics

— = nil or negligible trade.

APPENDIX 49

BENEFITS EXPECTED FROM USING MOTORWAYS WHEN COMPLETED
(SOUTH WALES MANUFACTURERS 100+ EMPLOYEES)

Percentages

Expectations	M.4 Bristol— London	M.4 West of Newport	M.5 Bristol— Gloucester	M.5 Bristol— Exeter
To use motorway	84	76	49	49
Save transport costs	49	42	22	22
Rationalise distribution	7	6	2	2
Speed delivery	64	54	27	31
Access to new market areas	5	5	5	5
Access to new sources of raw materials	3	2	2	1
Diversion of traffic from rail to road	6	4	2	2
Diversion of traffic from road haulier to own fleet	6	4	3	2

APPENDIX 50

BENEFITS EXPECTED FROM USING MOTORWAYS WHEN COMPLETED
(SOUTH WALES DISTRIBUTORS)

Percentages

Expectations	M.4 Bristol— London	M.4 West of Newport	M.5 Bristol— Gloucester	M.5 Bristol— Exeter
To use motorway	67	85	34	34
Save transport costs	29	54	17	19
Rationalise distribution	7	18	7	5
Gain access to new market areas	11	13	9	8

APPENDIX 51

BENEFITS EXPECTED FROM USING MOTORWAYS WHEN COMPLETED
(SOUTH WEST MANUFACTURERS 100+ EMPLOYEES)

Percentages

Expectations	M.4 Bristol— London	M.4 West of Newport	M.5 Bristol— Gloucester	M.5 Bristol— Exeter
To use motorway	88	68	75	58
Save transport costs	55	35	43	30
Rationalise distribution	9	5	6	4
Speed delivery	69	48	56	40
Access to new market areas	8	7	5	5
Access to new sources of raw materials	4	3	1	1
Diversion of traffic from rail to road	3	2	2	1
Diversion of traffic from road haulier to own fleet	7	5	4	3

APPENDIX 52

BENEFITS EXPECTED FROM USING MOTORWAYS WHEN COMPLETED
(SOUTH WEST DISTRIBUTORS)

Percentages

Expectations	M.4 Bristol— London	M.4 West of Newport	M.5 Bristol— Gloucester	M.5 Bristol— Exeter
To use motorway	78	59	84	73
Save transport costs	48	37	52	43
Rationalise distribution	13	11	16	13
Gain access to new market areas	11	11	12	9

M

Rail Freight Traffic from South Wales, 1966-1968

Something of the impact of the opening of the Severn Bridge on rail freight traffic can be seen from data generously made available by British Rail. This data concerns outward movements of freight from the Cardiff Division (which consists of the Newport, Cardiff and Swansea Districts) to Bristol and the West of England, to London, to East Anglia and to Portsmouth for March 1966, 1967 and 1968.

The overall pattern is shown in Table A.53.1 which gives the total tonnage moved (excluding coal) from each of the three Welsh divisions to each of the four English regions. The pattern is not very consistent. While there is overall a small increase in traffic between March 1966 and 1968, not all routes share this growth; there are for example significant reductions in traffic between both Cardiff and Newport and Bristol and the

West of England. Interpretation of the table is complicated by a number of factors: the restriction of the data to a single month; the 'lumpy' nature of some of the data, where a single contract generates a substantial tonnage for a short period and of course by variations in the general level of business activity.

The sharp changes in the fortunes of Newport to London traffic, Table A53.2, illustrate the influence of particular contracts. While there is a steady increase in steel there are reductions elsewhere. For Wood Pulp the 1967 figure is exceptional resulting from extra traffic between the Sudbrook and Dartford mills. The very sharp rise and fall in Slag, Cinders and Ashes and the Other Earths and Stone is much influenced by special contracts, particularly the completion of a London sewage works.

Freight Traffic, Newport to London in Certain Product Groups

		TONS		
Product Group	March 1966	March 1967	March 1968	TABLE A53.2
Finished Steel and Tinplate	8,474	12,037	15,149	
Wood Pulp and Esparto Grass	451	1,020	297	
Slag, Cinders and Ashes	0	1,529	0	
Other Earths and Stone	1,019	6,425	824	

The fall in traffic between Newport and Bristol and the West of England occurs mainly in a few products as shown in Table A53.3. The 1967 Animal Feeding Stuffs figure seems to have been a freak. The main traffic is in the opposite direction from the Bristol and Avonmouth mills. With the other two products there has been a change to road transport. Methods of packaging and handling timber have changed and facilitate transportation by road and the railways do not seem to particularly regret losing this business. The switch of Creosote etc to road between 1966 and 1968 in the continuation of a trend already discernable before the Severn Bridge opened.

Freight Traffic, Newport to Bristol and the West of England, in certain products

Product Groups	March 1966	March 1967	March 1968	TABLE A53.3
Animal Feeding Stuffs	18	1,839	0	
Creosote Pitch and Tar	1,904	1,368	0	
Timber (other than pit props)	436	290	73	

Between Cardiff and London the fall in traffic is most marked in the following products, Table A53.4.

Freight Traffic, Cardiff to London in Certain Products Groups

Product Groups	March 1966	March 1967	March 1968	
Other Earths and Stone	0	508	0	**TABLE A53.4**
Other Building Materials	809	969	167	
Paper and Paper Products	316	256	144	
Unclassified	416	334	167	

Over the period 1966—68 while the pattern of freight traffic that emerges is somewhat confused it does have some features very consistent with the earlier discussion of road haulage. The main impact of the Bridge on rail freight seems to have been limited to the shorter hauls between South East Wales and Bristol and the West of England, where a fairly consistent pattern of falling tonnages is found. The decline in traffic between Cardiff and Newport is also consistent but much of the fall here, as with Newport to London between 1967 and 1968 is the result of other influences than the Bridge.

Rail Freight, Excluding Coal, from South Wales to some English Regions, 1966–1968

tons

Origin By District	Bristol and West			London			East Anglia			Portsmouth			Total 4 Regions		
	March 1966	March 1967	March 1968	March 1966	March 1967	March 1968	March 1966	March 1967	March 1968	March 1966	March 1967	March 1968	March 1966	March 1967	March 1968
Newport	9,462	7,469	6,538	11,207	21,801	16,808	2,594	2,096	2,416	265	490	157	23,528	31,856	25,919
Cardiff	14,791	8,175	10,217	10,138	7,575	6,549	3,731	3,486	3,426	602	944	834	29,262	20,180	21,026
Swansea	9,849	9,377	15,822	7,029	7,135	5,991	3,380	6,358	6,843	129	502	734	20,387	23,372	29,390
Total	34,102	25,021	32,577	28,374	36,511	29,348	9,705	11,940	12,685	996	1,936	1,725	73,177	75,408	76,335

DESTINATION

TABLE A53.1

174

Map A

GENERAL STUDY AREA

Boundary of Study Area

Motorways, Existing (1969)

Under Construction
and Proposed

Trunk Roads

Main Railways

Major Ports

Special Development Areas (1969)

Development Areas (1969)

Intermediate Areas (1969)

© Crown copyright 1971

Welsh Office, Cardiff. January 1971

Based on the Ordnance Survey map

MILES

KILOMETRES

Bristol Channel

SWANSEA
Neath
Port Talbot
MERTHYR TYDFIL
Bridgend
Barry
CARDIFF
NEWPORT
Monmouth
Weston-super-Mare
Taunton
BRISTOL
BATH
Devizes
Warminster
Swindon
Cheltenham
GLOUCESTER
Severn Bridge

M5 M50 M4

A40 A465 A4061 A4042 A449 A479 A4059 A470 A48 A483 A40 A465 A470 A4119 A36 A38 A46 A4 A419 A417 A435 A449 A361

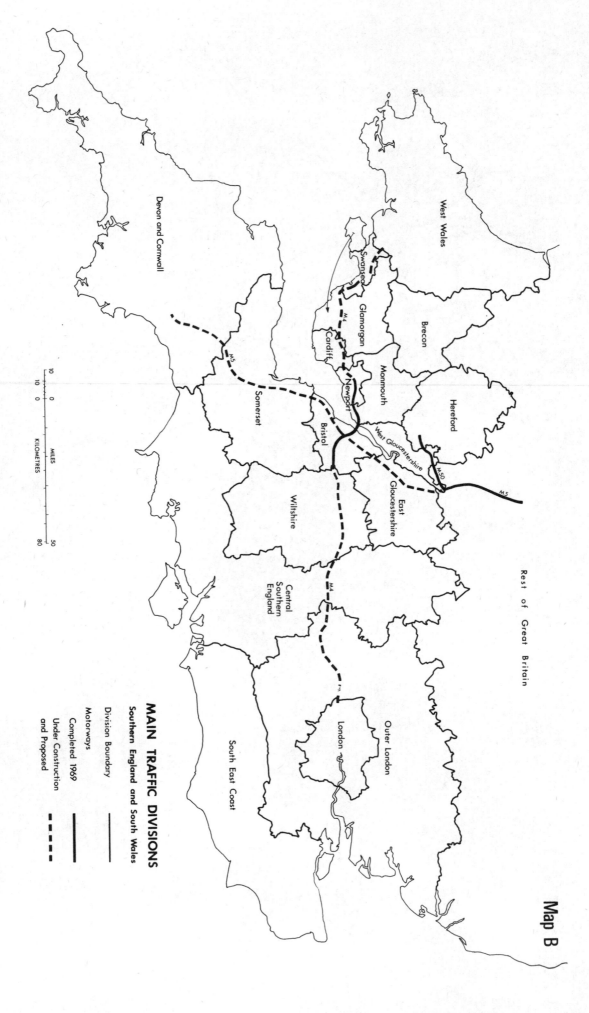

Map B

MAIN TRAFFIC DIVISIONS
Southern England and South Wales

Division Boundary
Motorways
Completed 1969
Under Construction
and Proposed

Devon and Cornwall

West Wales

Swansea

Glamorgan

Brecon

Cardiff

Monmouth

Newport

Hereford

Somerset

Bristol

West Gloucestershire

East Gloucestershire

Wiltshire

Central Southern England

London

Outer London

South East Coast

Rest of Great Britain

M4
M5
M50

MILES
KILOMETRES
10 10 0
0
10 10
50 80

Based on the Ordnance Survey map

© Crown copyright 1971

Welsh Office, Cardiff

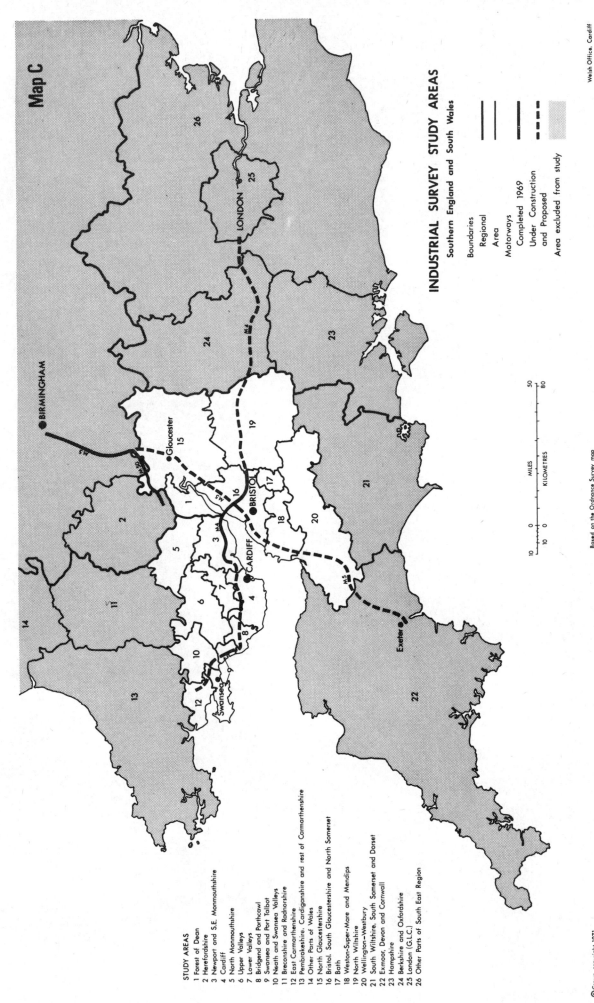

Map C

INDUSTRIAL SURVEY STUDY AREAS
Southern England and South Wales

Boundaries
Regional
Area

Motorways
Completed 1969
Under Construction
and Proposed

Area excluded from study

Welsh Office, Cardiff

STUDY AREAS
1 Forest of Dean
2 Herefordshire
3 Newport and S.E. Monmouthshire
4 Cardiff
5 North Monmouthshire
6 Upper Valleys
7 Lower Valleys
8 Bridgend and Porthcawl
9 Swansea and Port Talbot
10 Neath and Swansea Valleys
11 Breconshire and Radnorshire
12 East Carmarthenshire
13 Pembrokeshire, Cardiganshire and rest of Carmarthenshire
14 Other Parts of Wales
15 North Gloucestershire
16 Bristol, South Gloucestershire and North Somerset
17 Bath
18 Weston-Super-Mare and Mendips
19 North Wiltshire
20 Wellington—Westbury
21 South Wiltshire, South Somerset and Dorset
22 Exmoor, Devon and Cornwall
23 Hampshire
24 Berkshire and Oxfordshire
25 London (G.L.C.)
26 Other Parts of South East Region

MILES

KILOMETRES

Based on the Ordnance Survey map

© Crown copyright 1971

This report is a study of a major change in communications in Britain with implications not only for those who live and work in Wales and the West of England but for all interested in the impact of motorways on personal as well as business affairs — researchers, planners, administrators, politicians and the people of South Wales and the South West of England, as well as for those who may be affected in future by similar changes in communications.

It is the work of a team drawn from two universities — Bath and Swansea, and a technical college — Newport — and covers a wide range of academic disciplines. It deals with the problems of assessing the gains and losses arising from such a major change in communications and attempts to assess the gain to the community through cost-benefit analysis. The study of a change of this magnitude has few precedents and while a wide range of ideas from traffic studies and economics have been called upon, an integrated study of this type can bring together not only traffic forecasts — with all their implications for future highway planning but also the effect on industry and commerce both at the time and with some indication of future possibilities.

Inevitably the question has been asked who benefitted most? This is not answered in an inter-regional sense but it does show how the two communities along the Severn have each gained and how the nation as a whole has enjoyed the fruits of a very worth-while capital investment.

When Regional Economic Planning Councils were set up in 1965 one of their first tasks was to assess the longer-term position of their respective communities. This study was made possible by the joint initiative and sponsorship of the then Council for Wales and the South Western Economic Planning Council. Here is how the two communities are seen in the light of their new bond, itself a tribute to British engineers for all time, the Severn Road Bridge.